Religion and Science Fiction

Religion and Science Fiction

Edited by
JAMES F. McGRATH

☙PICKWICK *Publications* · Eugene, Oregon

RELIGION AND SCIENCE FICTION

Pickwick Publications
An Imprint of Wipf and Stock Publishers
199 W. 8th Ave., Suite 3
Eugene, OR 97401

www.wipfandstock.com

ISBN 13: 978-1-60899-886-9

Cataloging-in-Publication data:

Religion and science fiction / edited by James F. McGrath.

viii + 196 p. ; 23 cm. Includes bibliographic references and indexes.

ISBN 13: 978-1-60899-886-9

1. Science fiction—American—History and Criticism. 2. Science fiction television programs—History and criticism. 3. Religion in Literature. 4. Faith in Literature. I. McGrath, James F. II. Title.

PN3433.6 R45 2011

Manufactured in the U.S.A.

Contents

Contributors

TERESA BLYTHE is Coordinator of the Hesychia School for Spiritual Directors at the Redemptorist Renewal Center at Picture Rocks in Tucson, Arizona, and has served as a spiritual director and facilitator for the Fund for Theological Education's Volunteers Exploring Vocation program, Youth Specialties Sabbath, the Youth Ministry and Spirituality Project, and San Francisco Theological Seminary's Diploma in the Art of Spiritual Direction program. She frequently writes about religion in popular culture for *Beliefnet, Presbyterians Today*, and *Publishers Weekly*. She has coauthored two books on the subject—*Meeting God in Virtual Reality: Using Spiritual Practices with Media*; and *Watching What We Watch: Prime-Time Television through the Lens of Faith*. She is also the author of *50 Ways to Pray: Practices from Many Traditions and Times*.

ELIZABETH DANNA earned her PhD at the University of Durham in England. She is a native of the Toronto area, where she works for 100 Huntley Street, a large Canadian ministry. She is the author of *From Gethsemane to Pentecost: A Passion Study*, forthcoming from Wipf & Stock. She dedicates her chapter in this book to memory of her father, Frank Danna, who introduced her to science fiction in general and to *Star Trek* in particular.

JOYCE JANCA-AJI is Assistant Professor of French at Coe College in Cedar Rapids, Iowa. Apart from cultivating an interest in French science fiction films, she studies the influences of Eastern thought in French literature, particularly in Marguerite Yourcenar.

ERIBERTO P. LOZADA JR. is Associate Professor of Anthropology and Director of Asian Studies at Davidson College in North Carolina. He is the author of *God Aboveground: Catholic Church, Postsocialist State, and Transnational Processes in a Chinese Village* (2001). He has also published articles about his research on globalization and its impact on food and popular culture and on various issues in science and religion.

He is currently exploring the relationship between sports and civil society in China and the United States.

ALISON BRIGHT MACWILLIAMS is a visiting scholar at the University of Notre Dame. Her PhD in history from Drew University is on the subject of scientists in British fiction from 1830 to 1930.

JAMES F. MCGRATH is Associate Professor of Religion and the Clarence L. Goodwin Chair in New Testament Language and Literature at Butler University in Indianapolis. He is the author of *John's Apologetic Christology* (2001) and *The Only True God* (2009) as well as a number of articles and book chapters.

GREGORY PEPETONE is Professor of Music and Interdisciplinary Studies at Georgia College and State University where he has taught for the past fifteen years. A graduate of the Oberlin Conservatory of Music, Pepetone is a classical pianist who has performed extensively in England and the United States. Most recently he has been engaged in a performance of the complete cycle of Mozart piano sonatas as part of an international observance of the 250th anniversary of Mozart's birth. Whereas his achievements as a classical pianist are acknowledged, Pepetone has also been recognized for his contributions to interdisciplinary studies. He has received awards for best article of the year from *American Music Teacher* for two of his recent publications on the fine arts and spirituality: "A Fresh Look at the Authentic American Dream" and "Gothic Perspectives on Beethoven" (in *The Gospel according to Superheroes* and *Alcohol and Religion*). His book *Gothic Perspectives on the American Experience* (2003) explores American history as projected in gothic arts.

THE REVEREND CANON C. K. ROBERTSON is Canon to the Presiding Bishop of the Episcopal Church, and Executive Director for Film Clips Inc. Having formerly taught communications and ethics at Georgia College and State University, he presently serves on several national boards, works with the White House "Helping America's Youth" program, and speaks at conferences throughout the country. Robertson has written or edited several books and articles on religion and popular culture, including *Religion as Entertainment* (2002) and *Religion & Sexuality: Passionate Debates* (2006) as well as contributed chapters to other multiauthor volumes, such as *The Gospel according to Superheroes* (2005).

Religion and Science Fiction

JAMES F. McGRATH

THIS BOOK EXPLORES THE intersection between two topics that until recently seemed to many to be light-years apart, but which in our time have come to interact and overlap frequently and prominently. The connection between religion and science fiction is becoming a regular subject for discussion not only among academics but in the popular press. As I write this introduction, I am truly impressed as I think back on the number of books and articles that have been published over the past two decades or so, relating to at least some aspect the intersection between religion and science fiction. Yet a survey of this literature will also give an indication of how *fragmented* treatments of this topic are along disciplinary lines. Religion and science fiction is a subject of interest within the fields of literature, film studies, history, philosophy, religious studies, theology, cultural studies, and probably many more. If there is something lacking in previous publications on this subject, it is an attempt to bridge the gap not merely between different *works* of science fiction, different *subgenres*, and different *themes and issues* raised in the stories in question, but *also different approaches to and angles on the subject itself.* The present volume intends to take a first step towards remedying this situation, by bringing together in a single volume not merely treatments of a range of books and films, illustrating a range of topics and themes, but also a range of *areas of expertise*, providing an opportunity for students, scholars and indeed anyone fascinated by the subject to get a sense of the many different methodologies and perspectives from which one may approach it. If this volume takes you through territory both familiar and unfamiliar, it does so intentionally.

The story is often told, even though it is apocryphal, about Yuri Gagarin declaring that God does not exist, since he could not see him when looking out the window of his space capsule. For most of us today, at any rate, such a judgment seems trite—but perhaps that is only because of the extent to which human beings in general, and religious traditions in particular, have revised their view of the universe to incorporate scientific perspectives. Before the modern era, the heavens *were* the domain of religion, and stories about humans traveling there featured apocalyptic seers rather than astronauts. We need not look very far in order to encounter a point of intersection, where on the one hand science fiction takes on religious overtones, and where on the other hand religion takes on an aura of science fiction.

As an example of the former, some of the stories of contemporary UFO abductions (particularly those made popular on the TV series *The X-Files*) parallel the scenario set forth in ancient apocalyptic literature such as the Ethiopic Book of Enoch. For those unfamiliar with either storyline, both include interbreeding between humans and celestial beings, at least one person being taken up into the sky, a loner who warns that this human-celestial collaboration and hybridization program will end in disaster, beings from "up there" providing humans with advanced technology, and the list could go on.[1] And for an example of religion being expressed in a sci-fi manner, we do not need to turn to UFO cults or anything else that would be so obvious and yet so marginal. Books such as the Left Behind series have not inappropriately been categorized under the heading "science fiction." Indeed, if one watches the Left Behind movie, one might easily expect Mulder and Scully to appear on the scene at some point to investigate these strange goings on, and in doing so to catch a glimpse of the worldwide conspiracy that lurks beneath the surface.

Both religion and science fiction tell stories that reflect on the place of human beings in the universe, good vs. evil, humanity's future, and at times about the very nature of existence itself. But the parallels run much deeper than mere similarities of storyline. Science fiction scenarios often imagine the future of technology, and thus provide a wonderful starting

1. See further my "Religion, But Not As We Know It: Spirituality and Sci-Fi," in *Religion as Entertainment*, ed. C. K. Robertson (New York: Lang, 2002), 153.

point for ethical discussions. Moreover, at a deeper level, at least some science fiction provides an opportunity not only for discussion of specific moral issues and technologies, but of the very nature of good and evil itself. The Star Wars saga, to look at one classic example, began with an episode that, when taken on its own, might easily have seemed to be simply a re-telling of a classic and rather superficial story. A boy leads an insignificant life, dreams of adventure, meets a wise wizard, goes on a quest, rescues a princess, and so on through familiar territory. However, in the second installment (Episode V), the person viewers still thought of as the hero of the story, Luke Skywalker, was shaken from this complacent and superficial viewpoint, and learns that overcoming evil involves great dedication and not simply a desire for adventure. Over the course of the final install-ment of the original trilogy, it is revealed to us that this is a story not just about a boy, but about a father and a son, and we are confronted with the idea that ultimately evil is overcome not simply by "killing the bad guys" but by redeeming fallen heroes. The fallen hero in question, Darth Vader, is introduced to us in greater detail in Episodes I–III, where we learn that he (rather than his son) is the real main character of the story as a whole. More than that, we see how in times of conflict even "the good guys" (in this case the Jedi) can lose the moral high ground, with disastrous conse-quences. Anakin had been struggling with a number of issues, and we see how Chancellor Palpatine enticed Anakin to the dark side by manipulat-ing him in precisely his areas of weakness. We also see, however, how the blurring of right and wrong in the context of a time of war contributed to his fall, when the Jedi asked him to spy on the chancellor and so break the Jedi code, and when a member of the Jedi council member uttered words that had earlier been spoken by a Sith lord, claiming that their enemy was "too dangerous to be kept alive" and should thus be killed on the spot rather than made to stand trial. The persistent contemporary relevance of these issues is obvious, and the depth of insight and distinctive perspec-tive that these particular films offer is not to be overlooked.[2]

Science fiction also provides opportunities for tracing cultural trends. Although the setting of the stories is the future, like all fiction, sci-fi reflects and comments on the time in which it is produced. One well-known example is the development of *Star Trek* from the original series through its subsequent spin-offs. The original series adopted the

---

2. See ibid., 165–68.

view typical of "modernity," with the enlightened, sophisticated and apparently religion-free crew of the Enterprise encountering either similarly advanced cultures, or primitive ones that were still enslaved by religion/superstition. This is not to say that there could not be "gods" and the *apparently* supernatural: one needs to think only of Apollo from the episode "Who Mourns for Adonais?" or Q from *The Next Generation*. But in the end, for anything apparently supernatural, a reasonable, scientific, natural explanation is assumed to exist. However, as one moves into subsequent series such as Deep Space Nine, the cultural shift that has taken place in our time, from a modern to a postmodern perspective, is reflected. On the space station Deep Space Nine, every race has its own culture, and usually a religious perspective, and the human characters are invited to try them out. Perhaps most significantly, however, is the fact that no attempt is made to provide a scientific explanation for some of the apparently supernatural happenings—here the possibility that science may not have all the answers is seriously entertained. And so when one finally reaches the last series, *Enterprise*, Capt. Archer's claim to be open minded sounds far less impressive than Dr. Phlox's readiness to dive in and participate in other cultures, their beliefs and their ceremonies. *Star Trek* has from its very beginning engaged in cultural commentary, and it is not surprising to find the cultural shifts of recent decades depicted in its portrayals of the future.[3]

Over the course of the chapters of this book, the reader is invited to explore some of the many diverse points of intersection between religion and science fiction. This book is intended to be useful as an introduction to academic perspectives on this subject, suitable as a textbook, but of interest and accessible to any reader, even those who may not have read or seen all of the novels, stories, movies, or series mentioned. For that reason, each chapter seeks to engage and explore a major *theme* related to religion and science fiction. Although a chapter may focus on particular books or movies that a reader has not seen, each author attempts to use specific stories to illustrate more general *topics* of interest and *approaches* to the broader subject.

---

3. See ibid., 154–59, as well as more recently Michael A. Burstein, "We Find the One Quite Adequate: Religious Attitudes in *Star Trek*," in David Gerrold and Robert J. Sawyer, eds., *Boarding the Enterprise: Transporters, Tribbles, and the Vulcan Death Grip in Gene Roddenberry's "Star Trek"* (Smart Pop Series; Dallas: BenBella, 2006), 87–99.

Exploring dark, postmodern depictions of postapocalyptic futures, Janca-Aji finds within the complex intertextual play of postmodern sci-fi symbols of transcendence that lead to further explorations in the realms of chaos theory, panentheism and Gaia. This journey leads us to what Janca-Aji refers to as "the natural theology of children: a view of the world and nature as alive, magical, and with limitless potentiality." The female saviors of two French sci-fi films and Alien Resurrection are contrasted with the male-centered outlook of the movie Left Behind. Yet ultimately, it is suggested, the female-centered theological horizon of the films explored in this chapter has something positive to offer to Christianity, and is not simply antagonistic to it.

Continuing into the realm between the traditional novel and the graphic novel, Robertson's chapter introduces the importance of *myth*. Science fiction has, from its beginnings with a "modern Prometheus" to its recent big-screen epics inspired by the work of Joseph Campbell, treated and reenvisaged for new generations the key themes, characters and stories of classic mythology. Popular piety has always incorporated stories of super-human heroes, and a key moment in the blending of this traditional aspect of human religiosity with the science fiction genre is traced by Robertson in the surprising appearance of new mythmakers and new myths in small books "that only cost a dime." While comic books and the stories they tell may be scorned by defenders of "real literature," their expressions of and influence upon the worldview of the vast majority of human beings is no less worthy of serious investigation than those beliefs that scientists or theologians may regard with dismay and frustration, yet which a great many people nonetheless adhere to with deep devotion.

Robertson's chapter hints at the ways in which social relationships and organizations embody fandom in the real world, in ways that at times parallel religious modes of expression. Lozada's chapter brings social-scientific expertise to bear on the subject of how literature and film intersect with the lives of reader and allow for the exploration in a contemporary context of perennial human questions, focusing on the particular situation in today's China. If Janca-Aji's chapter explores the limits of the postmodern, Lozada's shows how the shock of the modern continues to be felt in parts of our world as an ongoing formative influence right up to the present day, as the classic modern view of science prevails (and is promoted) in a postsocialist context. In the process, Robertson's analysis of the mythological element in comic books finds its parallel in the mythological antecedents which have been identified for Chinese sci-fi. This chapter also explores the theme of nationalism in Chinese sci-fi, and compares it to the postnational "transgalactism" of Western science fiction.

The chapter by MacWilliams takes us back to the very roots of the modern science fiction novel. In addition to their pivotal role in giving birth to the genre as a whole, *Frankenstein* and *The Island of Dr. Moreau* gave rise to that subgenre of science fiction fixated on the disasters that may result when scientists "play God." Yet the actual novel *Frankenstein* is much more complex and nuanced than many of the comparatively simplistic treatments found in later literature and film—and even in movies based on the novel *Frankenstein* itself. When it comes to scientists playing God, does practice make perfect?

As the chapter before it began moving us into the realm of ethics (another major theme explored in science fiction), Danna's chapter seeks to penetrate deeper still, focusing not on the individual ethical issues raised by particular future technologies, but on *the nature of good and evil itself*. These questions are explored in connection with one of the most famous science fiction TV series of all time, and a somewhat less well known British series from the same time period, both of which were given a contemporary "reboot" in 2009. Star Trek's transporter provided more than one opportunity to split a person along moral lines, or switch the "same" individual between parallel universes, and in so doing raise the question of the very nature of human beings and our morality. But it is not enough to ask about the nature of evil—it is also necessary to reflect on appropriate ways to address it, to deal with it. Mirror opposites in science these fiction stories (which also featured prominently in the TV show *Lost*) provide a mirror that allows viewers to see themselves and reflect on these questions more clearly. Parallels and symbolism from Christian theology are prominent in this discussion, as are questions about free will, whether evil is primarily systemic or personal, and the use of violence in combating evil and/or seeking freedom.

The first part of my own chapter focuses on the ethical issues which will be raised if we are ever successful in creating a full-fledged artificial intelligence. We understand so little about the workings of the human mind, that any attempt to determine whether a machine has a similar subjective experience of self-awareness may be doomed from the outset. Nevertheless, we will not be able to forestall addressing *legal* issues regarding such technology until we have solved the relevant philosophical mysteries. Perhaps our relationship with these future creations of ours (and whether they turn around and enslave us, their creators) will depend less on our programming abilities, and more on our *parenting skills*. The second part of the chapter reverses the direction of consideration, and asks what artificial intelligences might make of some of our own human religious traditions.

Pepetone's chapter represents the perspective least commonly included in volumes on religion and science fiction, which most frequently focus on matters of philosophy, theology and ethics. Yet can there be any treatment of science fiction in film and television that does not enter the realm of the *fine arts* and the *aesthetic*? Not only that, but it is hard to imagine the epic story of Star Wars told without John Williams's incredible score, and the same could be said for many other science fiction films. Certainly one can tell the stories on their own, but the form in which they have made their monumental impact on human life and society is not as mere words, but as words, music, and images combined in a multifaceted sensory experience. Music and religion have been intertwined over the course of human history, and Pepetone explores the possibility that this may be because both give expression to archetypes deeply rooted in the human psyche. In dialogue with not only Madeleine L'Engle (whose personal faith is well known) but also Pythagoras, Origen, Bach, and many others, Pepetone engages in a reflection "on the relationship between religious truth and artistic truth"—a question at the very heart of the intersection between religion and science fiction, approached from a perspective all too infrequently included in the conversation.

The final chapter is deliberately placed last, since in it Blythe offers not simply insights into a particular film or topic, but guidelines for "detecting embedded theology in science fiction films," including at the end of her chapter a series of questions one can ask to facilitate this process. While for some readers this volume may simply be a compilation of writings by individuals with various areas of expertise relevant to the subject matter, for others it will be a starting point for *personal* reflection by readers attempting to integrate theory and practice, the intellectual and the spiritual, the fictional and the religious, life in the present and speculation about the future. Blythe's concluding chapter provides an example of that, but goes further, providing a helpful method for others who want to join in the same exploration.

Our aim in this book is to provide a broad treatment of, and diverse perspectives on, the topic of religion and science fiction. We write not only as scholars of religion and popular culture, but out of research and teaching interests ranging across a wide array of fields: history, literature, biblical studies, religious studies, theology, philosophy, anthropology, and music, among others. The intersection of religion and science fiction is a genuinely interdisciplinary field, with the range of approaches crossing the boundaries not merely between the humanities and the social sciences, for instance, but also between the liberal arts and the fine arts. In this volume, the aim has been to be *representative* rather than *comprehensive*, touching on a number of the major themes and perspectives in a broad historical and global context, and in the process discussing works that have already become classics, as well as ones whose long-term status is yet to be determined. Reading and writing the chapters of this book, and putting it together in this volume, has been a fun and fascinating adventure. I hope that you the reader will find your own experience every bit as enjoyable, stimulating, and thought provoking.

James McGrath

CHAPTER 1

The Dark Dreamlife of Postmodern Theology

Delicatessen, The City of Lost Children, and Alien Resurrection

Joyce Janca-Aji

The law of Nature is a spiritual law. It respects all life, for all life is equal. If we transgress it, the consequences will be dark and terrible.

—Chief Oren Lyons of the Iroquois

IN HIS STUDY ABOUT holy aliens and cyborg saviors, Anton Kozlovic argues that the majority of theological reflection on science fiction films has revolved around supporting the central claims of Christianity. However, the postmodern, postapocalyptic, postchristian and in some ways posthuman science fiction films of French directors Jean Jeunet and Marc Caro: *Delicatessen* (1991) and *The City of Lost Children* (1995), as well as Jeunet's later direction of the fourth Alien movie, *Alien Resurrection* (1997), give the viewer—and the theologian—pause. Although replete with biblical personas, themes, and narratives, their fractured and conflicted presentations disallow refuge in orthodox, or even coherent, theological narratives.

In *Delicatessen*, set after some unnamed natural holocaust, the lives of the residents of an apartment building revolve around the "communion" sacrifice of an ex-circus performer/hired hand, Louison, whose words on forgiveness echo those of Christ. However, not only does the sacrificial lamb fail to die, he escapes by calling forth a deluge that carries away the hungry mob like the Pharaoh's army. After the butcher who is called to perform the sacrifice of Louison (recalling Abraham and Issac) dies by his own hand, Louison and the butcher's daughter are free to sit among the clouds playing music, claiming a tiny piece of heaven for themselves at the end of the world. In *The City of Lost Children*, a fanatic Christianesque cult kidnaps young children to sell to the misbegotten creations of a mad scientist, who hook them up to a great machine to steal their dreams of Christmas. This cannibalistic consumption of souls only ends when the amnesiac creator makes an apocalyptic return and One arrives to save the children. In *Alien Resurrection*, Ripley is cloned by military scientists in order to reproduce the alien that was gestating inside her chest. Now both human and alien, redeemer and destroyer, Christ and anti-Christ, Ripley must outwit "Father" to kill the precious alien she has brought into the world.

One way to interpret the theological aspects of these films is to see them as postmodern critiques of the religious, phallocentric, and scientific cultures and discourses of Western modernity. Each film intertwines patriarchal biblical codes with a denatured nature and aliens of multiple types, linking Christianity and modern science with ecological destruction, dystopias, and apocalypse; each serves as an illustration of Jameson's definition of the postmodern condition: "what you have when the modernization process is complete and nature is gone for good."[1] While modernity tries to recreate a lost or mythical unity by constructing one linear totalitarian system after another to somehow encapsulate and express the whole of reality, deconstructive postmodernism, its other face, revels in a frantic undoing of modernism's conceptual scaffolds. Like the grandmother in *Delicatessen* who simultaneously knits and unknits the same skein day and night, the postmodern mode of thinking denies closure and completion, emphasizing the process of existence instead of unattainable absolutes. In *Delicatessen* and *The City of Lost Children*, this is performed in a ludic manner, playfully re-arranging and re-referencing

1. Frederic Jameson, *Postmodernism, or, The Logic of Late Capitalism* (Durham: Duke University Press, 1991), ix.

codes, symbols, and images, past and future, nostalgia and dread, the real and the imagined, as if everything is part of a dark fairy tale or dream. *Alien Resurrection*, which is more typically sci-fi and nightmarish, achieves similar reworkings through its emphasis on the hybrid and the feminine.

However, these three films have more to offer than postmodern recombinations of fragments from old and, as the films suggest, clearly failing systems. The dark, gray, artificial spaces devoid of nature do not just suggest the end of the world, but also the beginning of a new and corrected one. Unlike the assertions of Derrida and Barthes that there is nothing outside the text and no way to overcome metaphysics, these films are of interest precisely because they suggest that there is indeed something beyond endless intertextual referencing which deserves further attention. Through the postmodern play in the retro and neo-noir science fictions of *Delicatessen* and *The City of Lost Children* and the deliberate blurring of categories of being in *Alien Resurrection*, the directors obliquely suggest an alternative to dangerous apocalyptic perspectives. By highlighting the role of nondual interdependence in human and nonhuman interactions, Jeunet and Caro propose a more holistic and integrative view of nature and existence, suggestive of chaos theory, postmodern animism, and most particularly, James Lovelock's Gaia theory.

Delicatessen: *"Chacun pour soi et Dieu pour tous"*

The first image of the film is that of a blackened building standing among the bombed-out remains of a city cloaked in the permanent twilight of some postapocalyptic nightmare. The building, like the symbolic systems which led to this destruction, is a dead shell unlocatable in time and space ("Here or there, we are nowhere"). Nature, as the butcher tells the cab driver, is also dead and will never grow again. The grisly secret of the building is suggested by the menacing figure of the butcher in his bloody apron and the raspy echo of his cleaver being sharpened throughout the building. In the absence of all animal and plant life, the butcher's system of hiring handymen to transform them into small packages of meat—distributed with the reverence of a priest offering communion—allows for the continuation of life after the death of nature through the very literal body and blood of a sacrificial lamb. Yet for all his priestly and fatherly authority in the building, the butcher does not ascribe religious meaning to his system which he sees as not only fate but an improvement on other systems of survival: out "there" they draw straws.

The inhabitants of the building are no more appealing. Working class brothers Robert and Roger Cube handcraft small gadgets that nostalgically mimic the mooing of cows. Mademoiselle Plusse earns her living by selling her "hams" and "sucklings" to the butcher. Immigrant Claude Tapioca lamely tries to support his family by peddling rat callers and bullshit detectors on the black market. Living in the basement, the frogman has transformed his apartment into a swamp, replete with the snails and frogs he affectionately names before he eats while listening to military marches. Upper class Aurore hears "voices" begging her in quasi-Christian terms to free herself from this fallen, filthy world—which her hyperrational ultra-French husband somehow never seems to hear. Julie Clapet, the vegetarian and extremely near-sighted daughter of the butcher, at once rejects and depends upon her father's despotic system of food distribution. The wealth he gains from his enterprise, hoarded in large sacks of precious, irreplaceable lentils, buys her tea and biscuits. As Stephen Infantino describes it: "The postmodern/post apocalyptic being is a highly qualifiable situation, it has all come to this: a society . . . composed of rugbeating, nose-picking, snail-sucking, condom-patching, moo-making, people-eating survivalist slimeballs who would sooner trade Grandma for back rent than lose a single lentil."[2] As the frogman, who recalls the walrus of *Alice in Wonderland,* says before eating his pet snails: "Chacun pour soi et Dieu pour tous" (Everyone for himself and God for all).

In direct contrast to the social system of the predatory "surfacers" is an alternate and literally underground organization of Troglodytes: an egalitarian, vegetarian resistance group based on cooperation, solidarity, and sharing. Adopting a more amphibious existence, the Troglodytes can be seen as attempting to revert back to a premammalian, prehuman, and thus preEdenic world in the process of creation, unsullied by time, humanity, apocalypse and cannibalistic communion. However, as if to mock certain strains of New Age mysticism and green politics/spirituality, these men in wetsuits are ridiculously prepubescent in their idealism: from the secret handshake and the quasi-military discipline to their fear

2. Stephen C. Infantino, "Delicatessen: Slices of Postmodern Life," *Arachne: An Interdisciplinary Journal of the Humanities/Revue interdisciplinaire de langue et de littérature* 4 (1997) 98.

of being live prey, from their utter ineptitude in carrying out the plan to save Louison to the inability of a few of its members to discern the gender of a rather voluptuous woman.

The arrival of Louison, the latest handyman answering the ad, marks the beginning of the end of the butcher's reign. Instead of the rule of "chacun pour soi" or more literally, "eat or be eaten," Louison's love for his former circus partner, the monkey Dr. Livingstone, and his forgiveness for the crowd that devoured the monkey after a show, inspire the necessary change of heart first in Julie and Mlle Plusse which allows them to rebel against the butcher. Paraphrasing Christ, Louison tells Julie: "No one is entirely evil. It is circumstance. Or they don't realize what they've done wrong."

Although it is tempting to read Louison as a figure of Christ at the Second Coming, the butcher as the anti-Christ in the abjectly fallen world who prepares for the arrival of Louison, the hapless handymen as communion hosts, the virginal, protective Julie as Mary, and Mlle Plusse as a repentant Magdalene, the postmodern emphasis on the performative renders any attempt at allegorization futile. Circus music plays as the opening credits of the film roll. The menace of the building, the site of such cannibalistic evil, is mitigated by almost stereotypical scenes from classic horror movies (shots of the building like those of Frankenstein's castle, the residents breaking into Julie and Louison's bathroom hideout like peasants storming the castle's doors, and the frogman eating bugs like Dracula's lackey). Louison arrives at the building wearing clown shoes; his only luggage consists of memorabilia from his act. His escape from the butcher depends on circus stunts, acrobatics, Chaplinesque slapstick, and even lion taming techniques with a television antenna. If he has a dual nature, it is not so much human and divine as human and monkey—which would account for his ability to remain "natural" and to demonstrate basic mammalian compassion. As such, the reiteration of Christ's message of forgiveness can almost be seen as another remnant from a former reality, reconstituted and replayed, with just as much meaning as the gadgets that make sounds from extinct animals, or the endless series of cooking shows on television demonstrating the creation of dishes whose ingredients no longer exist. Indeed, the emphasis on the virtual nature of social reality (Louison is finally seen as human only after he appears on television) eliminates the possibility of taking any one particular narrative meaning seriously.

If viewers are asked to mistrust any overarching theological design, they are simultaneously invited to pay attention to the intricate series of interconnections, a kind of sympathetic magic which seems to suggest the existence of another kind of intelligence working behind the scenes. Although the film opens with the darkness of the building and landscape, there is also a light—without an identifiable source—which pours through the building like spirit streaming through dead matter. Behind the butcher sharpening his cleaver, the viewer is drawn toward and then into an illuminated vent pipe which connects, like the arterial labyrinth of a single organism, all parts of the building and suggests, quite literally, a light at the end of the tunnel. These early indications are reinforced by the series of coincidences throughout the film as if everyone were caught in a web of unseen connections and harmonies. For example, when the butcher and Mlle Plusse are having sex, the rhythmic squeak of the bed springs traveling through the air vents seemingly cause all the other activity in the building to keep time—Julie's cello piece, the beating of a rug, the pumping of a bike tire, Louison painting the wall, Robert drilling holes and the grandmother knitting—until the butcher climaxes, the springs stop, Julie's string breaks, and Louison falls over. A key dropped in a pipe somehow finds its way back to its owner's bedside. A dream of Louison being killed by Dr. Livingstone results in his toy monkey falling over. Louison's playing of a rusty saw strangely harmonizes with Julie's playing of her cello.

These coincidences and harmonics, however, cannot be contrived or used against the unseen order which binds them. When Aurore's voices convince her to kill herself, her suicide attempts, based on a series of causal relations, inevitably and comically fail. The ringing of the doorbell, which is supposed to engage the sewing machine and pull a piece of fabric to make a lamp fall into Aurore's bath, stops just before she would be electrocuted. Furthermore, once the pattern of interconnectivity is established, these coincidences seem to be motivated toward a positive end, driving the plot to its happy conclusion. Julie accidentally brews a sleeping tea that keeps Louison safely drugged—and off the stairs where the butcher waits. After a dream premonition of Louison's death, Julie unwraps some newspaper from a package in the refrigerator and stumbles upon an article on the Troglodytes which gives her the germ of her plan. Trying to escape the residents clamoring for their meat, Julie and Louison are forced into a bathroom—the only room which gives them a chance of escape. Through similar fortuitous circumstances, Louison and Julie are able to do away with their adversaries without causing them harm. The postman blows himself up trying to shoot Louison. When the butcher hurls Louison's boomerang at him, this time it is the butcher's head that is split in two. Aurore's last suicide scheme fails, but she then inadvertently sets fire to the building and dies as a result.

After the complete undoing of the cannibalistic scheme through the death of the father (the butcher) and the destruction of the building (his kingdom), the end of the film suggests the possibility of a return to an edenic innocence. Completely submerged in the flooded bathroom just before they escape, Julie and Louison enjoy an idyllic moment as they kiss. The last scene finds them playing their unworldly harmonies on a rooftop among the clouds, in a kind of postmodern version of angels with harps in the afterlife of a fallen world.

The City of Lost Children: The Interior of the Dream

If *Delicatessen* is Jeunet's foray into a possible postapocalyptic world, then *The City of Lost Children* is a study of evil from a postmodern perspective of childhood fantasies and fears. Yet despite the difference of focus, these two science fiction fantasies function as a diptych. Like its predecessor, *The City of Lost Children* relies on the same bleakness of landscape set in an imaginary retro postwar "France" and the same comic lightness of tone. The absence of nature, the denatured humans, and the undoing of an evil plot based on human consumption form the same contrast with circus motifs and the childlike innocence of the heroes.

The film begins with a child's dream of a Christmas morning set in the forties: a mechanical tin soldier with a porcelain face clapping cymbals, a wintry window, Santa coming down the chimney. As the music and scene begin to warp menacingly, a second, third, and tenth Santa come down, filling the room, making the boy run for his teddy bear and aged Krank wake up screaming. Because of a flaw in his design, Krank suffers from a complete lack of all imaginative faculties, which causes him to age at an accelerating rate. To save himself from death by lack of dream, Krank rebelled against the mad scientist who created him and threw him in the sea. Once he established himself as the head of his creator's floating lab, he begins, with the assistance of the other faulty creations (the dwarf Marthe, Irvin the migrained brain in an aquarium, and six narcoleptic clones) to steal the dreams of young children. Because the children's dreams inevitably turn into nightmares, Krank must continually replenish his supply with younger specimens freshly kidnapped by the apocalyptic cult of the Cyclops. This arrangement is only interrupted when an orphan from a gang of child thieves (run by a pair of Siamese twins) steals money from One (a sideshow strongman) and several of the Cyclops kidnap Denrée. One's search for his adopted little brother leads him to a young girl, Miette, who falls for the childlike giant and helps him rescue Denrée by revising Krank's dream.

As in *Delicatessen*, the haphazard allusions to Christian theology reveal a strange mix of biblical figures. Krank's inventor, the amnesiac Creator figure estranged from his creation, strolls the bottom of the port in a diving suit, spending his time gathering and tagging the rusty waterlogged treasures he finds for his collection. Finally, when a bottled message from Irvin causes him to remember his struggle with his wayward "son," Krank, he realizes that he must return to undo his foiled creation. Expecting his imminent arrival as the radar tracks the approach of an unidentified object to the lab, Irvin, functioning as a prophet, excitedly declares: "It's the messiah, it's the messiah who is coming to save us!" Marthe sardonically corrects him: "The messiah walked *on* water." The creator/messiah arrives in an apocalyptic frenzy, gathering dynamite, laughing wildly, and yelling truths from quantum physics: "Nothingness equals infinity!" When Marthe, his former disciple, recognizes his resurrected self, the professor does not affirm his identity or the arrival of a new world order, but denies his own existence and that of his creation: "There is no more professor, Marthe, there is just a terrible error that must be erased!" The clones, made in his image, realize that he is the "Original," but the professor, still unable to recognize his connection with his creations, cannot place them and vaguely says that they all remind him of someone. This absent-minded mastermind only remembers who he is when, strapped to a pole and wrapped in explosives, he happens to catch a sheet of his old notes flying in the air. Terrified, he orders, then begs Irvin and the clones to come and save him (from himself), but his last pleas fall on deaf ears as they row away toward freedom. Then, as if in a roadrunner cartoon, a bird happens to land on the switch and everything blows up.

Krank (meaning "sick" in German") first appears as a Lucifer figure: a masterpiece of creation turned fallen angel, out to revenge himself against his creator through corrupting the innocent. He introduces himself into the dreams of children as Santa Claus, a childlike representation of the goodness of Christ, but soon reveals himself to be Herod or a soul-stealing demon consuming them through their nightmares. Like an Adam newly expelled from paradise or Lucifer from heaven, he blames his creator for the soulless monster that he has become: "He is the only one responsible. I'm innocent. Innocent!" Although he is an "evil genius," this kind of anti-Christ who "suffers the little children" is terrified at the suggestion that his quest is in vain. A more literal translation of "Je suis pour rien. Pour rien!" suggests that his existence is forever without meaning.

Krank's evil counterpart is the fanatic leader of the Cyclops, a monastic cult of the blind who install a mechanical "third eye" which allows them to see "beyond appearances." Gabriel-Marie (whose name recalls the angel and the virgin present at the annunciation of the messiah) stands before an altar in ceremonial vestments with one arm raised and a fist over his heart, preaching among fire and brimstone, to his throng of converts:

> I, Gabriel-Marie, came down into the world with open eyes but saw a world of dogs. A litter of dogs! And so the creator sent me down here to Earth to recover the power that men have illegally seized. My brothers, you who have joined me in this struggle, understand that we must fight together human beings from their own grounds. The world of appearances! Only the third eye will enable you to enter the world of appearances. But beware because this sordid world of temptation and perversion is also the world of desire . . . My brothers, our race, our great superior race will reign once more on Earth! From that day on, our faithful third eye will become useless as the world of appearances will be abolished![3]

Babbling an apocalyptic mishmash about truth and appearances, purity and pollution, being chosen by God, and a special form of transcendence, Gabriel-Marie is a combination of fundamentalist preacher, cult leader, white supremacist and anti-Christ ushering in a false kingdom before the final apocalypse. However, any fright he may give is severely compromised as he is forced to interrupt his dire prophecies to haggle like a street vendor about the children he is selling. Denrée's well-timed burp also functions as a pointed commentary on his religious diatribes. Gabriel-Marie's order of the Cyclops is no less hypocritical. The mechanical third eye, which allows the faithful to see "truthfully," offers only

---

3. *The City of Lost Children*, screenplay (in French) by Gilles Adrien, Jean-Pierre Jeunet, and Marc Caro. Online: http://www.script-o-rama.com/movie_scripts/c/city-of-lost-children-script.html/.

two-dimensional black and white images and renders their entire visual field into a virtual reality. The entry into their secret complex requires mumbo-jumbo latinesque passwords; their robes are trench coats; and they do not hesitate from kidnapping children, stealing from orphans, selling information to the Siamese twins, or betting on whether One or Miette (destined to become "biscuits pour les poissons") will drown first.

The most likely true messiah figure is that of One, who, like Louison in *Delicatessen*, is the catalyst which brings about the end of the nightmare. However, despite his name, his ability to love, his desire to save the innocent from the machinations of Krank and the Cyclops, and the very Christian symbolism of his falling into a pelican nest, he is certainly not *the* One. Not only is this overgrown child lost without his adopted younger siblings, Miette ("crumb") and Denrée ("small change"), this sideshow freak of a strongman belongs more to the circus than theology. Furthermore, it is Miette who performs the actual work of saving Denrée and the other children through her deliberate self-sacrifice in a dream and resurrection back into waking life.

In place of biblical figures and narratives to advance a theological position, Jeunet and Caro resort to several series of interconnected coincidences—just as they have done in *Delicatessen*. Instead of a mechanistic universe or a God who is separate and distant from creation, instead of saviors or nihilistic despair, Jeunet and Caro posit reality as an active, intelligent web of mutual interaction in which all aspects of reality share and participate in arranging things for the highest good. In keeping with the themes of innocence and childhood, some of these co-incidences are presented with the logic of fairy tales and cartoons. To open a locked door, Miette uses a hairpin to push the key out, blows grated cheese under the door, and releases a mouse with a magnet tied to its tail who eats the cheese and then is chased back to Miette—with the key—by a cat. Other coincidences emphasize the profound interconnectedness of minute causes and effects as if an unseen spiritual force were tugging at the strings of the phenomenal world at just the right moments. For example, when One, drugged by the Siamese twins, suddenly turns on Miette and starts strangling her, the tear which falls from Miette's face ultimately saves her. The tear hits a spider web which wakes a parakeet who chirps as though giving a signal. This wakes a dog who begins to bark and who wakes a sleeping bum who throws a bottle which makes a pigeon fly. The pigeon poops on the windshield of a car which makes the driver crash into a fire hydrant which bursts like a geyser and floods the sewer. The flood makes a nest of rats float into the street and into the backdoor of a strip club, which frighten the strippers who run out of the club screaming. This distracts an electrician, perched on a pole above, enough to mistakenly cut off the electricity of the city and its lighthouses. The captains of an enormous ship, unable to see, crash into the docks and knock One and Miette into the water, which causes One to return to his senses and embrace Miette.

Not only does this mute but potent logic express itself through such interconnected activity, which demonstrates the intelligent cooperation of animate and inanimate, it also allows the pure of heart to imaginatively enter into the unseen fabric of reality itself in order to change the course of events. This is best illustrated in the pivotal episode when Miette consciously decides to enter and participate in Krank's dark dream to re-vision reality and save Denrée. The dream begins as they all do: Christmas morning, a toy soldier playing the cymbals, Santa about to arrive. But instead of Krank coming down the chimney, it is Miette in her red pinafore who runs to pick up Denrée. As the sound and image warp and the door in front of her turns to steel, the child she carries turns into Krank, who quickly ages back again. It is Miette's willingness to take Denrée's place in Krank's dream and die (symbolized by the ringer shaped like a noose which ends the dream) which allows the following transformation: as she ages and becomes an old woman, it is Krank who shrinks back into childhood and infancy. When Miette pulls the noose/ringer, Krank is caught between two recurring images of himself which nightmarishly alternate at an increasing rate until he falls over dead.

While there is resolution to the plot—the lab blows up, the children are saved, the Cyclops are put out of business and the Siamese twins attack each other and drown—there is no resolution to the competing binary opposites the film puts forth to viewers: good/evil, adult/child, self/other, original/copy, creator/creation, dream/reality are endlessly mirrored and reflected as if to suggest that there is no way beyond the circularity of such dualistic propositions except through more films, more dreams. Krank himself functions as the poster child of postmodernity. Having to steal images, dreams, and stories from others to construct his own artificial dreamlife, there is no way out of his dilemma until he is spun to death between two opposite and dizzyingly recurring images. However, neither Krank's death nor the way he dies is the most significant. Rather, Miette's entry into an altered state suggests that the only possibility for revising an apocalyptic script is to invoke a kind of magic sympathy which dissolves the fundamental dualisms of self and other, animate and inanimate, agent and action, divine and created. As such, *The City of Lost Children* ends much in the way *Delicatessen* does. Julie and Louison's music among the clouds and One's and Miette's rowing away from the burning lab both hint at possibilities beyond the nightmarish impasse of a cannibalistic postmodernity.

While nondualistic traditions of Buddhism, Taoism, Hinduism, and many indigenous religions can easily accommodate such perspectives by emphasizing the impossibility of separate or independent existences, theologians in the West must often forge more creative alliances. One intriguing option is provided by Jeunet himself. In an interview shortly after the release of *The City of Lost Children*, he describes how the episode of Miette's tear—and by extension all other examples of coincidences and synchronicities—is "a ludicrous illustration" of chaos theory.[4] Extrapolated from the impossibility of predicting weather systems beyond a certain point, chaos theory, also known as the "butterfly effect," posits that natural systems are not deterministic and outcomes are never fixed. Just as the flutter of butterfly wings can lead to a hurricane on the other side of the world (or the falling of Miette's tear can lead to the crashing of a giant rig), the interplay of causes and conditions gives rise to what appear as chance or random occurrences, but in fact form patterns. Theologically, chaos theory has largely been seen as a metaphysical principle incompatible with divine providence and purpose. On the other hand, in "Theological Reflections on Chaos Theory," John Jefferson Davis proposes a possibility for fusing science and spirituality: "Far from being a threat to a biblical understanding of providence, chaos theory can be seen as a new avenue for appreciating both the limitations of human ability to predict the future and the complexity and richness of God's creative power." This interpretation accounts for the ways in which the seemingly random synchronicities and sequences of events culminate in positive outcomes: Miette is ultimately saved by her tear, Louison overcomes the butcher, and One is reunited with Denrée.

---

4. Schlockoff, Alain, and Cathy Karani, "Excerpts from a conversation with Jean-Pierre Jeunet and Marc Caro," Image Refinery Productions, Inc. (1995) Online: http://www.sonypictures.com/classics/city/misc/interview.html.

However, even with Davis' theological bridge, there is much in the films which suggests that the use of chaos theory to understand the films' theological premises falls short. The seemingly magical intentionality behind the coincidences and interconnections that Jeunet and Caro foreground so insistently does not suggest either the workings of pure chance or of God, at least in the traditional (dualistic) sense. None of the characters appeal to heaven for help; no themes of divine providence are suggested. Instead, the numerous allusions to religion point to the failure of theology in light of social and ecological devastation. Science, represented by a natural holocaust, mad scientists, clones and soulless mutants, cannot be seen as fused (or infused) with spirituality.

Much closer to the implied theology of the coincidental sequences in *Delicatessen* and *The City of Lost Children* is David Griffin's explanation of a kind of postmodern animism. In *God and Religion in the Postmodern World*, Griffin argues that because of the split between spirit (a supernaturalist theism) and matter (a mechanistic view of nature as insentient and inanimate), modern thinkers have ignored the possibility of a third option: nondual interactivity.

> Once the idea of a supernaturalistic creation is fully overcome, the idea returns that the universe must be self-organizing and therefore composed of self-moving parts. Also, insofar as dualistic assumptions are fully overcome and human experience is accepted as fully natural, it begins to seem probable that something analogous to our experience and self-movement is a feature of every level of nature . . . According to this naturalistic theism, or panentheism, God is the soul of the universe, an all-inclusive unity of experience and agency which makes the universe a unity. Calling this theism *naturalistic* means that the fundamental relations between God and the world are natural features of reality, belonging to the very nature of things, not arbitrary features, based upon divine volition.[5]

Griffin's nondualistic approach which posits a God working not just through but *as* the world is much closer to the spirit of the films than Davis' version of chaos theory. Yet however well it may provide a theological explanation for the carefully coordinated synchronicities and coincidences, it is not as applicable to the apocalyptic undertones of a

---

5. David Ray Griffin, *God and Religion in the Postmodern World: Essays in Postmodern Theology* (SUNY Series in Constructive Postmodern Thought; Albany: State University of New York Press, 1989), 88–90.

denatured world where lentils are money and humans are food, where creation becomes the domain of mad scientists and mutants, or where spirit, as the capacity to dream, is co-opted, stolen, and sold.

Like Griffin's postmodern animism, James Lovelock's Gaia theory offers a nondualistic account of coincidental interactivity and an alternative to the transcendent and remote God of the Judeo-Christian tradition. It also provides a specific focus on the theology of the environment and its relation to gender. Named after the Greek goddess of the Earth, Lovelock's theory posits that the entire earth is an autopoeietic, self-regulating entity "endowed with faculties and powers far beyond those of its constituent parts."[6] More than just a host or context for life, the earth shares and *demonstrates* the properties shared by all life forms by maintaining a balanced metabolism through a vast array of feedback networks based on harmony, mutuality, and cooperation. While Lynn Margulis, microbiologist and a close colleague of Lovelock, considers Gaia as an important metaphor for Earth's symbiotic systems, others, including Lovelock himself, see the earth as "alive" and as the expression of a more intimate, immanent, and feminine version of God like the Virgin Mary or the Hindu goddess Kali.[7]

Other theologians have expanded on Lovelock's insights, making his theory a more legitimate vehicle of theological inquiry. In *Sacred Gaia*, Anne Primavesi asks:

> What can we say about God's relationship with the material environment that we share with other organisms, whether this be the air we breathe or the oceans and rocks which surround us, when they are all either the direct product of living organisms or else have been greatly modified by their presence? And in particular, what must say when we see the changes to the material environment caused by our presence, even within the relatively short lifespan of our species?" . . . The central theological task has become that of describing the paradoxical nature of this 'God' . . . both visible and invisible in the sacredness of the whole of existent reality.[8]

6. James E. Lovelock, *The Ages of Gaia: A Biography of Our Living Earth* (The Commonwealth Fund Book Program; New York: Bantam, 1990), 9.

7. James E. Lovelock, *Gaia, A New Look at Life on Earth* (Oxford: Oxford University Press, 1979), 206, 208.

8. Anne Primavesi, *Sacred Gaia: Holistic Theology and Earth Science System* (London: Routledge, 2000), xix.

Rosemary Radford Ruether calls for "a new consciousness, a new symbolic culture and spirituality" which transforms the ways in which we understand the earth, the divine, and humanity.[9] In *Gaia and God*, Ruether performs an extensive critique of the Western Judeo-Christian tradition, rereading seminal narratives of creation and destruction, domination and deceit, in order to assess how this legacy has contributed to ecological crisis and what theological resources might be found to aid in the healing of the planet. Such perspectives accord well with Jeunet and Caro's films. Gaia serves as a potent metaphor for the workings of the divine through the coincidental undoing of unnatural systems through the collaborations of the inanimate, animate and human in order to achieve a balance more conducive to life as a whole, restoring the original meaning of the frogman's dictum of "Dieu pour tous."

Gaia also has particular thematic relevance in terms of gender. In "Delicatessen: Eco-Apocalypse in the New French Science Fiction Cinema," Sean Cubitt finds that the conflict between denatured Man and Mother Nature not only structures the film's narrative resolution, it also highlights themes of lost childhood and motherhood: "The lost ability to dream, the disembodied brain, the . . . unfathered clones of *The City of Lost Children* are all aspects of technology as denaturing. If nature is to be recovered it will be through the restoration of paternity, traced in that film in One's relation to the little girl, his protégée. In *Delicatessen*, a similarly important role is played out in the relation between the clown Louison and the two young boys whose antics enliven the film's action and add depth to its conclusion."[10]

Another reading of gender and Gaia, however, would see Gaia as destroying denatured forms of paternity—as demonstrated by the butcher (particularly in his dysfunctional relationship to Julie), Krank the bad Father Christmas, the mad scientist as father/creator, and Gabriel-Marie, father to the brotherhood of Cyclops—in favor of relations based upon a more egalitarian siblingship. Louison and One are more like children playing adults; they establish innocently romantic relations with Julie and Miette respectively; both can be seen as older brothers protecting younger children. Most significantly, however, Julie and Miette can be seen as Gaia

9. Rosemary Radford Reuther, *Gaia & God: An Ecofeminist Theology of Earth Healing* (San Francisco: HarperSanFrancisco, 1992), 4.

10. Sean Cubitt, "*Delicatessen*: Eco-Apocalypse in the New French Science Fiction Cinema," in *Aliens R Us: The Other in Science Fiction Cinema*, ed. Ziauddin Sadar and Sean Cubitt (London: Pluto, 2002), 20–21.

figures in their own right. Once having renounced her father's authority, Julie begins to actively work to end his cannibalistic order with the help of the nature-respecting Troglodytes. Having pieced together what happened at the lab through Irvin's smoke-encrypted message and the fragmented memories of the amnesiac professor who finds her on the bottom of the sea, orphaned Miette leads One to the lab and rescues the children. As a result, the denatured paternal regimes of Krank, Gabriel-Marie, and the professor come to an end. As soon as the latent energy of Julie and Miette, both still in the age of innocence, is aroused against these destructive forces, the seemingly random web of interconnections and coincidences, the activity of Gaia herself, begins to revolve around them, actively furthering their causes.

Furthermore, Gaia theory can be seen as quite compatible with the films' foregrounding of innocence and childish fantasy. These postmodern fairy tales not only feature cannibalistic ogres, a blind princess, a clownish knight, a mad scientist, a misbegotten Frankenstein, twin witches, a giant, a dwarf and troll-like clones; they also recall hints of Little Red Riding Hood, Sleeping Beauty, Hansel and Gretel, and Rapunzel. This perspective allows Jeunet and Caro to focus their interest on the theological perspectives of the only characters who are not mutated, denatured, or alienated from themselves: Julie and Louison, One, Miette, and the children. More than postmodern animism or any other highly metaphysical, scientific or theoretical perspective, Gaia can be seen as consistent with what can be called the natural theology of children: a view of the world and nature as alive, magical, and with limitless potentiality. As such, Gaia can be described as a sort of theological birthright that can be reclaimed, as well as the most likely place to begin at the end of modernity and its apocalyptic narratives.

Alien Resurrection: "I'm a Stranger Here Myself"

As the culminating film of the Alien series, Jeunet cast *Alien Resurrection* in a different generic mode of science fiction/fantasy; however, there are distinct thematic and theological continuities between his film and his former collaborations with Marc Caro. As with *Delicatessen* and *The City of Lost Children*, the natural world is replaced by a bleak artificial environment ruled by science and technology; the humans are either denatured, artificial or hybrid; and the myriad biblical and theological allusions function as a critique of oppressive and paternalistic forms of Christianity in favor of a more Gaian perspective. Unlike its predecessors, however, *Alien Resurrection* is much more of a box-office thriller and as such, it is much less subtle in its approach.

The film opens with Newt repeating her famous line from the second Alien movie: "My mommy said there were no monsters, no real ones anyway, but there are." Here, however, the real monsters are the company scientists, who, in alignment with "Father," the ship's computer, create nightmarish postmodern nativity scenes: first the live caesarian birth of the alien from their chosen handmaiden and vessel, and later Ripley's own sticky, languid emergence from a cocoon. Although just a meat by-product of "Her Majesty, the Queen," her slicked back dark hair, fine bone structure, black leather and lithe body movements seem just as much a part of her genetic inheritance as her superhuman strength, green acid blood, and ancestral memory. When the Betty arrives with its pirated cargo (host bodies for the queen's eggs) and the slaughter of the company's crew begins, Ripley aligns with her human side to escape with the remaining crew members of the Betty in time to destroy the ship and avert an apocalypse on earth.

"God" in *Alien Resurrection* is represented as "Father," the ship's mainframe computer. At once transcendent and omniscient, Father manifests as the disembodied voice which controls the ship and disallows any deviation from the path he has provided for his crew. However, this hyperrational, hyperlinear, masculine divinity is not a God of justice, but of power and control. His high priests, the (mostly male) scientists, follow his apocalyptic plan of cloning Ripley. Specially created and chosen by Father, she serves as the demure (unconscious) handmaiden who will become the mother of the alien who will usher in a new kingdom through an "urban pacification" (weapons) program. Unlike Mary, however, she does not consent to this postmodern virgin birth, and when awakened, she seeks to destroy the very beings she has unwittingly brought forth. Neither does the resurrected Ripley allow herself to play the role of Christ sitting at the right hand of the Father, judging the living and the dead. Siding with her humanity over her alien divinity (Ripley is a hybrid of herself and the alien queen), she chooses to spare the earth from the wrath of the Father on high in the (intergalactic) heavens.

The linking of the mainframe Father with the image of God as distant, unappeasable judge is rendered even more explicit when Call, true to her name, must "prayerfully" call upon Father. However, unlike the scientists who have special codes of access to petition Father to act on their behalf, Call must manually patch in. With a holy fear and dread as if attending mass or preparing for the sacrament of confession, Call enters a small alcove like a chapel, makes the sign of the cross and genuflects (as she is programmed to do so). She opens a Bible in which there is a modem to insert in her arm like an I.V. Like a prophet, she first starts channeling Father's voice, reporting on the status of the ship. However, like Ripley, she too rebels against his divine authority to thwart his apocalyptic plans, replacing the will of the Father with her own. Speaking her own words with his voice, she proceeds to close off, one by one, the doors and passages around Dr. Wren, the head scientist and one most responsible for carrying out Father's plans. When Wren begins to panic, his pleas and then orders to Father are first met with silence—and then Call's channeled voice reverberating through the ship: "Father's dead, asshole." This thinly veiled allusion to the sterile and homoerotic aspects of male service to a male god—as well as to his ultimate defeat—is illustrated by the rape and death of the ship's authorities. The heads of both the captain (saluting as he dies) and Wren are penetrated from behind by the inner heads of the aliens, jutting out as screeching toothed phalluses. With Wren, it is particularly blatant. As one of the pirated members of the cargo feels the alien is beginning to emerge from his chest, he staggers toward Wren, knocks him over, beats him against the floor and positions himself behind him as the alien bursts from his chest and literally "fucks him in the head."

Free of the Father, God the Son in multiple guises is left to destroy the dangerous miscreations of the high priests and to save the world from its end. Of the thirteen aliens seeking their last supper (the remaining crew members), Ripley kills one to bring the number of the queen's "disciples" to twelve. At Call's shock that Ripley killed one of her own, Ripley offers Call the "gift of tongues" by ripping out the alien's tongue and presenting it to her. When Call comes to kill Ripley in her attempt to kill the alien and realizes that the alien was already taken from her, Ripley administers her own stigmata: driving Call's knife through her palm. Later, when Call rises again after being shot and Ripley realizes she is a robot, she gently opens Call's vest and places her hand in her side. Christi, a heavily armed, black, dreadlocked crew member of the Betty carries the dead weight of paralyzed Vriess like a cross on the way to Calvary. As he painfully climbs a ladder to escape, he is splattered by the alien's acid blood and sacrifices himself. Ripley's final redemption, and that of the world, is through her blood. Cutting her hand on the tooth of the Newborn, the live birth alien from the Queen, Ripley flings a few drops on the Betty's wall. The acid eats a hole in the metal and the Newborn is slowly sucked through the small hole in pieces and is dispersed into space, saving humanity and the world from destruction.

These allusions to Christianity in *Alien Resurrection* are clearly gender-conscious, foregrounding the female saviors alongside the dark apocalyptic designs and the servile high priests of the distant and authoritarian male god. In this regard, *Alien Resurrection* stands in sharp contrast to Jerry Jenkins and Timothy LaHaye's 1995 film, *Left Behind*, which quickly became one of the models for the emerging genre of Christian science fiction thrillers. Christian Thorne notes that *Left Behind* features a postapocalyptic world where women either disappear or become aligned with evil through their sexuality (becoming the whores of anti-Christ) and where the names of the rugged male protagonists sound like those of porn stars (Dirk Burton, Rayford Steele, and Buck Williams). Thorne sees *Left Behind* as advocating the thorough remasculinization of Christianity along with a world purified of the corrupting influences of the feminine, making the transformation of the world—and its theology—a more purely phallic, sterile, and almost homoerotic activity.

Jeunet's film, on the other end of the spectrum, revels in the feminine, the senses, the erotic, and the profane. *Alien Resurrection* opens with shots of Ripley being cloned: first cells clustering to organs, undulating, fluid red flesh, slowing changing and giving glimpses of recognizable human forms, deformities, and monstrosities; Ripley in the tube as a naked adolescent, her arms crossed over her chest like a modest virgin, her breasts just beginning to bud. After her "baby" is removed from her chest by caesarian section, Ripley slowly wakens in a gauzy white chrysalis, sensuously moving and touching her body to relearn it and herself. Her first word, a mispronunciation of "fork," is "fuck." When first presented as a character, Call is described as "severely fuckable." Elgyn's code for entry into the military ship is: EA TM E (a nicely defiant throwback to *Delicatessen*). The alien eggs beginning to hatch, sensing the warm meat of the human cargo, open and close like hungry, monstrous vaginas. Dr. Gediman, imitating the facial gestures of the alien, appears to be trying to seduce it through the glass. As a symbol of her alignment with the human half of her nature, Ripley births herself through a hole burned into the floor with alien blood. When Call comes to kill a supine Ripley and opens her vest with a knife only to find the scar, the two orchestrate, with remarkable symmetry, a play of submission and dominance: first Call leans over Ripley, then Ripley pulls herself over Call, slowly caressing her face and repeating her words with a languid and predatory sensuousness (as the Newborn will do to Ripley just after her birth), culminating in Ripley's penetrating herself (her hand) with Call's extended knife. Later, Ripley gently, and almost lovingly, slides her hand inside Call's gaping wound, seeping with white fluid. This "deviant" eroticism, surprising given Ripley's love objects in the previous Alien films (a cat, a little girl, and a prison doctor who is promptly killed), is clearly part of her alien inheritance. Not only is Ripley more animalistic, moving with a certain feline grace, sensing with the sharpness of a wolf, swimming like a sea lion, she responds to the queen in pain with a very visceral and almost automatic empathy which distracts her from her more human quest and affiliations. When an alien pulls out the floor under her, Ripley falls onto the massive maternal body of the queen and is slowly and almost unconsciously collapsing (while in a crucifixion posture) into the caresses of her oceanic undulations. In a series of broken stills, suggesting a departure from linear time, Ripley and the queen appear in various positions both maternal and almost sexual: carried by the queen like a baby, a lover, and in one pose, in a pieta.

This blurring of boundaries and desires has much to do with the profoundly postmodern and hybrid natures of the two female protagonists. At the end of *Aliens 3*, Ripley's crucifixion posture and her falling into fiery pit of the lead works as she births the alien ripping through her chest implicitly links her sacrifice to that of Christ on the cross. However, the Ripley resurrected two hundred years later consists of two constructed and split selves, Christ and anti-Christ—and both of dual natures. Reproduced from her own DNA, Ripley is at once herself and the queen, a human-alien and an alien-human as well as self and sister to the seven failed clones. Similarly, the human was not fully eradicated from the queen. After laying eggs, she added a second cycle. As Dr. Gediman cocooned inside the queen's nest croons: "This time there is no host, there are no eggs. There is only her womb and the creature inside. That is Ripley's gift to her, a human reproductive system. She is giving birth for you, Ripley, and now she is perfect!" The queen's newborn, Ripley's "granddaughter," is a more perfect human-alien hybrid and alternates between the sweet vulnerability of an infant and the terrifying rage of the aliens. Similarly, Call, Ripley's synthetic double, is also a "second gen[eration]" entity. As a robot created by other robots, Call finds her lack of human-ness "disgusting"; however it is precisely because of her compassion (a supposedly purely human trait) that Ripley realizes she is synthetic: "No human being's that humane." (As counterpart, Vriess, paralyzed from the waist down and strapped to a motorized chair, the most humane of the humans, functions as part machine).

The function of hybridity and gender in this film is not merely to stand in opposition to more masculine models of Christian sci-fi, but to present a viable alternative to their apocalyptic adventures. After the newborn is killed and the aliens are no longer a threat, Ripley announces: "We saved the Earth." Unlike Johner who referred to the earth as a "shit hole," Ripley finds it unexpectedly beautiful. As Ripley and Call gaze out the window onto heavenly cloudscapes (recalling the end of *Delicatessen*) and the approaching blue-green globe, the image of earth is reflected on the window and superimposed on their faces. When Call asks, "What happens now?" Ripley replies, "I don't know. I'm a stranger here myself." The ending, which suggests the possibility of renewal, also presents both Ripley and Call as Gaia figures, banished goddesses of the earth return-ing in their new mutated forms to reclaim and restore the natural world under siege from technology, greed and religious authoritarianism which have joined together to release a destructive life form which threatens ex-istence like a deadly virus. Not only do Ripley and Call embody the prin-ciple of interconnectedness which Gaia represents in their very hybridity, they come into being without the need for a male: self-generating as the earth itself and as in myths of the Great Goddess. As the (concentration camp style) tattoo of an "8" on her arm reminds viewers, Ripley's being symbolizes eternity amid the death that surrounds her.

Gaia: Not Just for Ecofeminists Anymore

Given the wealth of Christian theologies and perspectives, why might Jeunet (and Caro) privilege such a marginal theory such as Gaia? For one, such a position is completely appropriate to test out in the dark dreamlife of postmodern science fiction fantasy. Secondly, what else could be such a viable alternative to apocalyptic religious narratives and the ecological di-saster that threatens us? In his essay, "The Need for Transcendence in the Postmodern World," Vaclav Havel argues that because the current cultural conflicts far exceed those at any time of history, humanity needs a new model of coexistence and self-transcendence. As replacements for the modern scientific conception of the world, Havel proposes two postmodern possibilities of transcendence: the Anthropic Cosmological Principle in which "we are mysteriously connected to the entire universe, we are mirrored in it, just as the entire evolution of the universe is mirrored in us" and the Gaia theory. For him, both promote an awareness of not being separate from the universe and the divine; both allow for the possibility of enough self-transcendence to promote harmony and community and avoid extinction ourselves.

Does the suggestion of Gaia in these films—and the concurrent critiques of Christian motifs—mean that they are anti-Christian? The answer is yes if by "Christian" one understands certain theological tendencies aligned with the embrace of apocalyptic views and a mechanistic view of the world. A better way to understand the theological implications in these films is to ask how these films challenge us to examine the way we see the natural world and our place in it, as well as to imaginatively explore other possibilities beside the dark narratives which inexorably lead the world to its devastation. Although many Christians might see this as incompatible with their faith, Stephen Scharper argues that

> Gaia is significant because it fuses scientific insight and religious imagination in a potentially energizing and transformative way, challenging persons across a broad spectrum of disciplines to deal in an integrative fashion with the ecological crisis. Moreover, just as the Copernican revolution forced humanity to alter its self-proclaimed centrality within the universe, so may Gaia hold the potential for a similarly foundational cultural transition . . . As Lovelock himself comments, Gaia helps us to look at the world, not as a mechanistic Cartesian engine, but as an interrelated, vital, and cooperative enterprise in which interdependency rather than competition is the hallmark of life, revealing at the same time that the context in which human praxis is waged is also one of critical and unavoidable interconnectedness. Adding to the key insight of European political theology, Third World liberation theology, and feminist theology that a transformative theology must be contextual, Gaia forces us to expand our notion of context beyond social, economic, and political dimensions to include a critical planetary dimension.[11]

11. Stephen B. Scharper, "The Gaia Hypothesis: Implications for a Christian Political Theory of the Environment," *Cross Currents* 44.2 (1994) 1–7 Online: http://www.cross-currents.org/Gaia.htm/.

Delicatessen, *The City of Lost Children*, and *Alien Resurrection* seek to accomplish just such a widening of perspectives. Instead of God the Father as a distant, transcendent creator split from creation, spirit separate from matter, sacred split from the profane, male from female, these films suggest the overcoming of destructive fundamental dualisms by focusing on the complete interrelatedness of material and spiritual existence and by seeing the divine as embedded in and participating with creation. Likewise, salvation can also be seen as the ongoing promise inherent in being itself. Just as the physical body of Christ was comprised of the same stardust as the rest of the planet, and just as his human and divine natures were completely intertwined, we all share and are all called to act in accordance with the nature of the divine as expressed through the physical world.

These films also challenge the Christian tenet that post-Edenic nature is "fallen" by divine decree due to human disobedience to God. Given the stark shots of ecological devastation and examples of a very denatured humanity, it seems more likely that nature is fallen because humans made it so. The very will for mastery (which so displeased God when expressed by Adam and Eve's choice) has led to notions that human beings are apart from and above nature and that nature exists to serve them. Furthermore, it is precisely this understanding of "stewardship" that has led to such severe ecological malaise. It is particularly significant that *Delicatessen* and *The City of Lost Children* are mythically set in the post-war period, precisely the moment when it was believed that technology could rebuild the world. It is also noteworthy that *Alien Resurrection* takes place in a future where other planets are being colonized to replace Earth. What Gaia offers here is a larger planetary perspective and two important theological possibilities: that nature is God's body (as Sallie McFague has suggested), and that humans, made in the image of God, see themselves as interdependent with *all* of God's parts, participating in the rest of creation as it continues to unfold in ever greater multiplicity. Thus for Jeunet (and Caro), it seems that at the end of our apocalyptic narratives and the world as we know it lies not judgment and rapture, but rather a postmodern return to a premodern sense of being intimately intertwined with the sacredness of life itself. In other words, it is the possibility of resurrecting our basic humanity by resurrecting the divinity of the natural world and finding our place within it.

CHAPTER 2

Sorcerers and Supermen

Old Mythologies in New Guises

C. K. ROBERTSON

> There would be a day—there must be a day—when he would
> come back with a new Round Table which had no corners, just
> as the world had none—a table without boundaries between
> the nations who would sit to feast there. The hope of making it
> would lie in culture.
>
> —T. H. White, *The Once and Future King*

ARTHUR PENDRAGON WAS NOT considered a god, yet in his many and various tales he embodied the mythic ideal and introduced "mere mortals" to an extraordinary world, a world of wondrous triumph and heartwrenching tragedy, "a world which has more depths of reality to it than the daily world."[1] Science has long attempted to explain the *how* of existence, but it has been mythology, legend, and religion that have sought to explore the *why*. Not in the libraries of the intelligentsia, but around the campfire, tale after tale has been recounted of gods and goddesses, noble heroes and sinister demons, beings so far beyond us that an Asgard or Mount Olympus is required to house them, yet beings so like us that their petty wars and rivalries sound altogether familiar to human ears. "Here were worlds where we, too, could live, characters with whom we can

---

1. Madeleine L'Engle, "Foreword," in Paul F. Ford, ed., *Companion to Narnia* (New York: Collier, 1986), xiv.

identify."[2] Whether it was Beowulf, Odysseus, or the Knights of the Round Table . . . whether it is Spiderman, the X-Men, or Iron Man . . . these are iconic personages that are at once both transcendent and touchable.

The great heroes, the mythic heroes, have always reflected both what we are and what we desire to be. They both form, and are formed by, our continuous yet ever-changing culture. All that has changed is the media through which we encounter these immortals and thereby explore our understanding of self. This essay considers the legacy of the mythic hero and how that legacy reflects and informs the culture in which it has emerged, first in historical terms and then in the hero's present-day archetypal incarnations.

From Cave Paintings to the Batcave

> The first function of a living mythology . . . is to waken and maintain in the individual an experience of awe, humility, and respect.
>
> —Joseph Campbell, *The Masks of God*

> Welcome to a world of gods, myths, and dreams.
>
> —Hy Bender, *The Sandman Companion*

Although scholars have offered various definitions of *myth* through the years, it is usually assumed that it is "primarily concerned with the gods and man's relations with them."[3] The twentieth-century Oxford don and Christian apologist C. S. Lewis describes myth as a "real though unfocused gleam of divine truth falling upon human imagination."[4] The great myths of the ancient world provided for human beings lenses of imagination through which to see and understand—and relate to—their universe.[5] Through these stories, handed down from parents to children across the

2. Ibid.

3. Mark P. O. Morford and Robert J. Lenardon, *Classical Mythology* (New York: McKay, 1971), 2. Grant Morrison, "Saving Superman—Comic Book Creatives Try to Fix the Franchise." Online: http://www.comicbookmovie.com/superman_movies/news/?a=4932/.

4. Ford, *Companion*, 295.

5. The myths of old often served as reminders that life "is not accidental and meaningless but has value and purpose"; Charles Panati, *Sacred Origins of Profound Things* (New York: Penguin Arkana, 1996), vii.

generations, transcending official religious cults and organizations, the ancients were connected "not only to the gods but also to one another."[6] Within these tales listeners encountered the various deities of their culture's pantheon, figures such as the Greek Zeus and Hera, the Norse Odin and Thor, the Roman Jupiter and Venus, the Egyptian Osiris and Isis, the Babylonian Marduk. There were also the mythic heroes and demigods such as Gilgamesh and Heracles and Beowulf and Achilles. There were, of course, dark and shadowy figures in the mythic traditions, villains and beings so far beyond human comprehension that "villain" is too limiting a description for them.

From where did these mythic personages originate? The answer lies in the harsh realities of life for many ancient peoples. Some anthropologists have argued that "fear and denial of death" was the "primal motivating force" behind the creation of the various mythologies and, indeed, behind all religious tendencies."[7] In a time when the infant mortality rate was excessively high, when an individual's chances of outrunning war and disease to reach old age were slim, the concept of immortals was intriguing. The ancient myths and the characters who populated them, mirrored "the innermost stirrings of the people who created them,"[8] and gave human beings a sense of larger, greater worlds. As Joseph Campbell notes, "the paintings on cave walls and oral literature gave form to the impulse we now call religion."[9] Consider this Norse tradition of endings and new beginnings: "Deep in a wood two of humankind were left; the fire of Surtur did not touch them; they slept, and they wakened the world was green and beautifully again."[10]

Far from being totally divorced from this culture of the mythic, our Judeo-Christian ancestors took "well-known tales about Egypt's most important family of gods . . . and transformed them into stories about human

6. C. K. Robertson, *Conflict in Corinth: Redefining the System* (Studies in Biblical Literature 42; New York: Lang, 2001), 66.

7. Mark Woolverton and Roger Stern, *The Science of Superman* (New York: ibooks, 2002), 83.

8. Timothy R. Roberts et al., *Mythology: Tales of Ancient Civilizations* (New York: Barnes & Noble, 2003), 9.

9. Joseph Campbell, with Bill Moyers, *The Power of Myth* (New York: Anchor, 1991), xvii.

10. Padraic Colum, *Nordic Gods and Heroes* (New York: Dover, 1996), 282.

ancestors who founded the Hebrew nation."[11] Adam and Eve the progenitors, Noah the redeemer, Abraham the obedient patriarch and Sarah the miraculous mother, Jacob the rebel, Joseph the dreamer—all these find their roots or counterparts in the mythic culture around them, while tied intimately to the concept of the one Hebrew God over all.[12] Monotheism grew and flourished, but it could not obliterate altogether the fascination with the mythological pantheons. In port cities and urban centers of the first century CE, "where visitors and merchants were regularly passing through, it is not surprising to find a plethora of temples to gods of various origins."[13] The Apostle Paul learned this lesson the hard way as he moved through cities such as Athens, Thessalonica, and Corinth, attempting to convert faithful polytheists to "the unknown God" whom he proclaimed to them.[14] Even in the Christian communities Paul established, he recognized that "weaker" members had "become accustomed to idols" that represented the Greco-Roman deities with which their culture was saturated.[15] In the town of Lystra Paul himself was mistaken by some overly zealous residents as being Hermes, the messenger of the Greek gods, even as his companion Barnabas was understood to be Zeus, king of the Olympian pantheon: "The gods have come down to us in human form!"[16] Against all odds, Paul and companions like Barnabas made great headway with the new faith, and thanks to their foundation-laying and the courage shown in subsequent generations by Christian martyrs, idols were destroyed and pantheons of deities were superceded by the one invisible God.

However, in the centuries that followed the triumph of Christianity as the religion of the empire, "the images crept back, appearing under new names," so that "much of the pagan religion that their forefathers

11. Gary Greenberg, *101 Myths of the Bible: How Ancient Scribes Invented Biblical History* (Naperville, IL: Sourcebooks, 2000), 297.

12. It has been argued that Jewish eschatology, in fact, was heavily "influenced by Persian and Babylonian myths, in which battles between gods and demons would mark the end of earthly time" (cf. Panati, *Sacred Origins,* 381).

13. Robertson, *Conflict,* 67. Indeed, as noted by the author, "religion permeated all of life in the first-century empire."

14. Acts of the Apostles 17:23.

15. Paul's 1 Corinthians 8:7.

16. Acts of the Apostles 14:11–12. For more on the impact of Paul and Barnabas, see C. K. Robertson, *Conversations with Scripture: The Acts of the Apostles* (Anglican Association of Biblical Scholars Study Series; Harrisburg, PA: Morehouse, 2010).

had destroyed . . . was insensibly being restored."[17] In the Christendom of medieval Europe, reverence was given not to the old pagan deities but to saints—canonized heroes who became a curious blend of human and demigod, and who in many ways fulfilled the roles once held in pre-Christian times by the "*lares et penates,* little gods of house and home, whom pious people would venerate."[18] Mary, the mother of Jesus, evolved in popular imagination from doubting mother in Mark's gospel to faithful believer in Acts to *theotōkos* in the fourth-century Council of Ephesus to the immaculate and ever-blessed Virgin Mother in medieval times and beyond.[19] Here, too, it is possible to see congruity, however unintended, with pre-Christian mythological/religious figures such as the Great Mother of Eleusis. Underneath the theological arguments for the development of Mary as an almost goddess figure in Christianity is a very basic need for people for whom "the world can be a frightening place" to cling to "the image of a nourishing, nurturing mother."[20]

Theologians and scholars of our time can speak condescendingly of the "naïve polytheistic nature of religion of the simple people,"[21] but the fact remains that popular religious thought now, as in the past, remains something of a blend of institutional dogma and tall tales, codified commandments and fanciful fables. When asked about the existence of angels, seven out of ten Americans respond with "an unhesitant, unembarrassed, unequivocal yes."[22] If asked further to define or describe these heavenly beings, respondents often reply with answers developed more from childhood stories and Hollywood movies than from scriptural commentaries or

17. E. R. Chamberlin, *The Bad Popes* (New York: Barnes & Noble, 1993), 11.

18. Joseph F. Kelly, *The World of the Early Christians* (Collegeville, MN: Liturgical, 1997), 86.

19. It is interesting to note that the only two occurrences of dogmatic statements made via papal infallibility both concern the mother of Jesus, the first regarding the doctrine of Mary's immaculate conception (a retroactive recognition of an earlier statement immediately after the infallibility doctrine was established at the First Vatican Council in the late nineteenth century), and the second involving the assumption of Mary in bodily form into heaven without dying (made in 1954). The connection between the Vatican's reaffirmations of Mary's unique role in Christian faith and modernist challenges to traditional understandings of societal roles of women has been argued in many and various venues and need not be explored here.

20. Kelly, *The World,* 84.

21. Martin Hengel, *Judaism and Hellenism* (trans. John Bowden; 1974; reprinted, Eugene, OR: Wipf & Stock, 2003), 261.

22. Panati, *Sacred Origins,* 59.

denominational doctrines. Modern storytellers—authors and screenwriters—have understood this better than many religious leaders, and thereby tapped into the seemingly ageless human spirit of "campfire mythology." Roman Catholic J. R. R. Tolkien grasped this, and provided a mythology for Britain, a vision of Middle-Earth that has since captured the attention and praise of a vast number of readers and moviegoers alike. His fellow "Inkling," Anglican C. S. Lewis, similarly produced a mythological world in his Chronicles of Narnia, culminating with a final book that "has all the quality of the 'twilight of the gods,'"[23] echoing the "clear delineations of good and evil, light and dark" found in the ancient Norse world.[24] Tolkien and Lewis lived in a time that had already witnessed the "War to End All Wars," and were now witnessing the rise of a man named Hitler. In America, as in England, people were hungry for heroes like the ancient deities of Mount Olympus.[25] New myths—and new mythmakers—were needed. They came in a most unlikely form, in newsstand "funny books" that only cost a dime.

Four-Color Icons

> They're the successors to the stories that once came down from the hoe-down and the campfire and the wandering bard.
>
> —Elliot S. Maggin, "The New Bards," *Kingdom Come*

> The potency of the picture story is not a matter of modern theory but of anciently established truth.
>
> —William Moulton Marston, creator of *Wonder Woman*

The average comic book around 1938 "measured about 7 1/4 by 10 1/4 inches, averaged sixty-four pages in length, was glisteningly processed in four colors on the cover, and flatly and indifferently colored on the

---

23. Ford, *Companion*, xxxiv. Ford further speaks of "the proliferation of mythological themes and figures in the *Chronicles*" noting that this reflects Lewis's own "lifelong immersion in the wonders of mythology" (295).

24. Roberts et al., *Mythology*, 126. Edward Hunt notes that most people today, like the ancients, "need to view the world in terms of right and wrong, good and evil . . . There is right, there is wrong, and this matters" (Hunt, "Good and Evil in the Screenwriter or Filmmaker's Mind," *Screentalk* 3:4 [2003] 72–75), 75.

25. Mike Conroy, *500 Great Comic Book Action Heroes* (New York: Barron's, 2002), 15.

inside, if colored at all."[26] In their earliest forms, as bastardized children of America's beloved newspaper comic strips, comic books were little more than "reprint digests of the more popular strips, uprooted from their newspaper homes and forced, not without violence and scissoring, between a pair of cheap glossy covers."[27] From such inauspicious beginnings, comic books have evolved, matured, and grown in sophistication as well as price. Consider, for example, that *Action Comics* # 1, containing the first appearance of Superman, cost the local school kid ten cents. Although this was not an inconsequential amount in 1938, it is hardly worth comparing to the price tags of today's comics, with cover prices ranging from $2.50 for average comics to $24.95 for painted, hardcover "graphic novels." Then, of course, there is the back market, not the *black* market, though the money exchanging hands may appear to mirror some illegal trading. The aforementioned issue of *Action Comics* # 1, in near mint condition, has been listed for hundreds of thousands of dollars, not a shabby markup for a ten-cent magazine! Even by the time America entered the Second World War, comic books had "cemented their place in American pop culture . . . with 143 titles on stands and 50 million readers per month."[28]

Cynics may ask, "Why?" Dr. William Moulton Marston, the controversial creator of Wonder Woman, noted in 1943 how the "addiction" of comic book reading "puzzled" professional educators.[29] Wartime kids, however, understood the attraction, and their dimes paid the meager wages of a small, committed group of writers and artists. In a 1940 article appropriately titled "Don't Laugh at the Comics," Marston asserted: "The comics sections of Sunday newspapers long ago became the Sabbath-day bible of more than 100,000 children [and] now the comics magazines have become their weekday textbooks."[30] No one in Marston's time could have

---

26. Jules Feiffer, *The Great Comic Book Heroes* (Seattle: Fantagraphics, 2003), 5.

27. Michael Chabon, *The Amazing Adventures of Kavalier & Clay: A Novel* (New York: Picador, 2000), 75.

28. Jordan Raphael and Tom Spurgeon, *Stan Lee and the Rise and Fall of the American Comic Book* (Chicago: Chicago Review Press, 2003), 28.

29. From an article by William Moulton Marston in a 1943 issue of *The American Scholar,* cited in Les Daniels et al., *Wonder Woman: The Complete History* (San Francisco: Chronicle, 2000), 11. The controversy around Marston involved his rather unique home life as well as his apparent predilection for bondage, as seen again and again in the stories he told of Wonder Woman.

30. William Moulton Marston, "Don't Laugh at the Comics." *The Family Circle* (October 25, 1940), 10.

foreseen the fortunes that one day would be won and lost in comic books, but readers recognized something in the four-color magazines that made their imaginations soar. A man pressing forward, dressed in red and blue, holding a car above his head even as the mere mortals around him run and scream in terror. Thus, the 1938 cover of *Action Comics* # 1 heralded the arrival of the greatest comic book hero of all. While a real-life Hitler was spouting deadly propaganda about a race of supermen, here was a Superman of a different vein. He was "the ultimate embodiment of all childhood dreams of strength and power,"[31] yet it soon became clear that "the best in humanity [was] present in him as well."[32] Although his earliest appearances at times depicted a callous and even cruel side to Superman, his creators quickly saw that the greatest potential of the hero's character lay in his goodness. A transition occurred early in Siegel and Schuster's character, as he moved from being something akin to a pulp hero like Doc Savage to being the embodiment of "truth and justice," or, as comic book writer Grant Morrison states, "the American Christ."[33] Interestingly, even as his human kindness grew, so did his superhuman abilities. Once able to "leap tall buildings in a single bound," soon this god among humans was flying across the world. Here is a true mythic hero, both good and great!

Barely a year after the advent of Superman, *Detective Comics* # 27 introduced the Man of Steel's dark counterpart, an avenger of the night initially called "The Bat-Man." If Superman was the "champion, the inspiration," then Batman was "the bogeyman."[34] He was, however, a bogeyman on the side of good, feared primarily by "cowardly and superstitious" criminals such as the one who had gunned down his parents before his young eyes. Although it became quickly apparent that Superman needed to lose some of his more vicious personality traits seen in the earliest issues of *Action Comics* (such as nonchalantly throwing a man to his apparent death), Batman's character was wedded to the shadows.[35] Superman was draped in primary colors, Batman in grey and black. If Superman and his beloved Metropolis belong to the day, then Batman and his Gotham City very much belong to the night. "Batman represents

31. Ibid.

32. Woolverton and Stern, *The Science,* 256.

33. Grant Morrison, *Wizard* #143 (2003) 180.

34. *Batman and Superman* # 1 (New York: DC Comics, 2003), 3.

35. "Batman inhabited a world where no one, no matter the time of day, cast anything but long shadows—seen from *weird* perspectives" (Feiffer, *Great Comic Book,* 28).

what Superman, despite his name, can never be—the ultimate expression of human perfection in mind and body, the true 'Superman.'"[36] And yet what is in some ways most remarkable is the fact that both dwelt in the same literary universe. Without knowing it, the company that would one day become DC Comics had created the first two archetypal figures in its pantheon. Others, most notably Marston's own Wonder Woman, followed close behind. Competing publishers created iconic figures of their own, such as Captain America.

Similar to the pulp magazines that preceded them, comic books were soon full of colorful heroes and macabre villains.[37] However, though the new comic book heroes were in some way the progeny of pulp figures like Doc Savage and the Shadow, they soon overshadowed their literary antecedents, even as the Greek gods of Mount Olympus superceded their progenitors, the Titans. Why was this? Marvel Comics legend Stan Lee suggests that the difference might be one of timing, or it could be that the pulp heroes simply were not "super enough." They were, as Lee notes, "sort of one-note characters."[38] Comic book heroes quickly became more.

Parents who dismissed comics as "funny books" failed to understand the impact of the Depression and World War II—and, later, the Bomb—on the minds of the young. The adults could not perceive the paradox of a "psychological and in-depth dossier for characters in stories that would be read predominantly by kids."[39] For countless young boys like Joe Kavalier in Michael Chabon's coming-of-age novel, *The Amazing Adventures of Kavalier & Clay*, comics served to transfigure "their insecurities and delusions, their wishes and their doubts, their public educations

36. C. K. Robertson, "The True Übermensch: Batman as Humanistic Myth," in B. J. Oropeza, ed., *The Gospel according to Superheroes: Religion and Popular Culture* (New York: Lang, 2007), 84.

37. Like the comics that followed them, the pulp magazines of the early twentieth century "provided inexpensive entertainment for the masses who could not afford to buy pricey clothbound books"; Stan Lee and George Mair, *Excelsior! The Amazing Life of Stan Lee* (New York: Simon & Schuster, 2002), 23.

38. This and subsequent quotations from Stan Lee come from a personal interview, dated October 20, 2003.

39. Cf. Kimberly Shane O'Hara, "James Schamus Creates Ang Lee's Hulk," *Screentalk* 3 4 (2003) 40–45, 42: "Kids are more than capable when using materials and images available to them, and understandably, to process very interesting and complex psychological narratives."

and their sexual perversions, into something that only the most purblind of societies would have denied the status of art."[40]

Indeed, on this final point, sexual tension has played a part in the superhero genre from its inception. Unlike typical human relations, however, in the world of these new deities interpersonal issues took on unusual dimensions. For example, consider the unique love triangle involving Lois Lane, Clark Kent, and Superman, a theme that has been played out countless times by other heroes and their alter egos. As Lois pines for the heroic Man of Steel, Clark attempts to win her love in his more lackluster, wimpish guise of "mild mannered reporter," even as he secretly winks at the reader who knows what really lurks behind the suit and thick-rimmed glasses. There were echoes here of the mythic accounts of Zeus and Dionysus descending from celestial heights to meet (and bed) women while disguised as mere mortals. Although few ancients questioned how demigods such as Heracles (Hercules) could be the product of these divine-human liaisons, today's more sophisticated devotees debate whether Lois Lane could ever truly "handle" the Kryptonian physiology of her super paramour.[41]

Of course, a comic book character does not have to hail from another planet to be divinely "endowed," as is evident in the glaringly unrealistic physical dimensions of most female superheroes today, dimensions that are only accentuated by the creative costumes in which such characters have been placed from comics' earliest days. From earliest days, Black Canary had fanboys daydreaming of beautiful women in fishnets. The ultimate marriage of superheroes and sexuality is found in Stan Lee's most recent creation, *Stripperella*, a titillating late-night television series whose animated star is voiced, appropriately, by former *Baywatch* buxom beauty Pamela Anderson. Next to this "stripper by night, superhero by later that night," old-time goddesses like Aphrodite appear downright frumpy! As a young Robin is told by his mentor after noticing Wonder Woman's customary lack of clothing in the freezing temperatures of the Arctic in a now-classic Superman tale by Alan Moore: "Think clean thoughts, chum." Although the innuendoes are more blatant now, they were there from the beginning of comic books.

---

40. Chabon, *Kavalier & Clay*, 575.

41. Consider this and other similarly cynical queries in Kevin Smith's various films.

More than anything else, however, what separated the comic book archetypal heroes from their pulp magazine antecedents was adaptability. As the times changed, so did the comic archetypes, while at the same time staying true to their mythic roots. Superman, Batman, Wonder Woman, Captain America—the four-color heroes who have lasted through the years have remained recognizable in terms of their core elements, yet have evolved in many and sundry ways. Whenever the characters did stray too far from their essence—Batman of the 1950s and 1960s is an excellent example—a creative team would find a way to return them to greatness. Regarding the move in the mid-1990s to give Superman long hair, new powers, and a different costume, comic book painter Alex Ross argues for the iconic nature of the hero: "Superman should never reflect any fashionable trend or other affectation of a specific era . . . he is beyond that; he is out of time."[42] In short, as Batman scholar Will Brooker states, the archetypal characters' positions as "cultural icons" is due to "the extent that [they] can adapt within key parameters."[43]

In this sense, the primary superheroes resemble Arthur Rex, that figure who is more than human yet less than a god, a messiah-type legend of popular culture who has been viewed again and again with fresh eyes. From Mallory's *Le Morte d'Arthur* to T. H. White's *The Once and Future King* to Marion Zimmer Bradley's *The Mists of Avalon*, not to mention Boorman's film and Disney's cartoon, Arthur has been reinterpreted by each generation while remaining ever . . . Arthur. (As a passing note, it is little wonder that the great king would eventually work his way into the four-color medium. In 1986, when DC published the first comic book "maxi-series"—twelve issues printed on high-quality paper encompassing a unified story with a futuristic setting and adult themes—the subject of the series was not Superman or Batman, but their mythic ancestor, in a series appropriately entitled *Camelot 3000*.)[44]

42. From Chip Kidd and Geoff Spear, *Mythology: The DC Comics Art of Alex Ross* (New York: Pantheon, 2003), no page numbers listed.

43. Will Brooker, *Batman Unmasked: Analyzing a Cultural Icon* (New York: Continuum, 2001), 40.

44. Only a few years later, the myth of Arthur and the world of comic books collided yet again, this time in the form of two bestselling novels, *Knight Life* and *One Knight Only*, penned by Peter David, a fan-favorite comic-book writer with a record-setting run of consecutive issues on *The Incredible Hulk*.

Arthur has come a long way. So, too, have superheroes. Comic book versions of the biblical stories have never truly caught on. The Apostle Paul today might have as much trouble catching the attention of kids weaned on the family of Superman as he did with the Greeks who preferred Zeus and Hermes to his invisible God. Like Zeus, like Hercules, like Arthur, the steely-eyed, square-jawed, and gaudily attired heroes of comic books have gained an important place in our cultural imagination precisely because they are so highly visible, recognizable, and, ultimately, relatable. Whereas God can appear distant, these marvels are very much present. In many ways, they are the new household gods.

The Cult of the Supermen

The next century's task will be to rediscover its gods.

—André Malraux

Heroes are dangerous because we like them too much.

—Alan Moore

Although the last analogy may appear at first glance to be something of a stretch—after all, no one has created an official Cult of Superman—the fact is that there are indeed several ways in which the primary super-heroes fulfill a role not unlike that of ancient mythological characters. In an extended interview with Bill Moyers, Joseph Campbell notes the way in which myths are learned by human beings in childhood, only to be comprehended and appropriated at far deeper levels in adulthood.[45] Commenting on the difference between much of organized religion and a living mythology, Campbell asserts: "Our time has changed so fast that what was proper fifty years ago is not proper today . . . The old-time religion belongs to another age, another people, another set of human values, another universe . . . Our kids lose their faith in the religions that were taught to them."[46]

It is not insignificant that the sharp criticism and decline of comic books in the 1950s corresponded with a period of record-high church attendance by Americans. It was as if the four-color heroes were somehow antithetical to the Judeo-Christian beliefs of "God-fearing Americans." At

45. Campbell and Moyers, *Power of Myth*, 183.
46. Ibid., 16.

least, this is what Dr. Fredric Wertham insisted in a campaign that almost destroyed the comic book industry altogether. His 1954 book, *Seduction of the Innocent*, made several allegations against comic books in general and their chief iconic personages in particular. According to Wertham, the relationship between the Dynamic Duo, Batman and Robin, was "clearly" homosexual. Not surprisingly, Wonder Woman was for Wertham "the lesbian counterpart of Batman."[47] The doomsayer could find no such sexual accusations to make against Superman and instead came up with one that is far more fascinating . . . and insidious. On a deep psychological level, Wertham asserts, this visitor from another world in some way "undermines the authority and dignity of the ordinary man and woman in the minds of children."[48]

In this instance, perhaps Wertham was not so far from the truth. The fact is that for the two young Jewish boys who created the Man of Steel, the character represented something greater in themselves that was hidden, perhaps even repressed by the Protestant Christian American culture in which they lived. On so many levels, they were both Clark Kents, quiet "mild-mannered" reporters or observers of all the action that was going on around them, while hiding the Superman within. There is indeed something surprisingly subversive in their creation, a hero bearing the name of an Aryan myth that a madman an ocean away used to torture and kill young Jewish boys just like themselves. Superman himself would be adopted as an American symbol of patriotism and good citizenship in the war against Nazi fascism. In a time when so many felt so helpless against an evil that seemed so great, people were "hungry" for heroes from on high, even fictional ones; "Superman filled that need."[49] However, later, in the much chillier years of a war against "godless" Communism, it could be argued that a nation of Clark Kents was what Wertham and others like him truly desired. In a time when nationalism and religiosity appeared inextricably linked, when good children—Clark Kents— went to church, said their prayers, and obeyed their elders without question, Superman and the rest of his four-color pantheon might well have challenged the established order, had they not hidden their true identities behind facile

---

47. Fredric Wertham, *Seduction of the Innocent* (1954), cited in Les Daniels, *DC Comics: A Celebration of the World's Favorite Comic Book Heroes* (New York: Billboard, 1995), 114.

48. Ibid.

49. Conroy, *500 Great Comic Book Action Heroes*, 15.

tales of Gold Kryptonite, flying horses, and Bat-Mites. The majority of comic gods died in the Twilight of the 1950s, but Superman's (as well as Batman's and Wonder Woman's) adaptability allowed him to hide behind the Clark Kent guise of quiet conformity. To all, that is, but Wertham.

It has already been noted that in Christianity's earliest days, Paul and his fellow evangelist-apostles faced an enormous challenge in converting ordinary Greeks and Romans to the notion of a single invisible Deity who is over all. The Greeks "had long been ready to accept alien forms of the divine into their pantheon,"[50] but Paul and his colleagues were demanding a far more singular allegiance to a God that could not be seen. By the time of the Emperor Constantine's legalization of the faith in the 300s, Christianity faced the enormous obstacle of a reluctance on the part of average citizens to let go totally of gods and goddesses with whom they had a far more personal connection than with a God whose name was unknown to them and whose visage was not permitted to be set in stone or on canvas. Church historian Joseph Kelly notes the importance of "personalism" in ancient paganism. Ritual and visibility, in the form of "idols," helped make the spirituality and mythology that Paul confronted so familiar to so many. Ordinary people—powerless in an Empire in which decisions were made, taxes levied, and laws enacted without their involvement— found that initiation into so-called mystery religions made them feel "reborn, younger, stronger, more secure, and better able to face the world."[51]   RELIGION

As noted above, the Apostle Paul was keen to disassociate himself and his colleague Barnabas from the idolatry of the Lystrans in Acts 14. They could not deny, however, the influence of habitual immersion in "visible religion." The powerful combination of ritual and visibility was not lost on the apostles' successors in the medieval Church of both West and East. Iconography flourished as an integral part of public liturgy and private devotion in Orthodoxy, even as the pre-Reformation Roman Church represented the gospel and its heroes in stained glass, sculpture, and paintings. The extent to which many Christians clung to images in the face of extreme Reformed Protestantism is an indicator of the importance of "visible religion." To any today who dare to doubt the power of graphic storytelling, let them gaze upon the magnificence of Michelangelo's ceiling in the Sistine Chapel!

50. Hengel, *Judaism and Hellenism*, 266.
51. Kelly, *World*, 83.

In a similar way, in more recent years, fantasy author Madeleine L'Engle has remarked that behind the writing and, presumably, reading of fantasy works is an attempt to touch something of "particular personal concern."[52] This emphasis on the personal, on belonging, on the inherent meaning of an individual's life, was and is an attractive draw for seekers, especially those who feel they do not fit in elsewhere. Thus, Kelly speaks of the "obvious" appeal of mystery religions and mythological cults to "the socially marginalized" of the first century.[53] This understanding appears to resonate with diehard comic book readers, who describe themselves in seemingly denigrating fashion as "fanboys" or "comic geeks." Even Stan Lee's more positive vocabulary of "true believers" still emphasizes that comics fandom is a world of initiates set apart from others. What, then, happens when the myths of the insiders try to find their place in mainstream culture?

Marvelous Myths

> I really wasn't making an attempt at creating a mythology. I was just trying to write appealing stories about interesting characters with interesting powers. The mythology just seemed to develop on its own.
>
> —Stan Lee, in a personal interview

> I feel like I'm talking to Jesus here.
>
> —A fan, upon meeting Stan Lee

Stan Lee is arguably comics' most recognizable figure and the man who most visibly helped integrate the world of superheroes with the world of mainstream popular culture. Although nominally Jewish, Lee—born Stanley Lieber—co-created a virtual pantheon all his own for DC's chief competitor, Marvel Comics, while giving his creations a depth and complexity that set them apart from their longstanding rival. "Gone were the good cops and solid citizens of DC Comics' Main Street America, replaced by grotesque angels and sympathetic devils."[54] Marvel had entered the comic book scene almost at its inception. Martin Goodwin, a

---

52. L'Engle, "Foreword," xiii.

53. Kelly, *World*, 83.

54. Ibid., 95–96.

pulp magazine publisher, saw the profits to be made in comics and, thus, Timely Comics was born. With the company's first issue, it immediately was made clear that Timely's (later Marvel's) heroes were not going to be carbon copies of Superman. As startling an impression as Superman lifting a car overhead had been, as ominous an appearance as the Bat-Man swinging through the sky with a terrified criminal under his arm, the cover of *Marvel Comics # 1* (dated October 1939) offered readers an even more daring image. Bursting out of an iron tank through a still melting hole, a menacing-looking flame creature—complete with pointed ears, arched eyebrows, grim smile, and claw-like fingers—leapt toward a clearly frightened man shooting bullets that merely melted into nothingness as they hit their impervious target.[55]

Was this "Human Torch" a hero . . . or a menace? Listed simply as one of several original characters found within that issue's pages, here was a creature whose appearance and actions hardly made him an obvious hero. In fact, another character introduced in *Marvel # 1* would be equally complex, Bill Everett's creation, the Sub-Mariner. It was not surprising to find these two "heroes" battling each other, with innocent citizens around them taking the brunt of their primal battles. If Superman was in some way a "stand-in for Christ,"[56] then these Elementals were much more like the all too human and often petty mythological deities of Olympus and Asgard. It is true that with the coming of the company's third headliner in 1941, Joe Simon and Jack Kirby's Captain America, Timely Comics was able to join the country in a more black-and-white approach to heroism. Inasmuch as the mythological models we create have to be "appropriate to the time" in which we live,[57] it is not surprising to find that Namor and the Torch soon ceased trading blows with one another to join Cap and the nation in combating the Nazi threat. Stan Lee, a young man employed by Goodman in those earliest years, worked and watched and learned. "I was always questioning things," Lee admits.[58] It would take another two decades, however, along with an arguably more sophisticated and ambivalent readership, before Lee's questioning spirit and those roots of Marvel complexity would combine to form a pantheon of unforgettable figures.

55. Conroy, *500 Great Comic Book Action Heroes,* 16.

56. From Kidd and Spear, *Mythology,* no page numbers listed.

57. Campbell and Moyers, *Power of Myth,* 16.

58. Stan Lee, in a private interview, October 20, 2003.

To put it more succinctly, using Lee's own words from the introductory words of *The Avengers*, "And there came a day unlike any other . . ."

As the 1960s exploded in the minds of America's youth, "marvelous" new four-color characters appeared—one after another in glorious majesty—written by Lee and brought to dynamic life by the great Kirby or the more reclusive, yet equally amazing Steve Ditko. The Fantastic Four, Hulk, Thor, Spider-Man, Doctor Strange, Daredevil, Ant Man and the Wasp, Iron Man, the X-Men—these strange new heroes caught on with a new generation of American comic book readers, mirroring the national and personal tumults that were everywhere. Once upon a time, ancient peoples stood by as helpless spectators before creative and destructive forces far beyond their control or even their comprehension. Spectators became narrators as they related tales of epic mythological battles between "the Giants who would have destroyed the world and the race of men, and the gods who would have protected the race of men and would have made the world more beautiful."[59] In a similar way, the world following World War II and the advent of the Atomic Age, was "a frightening place."[60] American youths watched in confusion while their parents, members of that "greatest generation" who had faced the Nazis head-on, now were busy "digging holes in their backyards to save themselves from potential Russian A-bombs."[61]

Some among the baby boomers did respond to the anxieties all around them by turning to the very things against which Dr. Wertham had once warned: promiscuous sex and illicit drug use. Others, however, found in the world of comic books not temptation to such vices, but rather a different kind of escapism, solace in the form of relatable gods. It had been "a long road from the patriotic trust and respect for the established order at the close of World War II,"[62] but comics somehow kept pace with the ever changing society in which they were read and discussed. Superman, Batman, Wonder Woman, and a new generation of DC heroes, collectively known as the Justice League of America, continued to hold an iconic place in American culture, but it was Marvel Comics who, in the 1960s, offered "the combination of a common need/interest and a focal

---

59. Colum, *Nordic Gods*, 6.

60. Kelly, *World*, 84.

61. Lee and Mair, *Excelsior!*, 79.

62. John W. Gamble, "When East Meets West: The Rise of Meditation," in C. K. Robertson, ed., *Religion as Entertainment* (New York: Lang, 2002), 86.

individual [Stan the Man himself] that could connect different persons through a relational network."[63]

Although professional rivals, Marvel and DC, the "Distinguished Competition," both profited by the networking skills and Bullpen chats of Lee. Soon, comics fandom came into its own and countless independent yet interconnected cell groups of fans began conversations about things both profound and pedestrian, philosophical and political, always in the context of heroes who were as human in their personal struggles as they were mighty in their power. When he was not swinging through the Manhattan skyline, Peter Parker was constantly trying to keep a job or get a girlfriend. Similarly, Ben Grimm, the rock-encrusted member of the Fantastic Four known appropriately as the Thing, joked and scrapped simply to keep himself from falling into despair over his seemingly eternal plight. Superman and Batman had always had to wrestle with the struggles that came with their secret identities, but Marvel heroes found their powers to be a curse more than a blessing. With the long-standing DC heroes, great power and great responsibility seemed to come hand in hand. With Marvel characters, however, any lessons that were learned always appeared to be learned the hard way. If these were modern-day deities, they were appropriate ones for the 1960s, very human and far from perfect. Of all of Lee's creations, four deserve special mention, inasmuch as they directly involve mythological or supernatural themes. These characters are the Mighty Thor, Dr. Strange, the Silver Surfer, and Galactus, Devourer of Planets.

Lee and Kirby had enjoyed great success already with the Fantastic Four and the Hulk. These were concepts grounded in the world of science, with characters whose extraordinary powers resulted from exposure to cosmic rays and gamma radiation. With the FF's Thing, the result was a man trapped in the body of a monster; with the Hulk, the result was a man who actually became a monster, the mightiest mortal to walk the earth. What could possibly top that? Suddenly, the Mighty Thor appeared! For Kirby, a mythology buff, Thor was a delight. Lee, however, is quick to deny any intentional desire at the time to "say anything deep or meaningful" about mythological characters like the Norse god of thunder. "I had done so many superheroes with super powers that I was just trying to think of a different kind of superhero, and thought it would be fun to try a god

63. Robertson, *Conflict*, 67.

from mythology."[64] Indeed, Lee goes on to assert that the only reason for choosing a *Norse* deity is the fact that "people were more familiar with the Greek and Roman gods and I wanted my strip to seem really new." This may well be true, but the choice of Thor and his Asgardian comrades over, for instance, Zeus and the Olympian deities, was not insignificant given the period in which Lee and Kirby were working. A "characteristic of the Norse canon that differentiates it from practically any other ancient canon is its inherent bleakness . . . The most a Norseman could aspire to was to die fighting against the world's evils."[65] Many readers in the 1960s, particularly as the decade wore on, must have felt a similar degree of doomed heroism. It might have appeared as if Ragnarok was only a thunderclap away. Unsurprisingly, Lee's Thor, Odin, Loki, and company, though sharing the names and basic themes of the ancient Norse deities, often did "not correspond to the literary exemplars."[66] In fact, it can be argued that as the stories progressed, Thor and his mythological clan in the Marvel universe actually appeared more impressive and infinitely more interesting than their ancient namesakes. The "exaggerated Elizabethan dialogue" given to Thor by Lee made him appear larger than life and outside the normal mortal realm.[67] Indeed, Lee "liked rearranging typical sentence structure to give it more drama and replicate the English used in days of yore, particularly Biblical times."[68] Despite Jules Feiffer's assertion that "once you've made a man super, you've plotted him out of believable conflicts,"[69] Thor's fabled powers, in conjunction with the exalted language that flowed from his mouth, simply demanded conflicts of divine proportions, including war in Asgard itself! To readers tired of a real-life conflict in Southeast Asia, such tales were escapism at its best.

Doctor Strange touched readers on a very different level, tapping less into the mythological and more into the mystical and supernatural.

64. From a private interview, October 20, 2003.

65. Roberts et al., *Mythology,* 125–26.

66. Kelly, *World,* 94.

67. Raphael and Spurgeon, *Stan Lee,* 4.

68. Craig Shutt, *Baby Boomer Comics* (Iola, WI: Krause, 2003), 42. Shutt, "Mr. Silver Age," notes that Lee's protégé, a former English teacher named Roy Thomas, adopted a similar usage of dramatic phraseology. Specific examples of titles from consecutive issues of a comic that Thomas took over from Lee, *The X-Men,* include "And None Shall Survive" (#17), "If Iceman Should Fail (#18), "Lo, Now Shall Appear the Mimic" (#19), "I, Lucifer" (#20), and "From Whence Comes Dominus" (#21).

69. Feiffer, *Great Comic Book Heroes,* 15.

To a generation that was growing increasingly disenchanted with organized religion while turning instead to spiritualism of a far different and
more esoteric kind,[70] Dr. Strange was a welcome addition to the growing marvel pantheon of heroes. Stephen Strange, "Master of the Mystic
Arts," was brought to life by Lee and Spider-Man co-creator Steve Ditko.
Here was a seemingly omniscient character who used magic as a weapon
in his battles against evil. With this hero, Lee tried to "keep everything
mystical." Thus, the foes Dr. Strange fought were not just "ordinary gang-
sters or war mongers," but rather "demonic opponents" like the devilish
Dormammu.[71] Lee filled the world of Dr. Strange with "gibberish totems,
secret idols, and heathen gods called on in spells that amused readers
with their tongue-twisting quality without going so far as to spoil the
moody atmosphere provided by Ditko's art."[72] If Thor's language was
exalted and godlike, then Stephen Strange's self-expression simply con-
firmed that this character was not fully on our plane of existence: "For
many can be the forms, and many the faces, of The Man Called Doctor
Strange!"[73] It is little wonder that some have claimed that Strange was
"aptly named."[74] Others, however, experimenting with both substances
and esoterica, might have found themselves similarly struggling to be
understood by establishment types.

The Silver Surfer, arguably Lee's personal favorite of the characters he
co-created, was born out of the pages of Fantastic Four #48. Initially a mysterious herald from the stars imbued with the "power cosmic," the Surfer
arrived on earth with ominous news of the coming of Galactus, Devourer
of Worlds. After being shown the paradoxical wonder of humanity by the
Thing's blind girlfriend, Alicia Masters, the Surfer eventually turned on
his godlike master, taking his place beside the humans and earning for
his actions a seemingly eternal exile. The character was popular enough
to graduate to his own title, where Lee revealed in much greater detail the
tragic background of this noble hero, as Norrin Radd willingly gave up his
freedom and mortal life to save his home planet and the woman he loved.
Consciously or not, Lee had "taken a character with godlike abilities" and

70. Gamble, "When East Meets West."

71. From a private interview, October 20, 2003.

72. Raphael and Spurgeon, *Stan Lee*, 104. Kelly, *World*, notes our "fascination" with
the apparent ability of the magician "to be able to overcome the laws of nature" (88).

73. *Dr. Strange* #177 (February 1969), 13–14.

74. Cf. Shutt, *Baby Boomer Comics*, 127, which describes the good doctor as "bottom-
line strange."

recast him in "traditional humanist fashion."[75] Lee insists that "the only religious/philosophical themes I tried to insert in anything I wrote could be summed up in the one code I've always tried to live by: 'Do unto others as you'd have others do unto you.'"[76] Perhaps more than any other Marvel hero, it was the extraterrestrial Surfer—not unlike Steven Spielberg's later cinematic creation, ET—that allowed Lee the greatest vehicle for sharing his optimistic, humanistic views. More than Superman, here is a messiah who casts his lot with a flawed humanity against a cruel, heartless god.

In calling Galactus a god, however, it must quickly be said that Lee himself categorically denies such a definition. "I did not really think of Galactus as a god. He was just so much more powerful than anyone else that he seemed to have the status of some sort of demigod. . . . I was always trying to top myself in the creation of villains, and I wanted Galactus to be as powerful as possible."[77] This may well be true, but there are certainly mythic resonances in the clash between seemingly helpless humanity (represented by Reed Richards) and the nigh-omnipotent Galactus. Intentionally or otherwise, Stan Lee had taken the story of Prometheus and made him—made humanity—the winner.

Of course, an elaborate origin story has since grown up around the "Devourer of Planets," but it is in Galactus's initial appearance that we see the greatest evidence of a "new mythology" being created in the world of comics. This mythology is humanistic, holding an inherent suspicion (though not necessarily outright rejection) of much of organized religion while at the same time clinging to the hope of an intrinsic goodness and shared wisdom in humankind. In many ways, then, Galactus can be said to represent a visual image of the worst kind of religion: Intolerant, demanding, unfeeling. Counterbalancing such an image is faith in the ever-evolving development of humankind, personified in Reed Richards, as well as recognition of humans' inherent nobility by the repentant, compassionate Surfer. In a three-issue tale that raised the bar for comic book scope and profundity, Lee and Kirby gave to comic book readers of the 1960s a mythology that humanized cosmic deities while lifting up humanity. Two decades later, the myth-making work of comic creators would begin to reach a much larger audience.

75. Raphael and Spurgeon, *Stan Lee*, 123.
76. From a private interview, October 20, 2003.
77. Ibid.

Marvelous Movies

The world of comics was a form of visual shorthand.

—Jules Feiffer, *The Great Comic Book Heroes*

Comic books litter the offices of Hollywood.

—Gerard Jones and Will Jacobs, *The Comic Book Heroes*

As comics' most recognizable figure, Stan Lee was the obvious choice to bring the four-color heroes to Hollywood . . . and that is exactly what he attempted to do. Unfortunately, Lee's, and comicdom's, best efforts were lost on the Dream Factory. There were, of course, several low-budget movies with B-list actors and directors involved: Spiderman, Captain America, the Punisher all suffered an ignoble fate they did not deserve, as the noncomics public simply shook their heads and laughed.[78] It actually started in the 1960s, with Batman's "immersion in late 1960s culture" through the ABC television series starring Adam West and Burt Ward.[79] Invariably dismissed as "camp" by comic book fans, the show is a great example of how a four-color iconic figure can be understood in one way by the faithful, and in a much different way—"Holy Bat- Shark Repellant!"—by the uninitiated. It actually took the grandfather of comics icons to bring comics mythology to the silver screen.

"Forget that [*Superman: The Movie*] made America believe a man could fly. The film's greatest achievement remains that it convinced average moviegoers, Hollywood, and comic book fans that an impressive comic film could be made through acting and special effects."[80] Indeed, while there had been several on-screen depictions of the Man of Steel throughout the decades, most notably the George Reeves television series, it was Richard Donner's film that now stands as "the template by which today's superhero films are judged."[81] The story was told in three acts, with a serious, nigh-operatic dimension given to the first two parts of Superman's story: A father from beyond the stars sends his only son, imbued with mighty powers, to earth, there to learn the lessons of being

78. "When it comes to comic book movies, every rose has its thorn. Most of the time, those thorns are made-for-TV movies with cheap production values and even cheaper stars"; cf. "The Top Comic Book Movies of All Time," *Wizard* #143 (August 2003), 82–94, 90.

79. Brooker, *Batman Unmasked*, 234.

80. "Top Comic Book Movies of All Time," 92.

81. Ibid.

truly human and truly heroic from a kindly, salt-of-the-earth Midwestern couple. Although it was decided to alter the third part of the film, the section dealing with Superman/Clark Kent in Metropolis, to have a lighter, less serious feel to it, the film as a whole brilliantly tapped into the mythological/iconic status of its title character. Even with the star power associated with the film, headlined by Marlon Brando and Gene Hackman, with a magnificent score by John Williams, the intentional decision to cast a then unknown Christopher Reeve as Superman added to the sense that Superman is bigger than any lead actor who could be chosen to portray him. Here was the great American myth brought to celluloid life: God, the flag, and apple pie all wrapped up in red and blue, soaring through the starlit sky. This was no Paul Bunyan or Pecos Bill; Superman had already become far more renowned than they and, thanks to Hollywood, would become more iconic still. And just to make sure that no one could forget the roots of this All-American god in spandex, the film opens with the turning of pages of a 1938 comic book while an offscreen narrator introduces the coming of the mighty one disguised as a mild-mannered reporter of a great metropolitan newspaper. Along with an equally impressive sequel, *Superman: The Movie* (sadly, *Superman III and IV* did not continue the quality and success of the first two films) opened the doors of Tinseltown to the other members of the four-color pantheon of heroes.

Not surprisingly, at the close of the 1980s, DC's other archetypal figure received the nod to join the Man of Tomorrow at the box office.[82] Tim Burton's dark and edgy *Batman* was a far cry from the television series of two decades past, much closer in both themes and tone to recent graphic novels such as Frank Miller's *The Dark Knight Returns* and Alan Moore's and Brian Bolland's *The Killing Joke*. Despite becoming a box office bonanza and spawning a franchise (albeit one that repeated the disappointing trend toward mediocrity and camp of the Superman films), Burton's and Hollywood's treatment of the Dark Knight did not meet with unanimous praise from the insiders of comics fandom. The director's admission that, with the exception of the two titles just mentioned, he did not care much for comic books, his choice of casting "Beetlejuice" Michael Keaton in the lead role, and clear departures from the "canon" of Batman mythology (naming the Joker, revealing him to be the murderer of Bruce Wayne's parents, and killing him at the end) seemed to be too much for

82. DC's other two "great ones," Wonder Woman and Captain Marvel (Shazam), had by this time appeared in their own television series, though not in feature films.

many faithful comics readers. "To many fans, they got it wrong. They blew it. And, worse, they didn't care."[83] Marvel Comics witnessed all this and, a decade after *Batman*, took action.

"It takes a special kind of comic flick to connect with both mainstream audiences and continuity-privy comic aficionados."[84] Marvel Studio's former CEO, Avi Arad, showed how it could be done in the late 1990s, first dipping Marvel's toes in the water with a lesser-known character, Blade. With a well-known action star, Wesley Snipes, and a script written by comics creators, the film was a clear success, resulting in two more *Blade* movies and, more importantly, the green light for the release of other, more prominent Marvel properties. The mutants of *X-Men* were the next to get Hollywood treatment, with director Bryan Singer and an impressive array of stars who were received well by comic book insiders and the general public alike. Sam Raimi's *Spider-Man* came next, followed by franchise-building X-Men and Spider-Man sequels and several more films highlighting other members of Marvel's pantheon, including Daredevil, Elektra, the Hulk, Ghost Rider, Fantastic Four, Wolverine, Iron Man, Thor, and Captain America—all culminating in the ultimate fanboy's (and producer's) dream team: The Avengers, with the characters and their corresponding top-name actors all together in one film. Marvel has clearly learned how to make superhero movies.

It can be argued that one of the prime reasons that these movies have been so "marvelous" is that they have followed the example of Richard Donner's *Superman* in staying true to their comic roots. Spider-Man's classic lesson, "With great power comes great responsibility"—a major part of the character's mythos—not only made it into the box office hit, but became a mantra that viewers would take with them as they left theatres. Marvel Studios introduces each of its movies with a lightning-fast montage of comics panels featuring the hero in focus, thus bridging the worlds of film and comics. Marvel has even gone so far as to add a cameo of Stan Lee in every film, in tongue-in-cheek moments such as when Lee, looking very much like talk show guru Larry King, tries in vain to interview Tony (Iron Man) Stark. Marvel learned that comic creators and fans alike now share a life experience that "includes a substantial amount of exposure to film."[85] DC has tried successfully (with Christopher Nolan's *Batman Begins*) and not so successfully (with Bryan Singer's *Superman Returns*) to emulate Marvel's onscreen magic. The impact of comic book films has invariably changed the way in which these four-color heroes are now understood.

Conclusion

> Myths inspire the realization of the possibility of your perfection.
>
> —Joseph Campbell

> Superheroes were created to represent the best in all of us.
>
> —Gerard Jones and Will Jacobs

When the dream of two young boys was first introduced on the cover of *Action Comics* #1 in 1938, it was impossible to foresee the iconic status that their character and his progeny would gain. However, looking back in hindsight, it is easier to agree with Jules Feiffer: "Our reaction was less 'How original!' than 'But, of course!'"[86] In an age of uncertainty, in a time of disappointment with the present and worry about the future, it was predictable that someone would revitalize the ancient notion of a god among mortals, a mighty power who righted wrongs and stood on the side of justice. What was not possible in the realities of the Depression and World War II was made possible within the pages of a ten-cent magazine. Add to this the notion that hidden behind the façade of every mild-mannered reporter—or every mild-mannered comic book reader for that matter—might exist someone infinitely special and incredibly heroic, and a lively, engaging tradition was created. It is a tradition that has been modernized and enhanced, most notably by Stan Lee and Marvel during the 1960s, and it is a tradition that has been disseminated through the electronic media, especially film, to the mainstream public.

That this superhero tradition is not specifically religious in nature is obvious; comic readers are not holding worship services to Superman or Thor. However, on a much more subtle level, there are large gatherings of the faithful at comic book conventions and "cell groups" that come in and out of specialty comic shops every week, bringing with them their

85. Ibid., 72.
86. Feiffer, *Great Comic Book Heroes*, 9.

offering of money—much more than ten cents now—and receiving not only their tangible sacraments, the comics themselves, but also news and announcements of the comings and goings of their favorite mythical beings. The tradition is not religious, but the people who find themselves in the comics subculture treasure it with near-religious devotion. There is in this tradition, in this subculture, in this devotion, a living mythology.

Even as in ancient times the "Great Mother of Eleusis admitted men to her mysteries,"[87] so the mysterious, mythical world of comic book gods and goddesses has appealed to children and adults alike, especially in times as uncertain as when the Supermen first appeared. When people tried with all their might to believe that "the only thing we have to fear is fear itself," the four-color mythology was embraced and millions of issues were bought. When the war was over and the economy was booming and certainty reigned in America, the four-color mythology was discredited and dozens of publishing houses were killed off. When a new war far away and race riots close at home divided the nation, the four-color mythology was revitalized and hundreds of new comic titles emerged. And when a new century was ushered in with international terrorism and national anxiety, the four-color mythology was transformed, and billions of dollars were spent by an untold number of new initiates on silver screen adventures of these now familiar icons.[88] Jules Feiffer claims that comic books were "our booze,"[89] but the fact is that in 1938 and 1943 and 1968 and 2001 and beyond, it was not only addiction and escapism that they provided, but hope for the heroic within our own selves.

The mythology of comic books has always suffered most at the hands of certainty and "grown-up thinking." Madeleine L'Engle offers a reminder that as children, "we are aware that there is an infinite amount to learn," and as we exchange our "real world of fantasy" for the phony, pretentious world of painful certainty, we lose the precious gifts of imagination and hope that always accompany a living mythology.[90] Indeed, Chronicles of Narnia author C. S. Lewis argues that "grown-up" can be "a synonym for wrong thinking" and that such persons have "lost their imaginations."[91]

---

87. Kelly, *World,* 84.

88. "Spider-Man 2," *Wizard* #141 (2003) 103.

89. Feiffer, *Great Comic Book Heroes,* 77.

90. L'Engle, "Foreword," xii.

91. Ford, *Companion,* 1.

Even amongst Christians, more than any other book of the Bible, "the book of Revelation continues to capture the popular imagination,"[92] precisely because it offers mythical elements that the child in each of us can play with and view in our mind's eye. Even so, from 1938 onward the mythology of comic books has been "unfettered by the confines of realism,"[93] and remains now, as then, something best accepted and appreciated by those whose childlike imaginations continue to soar, by those who still dare to believe that a man can fly.

92. Panati, *Sacred Origins*, 389.

93. Eisner, *Graphic Storytelling*, 73.

CHAPTER 3

Star Trekking in China

Science Fiction as Theodicy in Contemporary China

ERIBERTO P. LOZADA JR.

Science fiction is the people's—especially the young people's—sweetest spiritual nourishment. It can liberate their thoughts, lead their exploratory desire, increase their innovation, and can also impart to them scientific knowledge.

—Pan Jiajing, Chinese hydrological architect
and science fiction writer[1]

IN CONTEMPORARY CHINESE CITIES, internet cafés are everywhere, crowded by hordes of young adults playing online computer games such as "World of Warcraft" or socializing with others online; rarely do I see people working or reading news on the computer.[2] Most internet cafés, for example, do not have printers to produce schoolwork or reports; there are different stores for people who need to print, and of course of-

---

1. "Author Bios." Online: http://replay.waybackmachine.org/20060907111728/http://zhwj.livejournal.com/3944.html/.

2. See Eriberto P. Lozada, "Computers, Scientism, and Cyborg Subjectivity in Postsocialist China," *Asian Anthropology* 2 (2003) 111–37.

fices and school laboratories are full of people using computers for work and to exchange information. This mixed usage of computer technology has resulted in a social ambiguity towards the impact of computers in contemporary Chinese society. Nonetheless, computers have become an important symbol of Chinese modernity—of a belief in science and rationality that supports an emerging Chinese global economic and political power. Science fiction, as I will argue below, has been an important component of the popularization of such a belief in science, and science fiction writers (many of whom are scientists or engineers themselves) are very conscious of their role in promoting this vision of Chinese modernity.

As science and technology have become the dominant authority in globalized everyday life throughout the world, science (and science fiction) has to a large extent displaced religion as the domain for both the exploration of "the big questions" of life and the explanation of why things are the way they are. This is especially the case for people in the contemporary People's Republic of China, who in their lifetimes have witnessed tremendous ideological, material, and social change in the latter part of the twentieth century and the dawning moments of the twenty-first century. While such change is explained locally in ideologically-charged Chinese categories (superstition:civilized; backwards:modern; religious:scientific),[3] in this essay I will argue that these categories mask the processes by which people find meaning in their lives, plan for an imagined future, and make sense of the changing world around them. By exploring the Chinese science fiction scene from two concepts—scientism and theodicy—I will illustrate how science is used symbolically by people in contemporary China to give meaning to their lives, and in so doing explain why Chinese internet cafés are crowded with young adults.

Contemporary Chinese Culture and Scientism

Contemporary China continues to be shaped by the traumatic encounter with the modern West since the mid-nineteenth century, when European traders, diplomats and soldiers, and missionaries began to penetrate into wider Chinese society. This encounter created tremendous intellectual and cultural shifts (and traditionalizing responses) for the Chinese zeitgeist.[4] The raw political and technological power demonstrated by

3. See Maris Gillette, *Between Mecca and Beijing: Modernization and Consumption among Urban Chinese Muslims* (Stanford: Stanford University Press, 2000).

4. This "contact with the West" is well documented and explored in a number of classical Chinese historical accounts, including John K. Fairbank, *China Perceived:*

these Westerners shattered the traditional conception of China as the "central kingdom" (the literal meaning of the Chinese term for China) and created a cultural environment that sought to find the answers to this cultural crisis in a diverse array of problems in foreign ideologies and practices or re-interpreted Chinese tradition. As can be seen in the ideas expressed in the May Fourth Movement,[5] a wide variety of Western ideologies—everything from Spencer's Social Darwinism and Dewey's philosophical pragmatism to Marx's historical materialism—mobilized a critical re-examination of the corpus of Chinese thought. The need for China to develop Western science became the focal point for early twentieth century intellectuals, political reformers and revolutionaries, and even Christian missionaries. As Western imperialists further challenged Chinese sovereignty on the littoral (the areas most affected by contact with foreign people, ideas, and technology), "Mr. Science and Mr. Democracy" became a rallying symbol for reformers and revolutionaries. Hu Shi, one of the intellectual leaders of the May 4th movement, wrote: "During the last thirty years or so there is a name which has acquired an incomparable position of respect in China; no one, whether informed or ignorant, conservative or progressive, dares openly slight or jeer at it. The name is Science. The worth of this almost nationwide worship is another question. But we can at least say that ever since the beginning of reformist tendencies (1890s) in China, there is not a single person who calls himself a modern man and yet dares openly to belittle science."[6]

Images and Policies in Chinese-American Relations (New York: Vintage, 1976); Benjamin Schwartz, *In Search of Wealth and Power: Yen Fu and the West* (Cambridge, MA: Belknap, 1964); Chow Tse-tsung, *The May Fourth Movement: Intellectual Revolution in Modern China* (Harvard East Asian Studies 6; Cambridge: Harvard University Press, 1960); and in more recent works such as Paul A. Cohen, *History in Three Keys: The Boxers as Event, Experience, and Myth* (New York: Columbia University Press, 1997) and Jonathan Spence, *The Search for Modern China* (New York: Norton, 1990), to name only a few.

5. The May Fourth Movement, sparked by the unfair treatment of China by the Western powers and Japan at the 1919 Versailles Peace Conference, is shorthand for a wide variety of intellectual and sociopolitical reforms that sought to rebuild Chinese society and culture. Some of its salient goals were the use of the vernacular language in written form, the development of a strong Chinese nationalism, and a move away from traditional cultural practices that were seen as imprisoning the individual Chinese spirit.

6. Hu Shi, quoted in Shiping Hua, "Chinese Scientism and Political Culture," *Asian Thought and Society* 19:55 (1994) 5; also in Shiping Hua, *Scientism and Humanism: Two Cultures in Post-Mao China (1978–1989)* (Albany: State University of New York Press, 1995), 145.

The development of Western scientific institutions, such as the chemistry educational system and industry described by Reardon-Anderson,[7] reflected deeper shifts in Chinese society towards the Chinese Communist Party's (CCP) new regime that was ultimately characterized by "scientific socialism"—the application of Marxist historical materialism and the development of a new culture based on science was seen (and used by the CCP) as a way of delegitimizing traditional Chinese structures of authority such as "superstitious" religious and kinship groups.

As part of the program of scientific socialism, religion as "the opium of the masses" was specifically targeted by the Chinese Communist Party (CCP) as one of the cultural practices that kept the Chinese backwards and irrational. This included both world religions such as Christianity (seen by the PRC state as a tool of Western imperialism, especially through the activities of foreign missionaries) and traditional Chinese religions, which were seen as supporting the bourgeois elite. Initially, religion was not specifically targeted (especially the religious traditions of minority groups in China) to maintain a "united front" in the 1950s, but private religious institutions such as churches, schools, and hospitals were nationalized by the state. With collectivization in the late 1950s, and campaigns against "rightists" (which included religionists), however, state controls over religion became more stringent; in the Cultural Revolution (1966–1976), all public religious activity ceased as Red Guards targeted religions to wipe out the "Four Olds" that were preventing Chinese society from attaining true socialism. With the "reform and opening" program initiated by Deng Xiaoping in 1979 that re-introduced the market and pulled the state back from management of everyday life, religions gradually resurfaced into the public sphere. Through all these changes, science remained the dominant ideological basis for the postsocialist Chinese state.

Science and technology as a discursive system is of course a "cultural invention, in the sense that it brings forth a world; it emerges out of particular cultural conditions and in turn helps to create new ones."[8] It is, however, a particularly powerful cultural invention because science and technology *naturalizes its epistemological origins.* The laboratory (or

7. James Reardon-Anderson. *The Study of Change: Chemistry in China. 1840–1949* (Studies of the East Asian Institute, Columbia University; Cambridge: Cambridge University Press, 1991).

8. Arturo Escobar, "Welcome to Cyberia: Notes on the Anthropology of Cyberculture," *Current Anthropology* 35 (1994) 211.

by extension the factory, the market, and other territorial spaces where scientific and technological knowledge is produced) is portrayed as an "objective space."[9] These spaces artificially reconfigure natural objects by transforming or making partial versions (reducing), taking them out of context, and controlling the timing of particular occurrences.[10] Knowledge thus produced through the social institutions of science and technology asserts a universalistic applicability that masks the particular cultural conditions of scientists and technologists. In the case of postsocialist China, science and technology hides the dominant political hold of the CCP and its nationalist project of modernity; in fact, the growth of the Chinese market economy and the heightened consumption lifestyle of urban, coastal economic elite paradoxically legitimizes the CCP's rule in China.

But for most people in Chinese society, those with limited education in science and technology, the "worship of science" quoted above by a prescient Hu Shi, is better understood using the concept of *scientism*: the "propensity to idealize science, to reify and universalize its precepts, thereby elevating it from a method of inquiry to the status of canonical dogma."[11] In his examination of Chinese reform-era intellectual thought, Shiping Hua concludes that scientism has taken a strong hold among intellectuals because of science's claim to a unitary truth within a climate of political and cultural fragmentation. Both Baum and Hua claim that scientism is particularly appealing because of certain propensities of Chinese culture: Baum asserts that contemporary scientism complements the "cognitive formalism" found in the categorical thinking of both Daoist and neo-Confucian metaphysics, while Hua claims that contemporary scientism is "continuous with the holistic-monistic intellectual-political modes of thought in the Chinese tradition."[12]

Because of science fiction's *speculative* nature, science fiction structures and propagates scientism. In a study of scientology, Harriet

9. Pierre Bourdieu, "The Specificity of the Scientific Field and the Social Conditions of the Progress of Reason, in Mario Biagioli, ed., *The Science Studies Reader* (London: Routledge, 1999).

10. Karin Knorr Cetina, *Epistemic Cultures: How the Sciences Make Knowledge* (Cambridge: Harvard University Press, 1999).

11. Richard Baum, "Science and Culture in Contemporary China," *Asian Survey* 22:12 (1982) 1172; cf. Shiping Hua's definition of "scientolotry," *Scientism and Humanism*, 15.

12. Hua, *Scientism and Humanism*, 7.

Whitehead explored the background of its founder (science fiction writer L. Ron Hubbard), the consolidation of this religious movement, and some of its major tenets to show how the specific historical and cultural context of post-war America intertwined together historical strands of occultism and positivism. According to Whitehead, occultism (a popular metaphysics based on transcendentalism and historical esoteric practices such as Tarot, Qabbalah, and Gnostic traditions) was re-contextualized within a positivism (which she defines as a belief in the eventual human mastery of reality that uses science as the medium for truly understanding the world) that accompanied the scientific and technological advances in the mid-twentieth century.[13] The scientific and technological advancements created a sense of Weberian disenchantment of the world that science fiction was able to undo because of its transcendence, in the sense that the "realm of the extraordinary"[14] is accessible through innovations in science and is explicitly explored by science fiction: "The unarticulated charisma with which the Positivist endowed science and technological achievement was but a hair's breadth away from the more expressly magical fantasies which the science fiction writer wove into it. In science fiction creations the Positivist could entertain himself by hovering on the brink of the fantastic while the Occultist could find in the same creations the possibility of bringing the supersensible realm down onto the plane of hard, commonsense factuality."[15]

In other words, science fiction was able to counter the numbing "iron cage" of modern postwar America that resulted from the rationalization of culture brought about by the increasing bureaucratic authority of science, at least for those involved in scientology in the example studied by Whitehead. While science can be described as charismatically sterile,[16] science fiction, with its narratives of the fantastic and its speculation about the future, is charismatically fertile. In a postmodern world, science fiction can "revitalize, . . . reactualize, . . . rebanalize fragments of simulation—fragments of the universal simulation which our presumed

---

13. Harriet Whitehead, "Reasonably Fantastic: Some Perspectives on Scientology, Science Fiction, and Occultism," in Irving I. Zaretsky and Mark P. Leone, eds., *Religious Movements in Contemporary America* (Princeton: Princeton University Press, 1974), 555.

14. Ibid., 553.

15. Ibid., 569.

16. As Whitehead notes in ibid., 562.

'real' world has now become for us."[17] As I will argue below, I believe this property of science fiction can be extended to exploring scientism in contemporary China. Moreover, as Whitehead emphasizes in her analysis, the impact of science fiction—its hypothesized futures and the stimulation of the cultural imagination[18] it engenders—is tightly linked to the specificities of historical and social experiences, as I will argue in the case of Chinese science fiction.

Science Fiction in China: Science Fiction and Chinese Nationalism

Chinese science fiction has been traced by some analysts back to premodern literary genres such as mythology, resulting in a particular emphasis on certain science fiction genres. For example, Wu Dingbo, in an article on the history of Chinese science fiction, points to such Chinese mythological classics as the *Huai nan zi* or classical novels such as the *Xi you ji* (Journey to the West) as local precursors to science fiction. The *Journey to the West*, the putative story of the monk Xuanzang's journey to India for Buddhist scriptures, continues its popularity in contemporary Chinese culture. One of the more memorable characters who accompanies Xuanzang is Sun Wukong, the Monkey King; Chinese children all recognize the Monkey King, in ways similar to Mickey Mouse's hold on American (and increasingly, Chinese) children. Another intriguing premodern example is a story of a robot in the *Lie zi*.[19] In this story, a craftsman constructs a robot that can sing and dance for the emperor, but because the robot is so lifelike, and appears to stare at the empress, the emperor becomes enraged with the craftsman, until the craftsman opens up the robot and shows the artificial mechanisms at work.

17. Jean Baudrillard, "Simulacra and Science Fiction," *Science Fiction Studies* 18:3 (1991) 3.

18. I use the term "imagination" following Arjun Appadurai's (1996) use, denoting that area of culture which provides a staging ground for choosing strategies and criteria for what constitutes "the good life." Appadurai argues that the "work of the imagination," an increasingly complex and diverse repertoire because of globalization, is the fundamental drive that structures cultural practices and social relations by providing the range of possibilities that people have in making everyday and life-changing decisions; the imagination must be understood, in Appadurai's model, as being culturally specific and greatly shaped by historical and social experiences.

19. Wu Dingbo and Patrick Murphy, eds., *Science Fiction from China* (New York: Praeger, 1989).

But science fiction as a modern literary genre[20] in China is most often traced back to the early twentieth-century Chinese reformers and literary figures of the May 4th movement—most notably, Lu Xun—and the Chinese encounter with Western science.[21] Lu Xun was originally trained as a medical doctor in Japan. But when he saw a news picture of a Chinese peasant being executed as a spy by a Japanese soldier in north China, Lu Xun was moved by nationalist sentiments—sentiments widely shared among overseas Chinese students studying sciences—to transform what they saw as inherent failings in Chinese culture. Arguably one of the best writers of modern Chinese literature, Lu Xun is best known for his short stories critiquing Chinese traditions, such as "A Madman's Diary" and "Medicine," which portray Chinese traditions as superstitions that weaken the Chinese spirit. Lu Xun also translated Western science fiction to help stimulate the scientific imagination of his compatriots, as he indicates in his 1903 preface to a translation of Jules Verne's *From the Earth to the Moon*: "Only science fiction is as rare as unicorn horns, which shows in a way the intellectual poverty of our time. In order to fill the gap in the translation circles and encourage the Chinese people to make concerted efforts, it is imperative to start with science fiction."[22] Many of Jules Verne's works and other Western science fiction novels were translated by Chinese intellectuals who were searching for ways to build a "New Culture" (another name for the May 4th movement) that would form the basis for a strong and modern Chinese society.

Lu Xun was not the only prominent Chinese writer to translate and promote science fiction; another important literary figure of the Republican period (1911–1949) Lao She wrote a novel called *Cat Country*,

20. Because of space limitations, I will not go into detail about the differences between myths, fantasy, and science fiction as genres—in China, there is a distinction made between "science fiction" (*kehuan*) and "fantasy" (*qihuan*), although like in American literature categories, the two are often grouped together as science fiction-fantasy. What I refer to as modern science fiction follows from the following definition: "Science Fiction is the branch of literature that deals with the effects of change on people in the real world as it can be projected into the past, the future, or to distant places. It often concerns itself with scientific or technological change, and it usually involves matters whose importance is greater than the individual or the community; often civilization or the race itself is in danger" (James Gunn, *The Road to Science Fiction*, vol. 1, *From Gilgamesh to Wells* [New York: New American Library, 1977], 2).

21. Wu and Murphy, *Science Fiction from China*; Jie Lu, "A Report on the World's Largest Science Fiction Magazine" *Extrapolations* 43 (2002) 219–25.

22. Quoted in Wu and Murphy, *Science Fiction from China*, xiii.

a work that is considered a classic of Chinese science fiction. Set on Mars, a person from Earth is stranded in a country of cat-like people whose mannerisms depict the chief vices that the New Culture intellectuals strongly critiqued: opium addiction, official corruption, and an inability to unite together to combat foreign invasion. Many other science fiction works were published during the Republican period, but as Wu asserts, the chaos of the period (notably the Japanese invasion of China starting in 1936 and the civil war between the CCP and the Republican government) resulted in the relative underdevelopment of native Chinese science fiction.[23]

With the establishment of the People's Republic of China and its initial pro-Soviet ideology, science fiction in the Maoist period (1949-1976) was, as expected, heavily influenced by Soviet science fiction, replacing Western authors as the primary source for translated works. According to Wu, science fiction from the Maoist period was heavily structured by Soviet science fiction styles and techniques, such as the preference for stories that explore the uses of current science and technology instead of hypothetical scientific advances.[24] Maoist ideology functionalized many aspects of culture in relation to its political program of building an industrial, socialist society, and science fiction was not an exception; science fiction stories were part of an effort by the state to popularize science. As a result, science fiction stories from this period were completely targeted towards Chinese youth; science fiction itself was considered a category of children's literature in Maoist China. With the chaos and iconoclasm of the Cultural Revolution, however, science fiction disappeared (along with other forms of literature that were not explicitly political tracts).

Like the re-emergence of religion after 1979, Chinese science fiction experienced a revival with the political pronouncement of "reform and opening." After the creative vacuum of the Cultural Revolution, there followed an explosion of Chinese science fiction writers producing their own stories. One famous story from this period is Tong Enzheng's "Death Ray on a Coral Island" (*Shanhudao shang de siguang*) initially published in a mainstream literature magazine. This story is about a Chinese scientist who is deceived by a foreign consortium that wants to develop a military laser weapon. After learning about the deception, the scientist sacrifices himself so that a younger colleague is able to escape the island and return

23. Wu and Murphy, *Science Fiction from China*, xviii.
24. Ibid., xix–xxii, xxv.

back to China with the prototype. This story was later converted to a film of the same name.

Although science fiction authors of the reform period were increasingly becoming more creative with their stories, most of the authors continued to write science fiction as a way of promoting science in wider Chinese society. In the 1980s and 1990s, most science fiction writers were scientists and engineers who wrote stories as a hobby, whose goal continued to be the same as writers from the May 4th period—to popularize science. For example, Zheng Wenguang, referred to in Chinese circles as the "father of Chinese science fiction," was a research fellow with the Beijing Astronomical Observatory.[25] Another noted science fiction author and hydrological engineer Pan Jiajing stated in an interview that "science fiction is the people's—especially the young people's—sweetest spiritual nourishment. It can liberate their thoughts, lead their exploratory desire, increase their innovation, and can also impart to them scientific knowledge. Good science fiction allows all of this to go on in the midst of pleasure reading, bringing them to a world where all matter evaporates without a sound."[26]

Unlike Western science fiction authors like Heinlein, Asimov, or Clarke, these writers did not push the boundaries of science or provide alternative models of society and culture. In fact, as part of its political campaign against "spiritual pollution" from the West (a retightening of state control in the mid 1980s following the creative explosion and cultural experimentation with the implementation of the reforms), the CCP continued to monitor science fiction to ensure that science fiction writers were not promoting superstitious pseudoscience. One writer, Ye Yonglie, was criticized by the CCP in the mid 1980s for his story about a group of scientists who hatched a dinosaur egg (ironically, this is exactly what biochemists from Peking University, China's premier research institution, tried to do later in 1995).[27]

As Tong Enzheng's story depicts, Chinese nationalism also continued to be an important theme in later Chinese science fiction. This is clearly evident in another science fiction story from the 1980s, Wang Xiaoda's "The Mysterious Wave." The main character, a military science and technology news reporter, visits a military research base that is devel-

25. "Nurture Nation's Fiction Writers," *China Daily*, July 23, 2003.

26. "Author Bios."

27. See Unsafe Powerbase Alpha 2004, "Chinese Science Fiction." Online: http://www.well.com/~tux/unsafe/articles/018.html/.

oping holographic technology. There he witnesses a military incursion by American top-secret military aircraft, whereupon one pilot and his plane are captured using the holographic technology. He then visits the scientist (and his daughter, with whom he develops a romantic relationship) who developed this "mysterious wave," and with help from the holographic technology, thwarts a foreign spy who has infiltrated the scientist's laboratory. Like Tong's story, in Wang's "Mysterious Wave," Chinese scientists and other adventurers are able to subvert intrusions for the benefit of China's defense against predatory foreigners.

This theme of nationalism is a major distinguishing characteristic of Chinese science fiction, especially when compared to the science fiction from the United States and Europe. As Csicsery-Ronay concludes, Western science fiction as a genre is marked by a post-nationalist theme: [Western science fiction has a] "globalizing imaginary . . . based on a notion of history and historical innovation that systematically, though unconsciously, ignores the role of nationality in the development of individual consciousness, to the extent that science fiction cannot imagine a future society in which nationality has any significance. This "post-nationalist"—or antinational—orientation forms the basis for some of the most powerful world-construction models in the genre's treasury, models that disavow national particularity and bypass the cultural tensions that might emerge in the relationships of self-distinguishing national cultures in the future."[28]

In an overview of a wide corpus of mostly Western science fiction, Csicsery-Ronay argues that the rationality of the *science* in science fiction results in a rejection of nationalist ideologies based on the irrationalities of a constructed historical memory. He further shows that there are five different strategies that science fiction takes in "dis-imagining" the nation: transgalactism/transglobalism; corporate globalization; apocalyptic winnowing; biological displacement; and archaicization. Transgalactism appears in Asimov's *Foundation* series, where issues of national difference are subsumed in the wider backdrop of galactic politics or reduced into matters of charismatic leadership. Corporate globalization has multinational corporations overshadow the authority of nation-states—

---

28. Istvan Csicsery-Ronay, "Dis-Imagined Communities: Science Fiction and the Future of Nations," in Veronica Hollinger and Joan Gordon, eds., *Edging into the Future: Science Fiction and Contemporary Cultural Transformation* (Philadelphia: University of Pennsylvania Press, 2002), 1.

global capitalism run amok, a strategy that Csicsery-Ronay attributes to cyberpunk genres such as Riddley Scott's film *Blade Runner* or Gibson's *Neuromancer*. Apocalyptic winnowing, such as in Le Guin's *Always Coming Home*, reduces human civilization through a particular catastrophe, resulting in a reduction of societies to smaller-scale structures such as tribes. Biological displacement, for which Csicsery-Ronay cites the *Star Trek* series as an exemplar, translates all manners of human differences (cultural, racial, national) into human/alien dichotomies. Archaicization reflects a throw-back of social structures to archaic forms (feudalism, tribal) not as allegories for national differences, but to provide alternative ways of connecting people together.

Csicsery-Ronay concedes that while these categories may largely hold in Western science fiction, such is not the case for science fiction from the former second world (with its postsocialist transformations) nor for Japanese science fiction. Csicsery-Ronay argues that Japanese science fiction does not reflect as deep a post-nationalist theme because of Japan's own alienation from its nation-state, a foreign structure that was imposed by a victorious America after the end of World War II. Despite its modern economy and institutions, according to Csicsery-Ronay, science fiction in Japan is still markedly postcolonial, and thus the identification with a Japanese vision of the state is negotiated in its literature. As the continuing emphasis on nationalism in Chinese science fiction shows, Chinese science fiction also reflects an ongoing negotiation with both postsocialist changes to the Chinese state and society, and a resolution of the postcolonial experiences that China faced since the mid-nineteenth century. China of the early twenty-first century is only now realizing the dreams and promises of the May 4th movement, of building a modern and powerful Chinese nation that has science and rationality at its center, instead of age-old superstitious traditions that limit the creativity and social mobility of its people. In China, science (and science fiction) is not driven by a universalism that hides the social agency that people in China feel they are only now beginning to claim, but by the search for a modern Chinese society and its place in the world.

The impact of nationalism on science and science fiction can be clearly seen in the euphoria after the successful Chinese manned spaceflight in October of 2003. Two weeks after the 2003 National Day celebrations of the establishment of the People's Republic on October 1, 1949, China launched the Shenzhou V ("divine ship") into space, carrying

Colonel Yang Liwei into orbit for twenty-one hours. Yang Liwei became an instant hero and celebrity, later touring the country as a symbol of China's scientific and technological prowess. Chinese science fiction benefited greatly from the space launch; one science fiction author was at mission control for the flight, while two others were featured in television coverage. Two Chinese technology companies (Lenovo Computers and Sina.com) held a science fiction contest in honor of the successful launch. But more importantly, the Shenzhou V was also a powerful political symbol, demonstrating the legitimacy and wisdom of the CCP and China's political leaders, for both China's then-new president, Hu Jintao, and his predecessor, Jiang Zemin, who initiated the program in 1992. Building on this success, China planned to launch a vehicle to the moon by 2010, and to ultimately build a station on the moon and to carry out a mission to Mars. There are even claims (though unofficial) that China may have tried an earlier attempt at a manned spaceflight in the middle of the Ming Dynasty (in the sixteenth century). Legend has it that a local government official and stargazer named Wan Hu built a spacecraft around a sturdy chair, two kites, and forty-seven gunpowder rockets.[29] He then had his servants light the fuses, and after a tremendous explosion, Wan Hu and his sedan chair were gone. Although this humorous legend is undoubtedly not a documented space flight, such popular Chinese claims that "it was first invented in China" are common and depict the vibrancy of Chinese nationalism.[30] Seen in a wider historical context, Yang Liwei's successful spaceflight looks, for people in Chinese society, like the realization of the dreams of Wan Hu and the promises of science fiction, from the very first translation of Jules Verne's *From the Earth to the Moon.*

From the perspective of the state, such dreams of conquering space help support the legitimacy of a communist party that increasingly must manage such contradictions as "socialism with Chinese characteristics" (the official ideological explanation of market capitalism in China) and

29. Joe Havely, "Legendary Ming Dynasty Official Was Space Pioneer," *CNN* (Hong Kong), September 30, 2003. Online: http://edition.cnn.com/2003/TECH/space/09/30/china.wanhu/index.html/.

30. During the 2002 FIFA World Cup, there were popular reports in Chinese newspapers about historical documents from the second century BCE that depict a game where feet were used to control a leather ball kicked through a goal; the FIFA chair's acknowledgement of the possibility that soccer was invented in China set of a storm of popular debates in Europe and Asia over this issue (especially with the complete failure of the Chinese team in that competition).

tensions arising from heightened social stratification, the urban-rural divide, and labor problems. As a result, successful space missions serve to further its promotion of scientism as an alternative to other religious-like movements that have also been rising such as Falungong and evangelical Christianity. In her study of *qigong* associations like Falungong, Nancy Chen concluded that such groups are fluid, spanning a continuum between state-recognized groups incorporated into the state bureaucracy, and groups unrecognized by the state centered around charismatic leaders.[31] The charismatic *qigong* groups are seen by the state as the biggest challenge to state authority because of their resemblance to popular soteriological religious movements that in the past have torn China apart (such as the White Lotus or Taiping Heavenly Kingdom).[32] The beliefs of Falungong, furthermore, are seen by the state as irrational: Falungong centers around a system of *qigong* beliefs and exercises that enable practitioners to develop "moral character" (*xinxing*) so as to tap into the power of the supreme cosmic quality that Li refers to as "*zhen-shan-ren*" (truthfulness, benevolence, and forbearance). Falungong's beliefs and exercises are designed for healing, stress relief, and health improvement, with an ultimate goal of personal enlightenment. Founded in 1992, Falungong was initially recognized by the state-sponsored Chinese Qigong Research Association in 1993, but was later expelled in 1996 for Li's unscientific cosmological ideas—unlike astronaut Yang Liwei, Li Hongzhi claimed he could fly through space without the technological and economic infrastructure of the state. From the Chinese state's perspective, their distrust of such popular religious groups was validated in Falungong's April 1999 demonstration held in Beijing.

On April 25, 1999, over 10,000 people gathered in silent protest outside Zhongnanhai, the walled compound in Beijing where the Chinese top leaders live, in the largest demonstration since the 1989 student demonstration in Tiananmen. The protesters were from all over north China, gathering together to petition for state recognition of the cult. The protest was initiated by an earlier incident in Tianjin, where Falungong practitioners were assaulted by police when they protested against an article critical of Falungong. The protest in Beijing terrified the top leadership of the

31. Chen, "Urban Spaces and Experiences of *Qigong*," in Deborah Davis et al., eds., *Urban Spaces in Contemporary China* (Cambridge: Cambridge University Press, 1995), 347–61.

32. See Lozada, *God Aboveground: Catholic Church, Postsocialist State, and Transnational Processes in a Chinese Village* (Stanford: Stanford University Press, 2001).

Communist party because it demonstrated that popular religious groups like Falungong were well organized and could mobilize large groups of people. Practitioners represented a wide segment of Chinese society, and more importantly, the top leadership later discovered that many party cadres and members of the army were active practitioners of Falungong. By July 22, 1999, the PRC proscribed participation in Falungong, and actively persecuted Falungong leaders. This is the kind of science fiction that the state does not want to promote, and in the world of Chinese science fiction, such fantastic musings are also rejected as "unscientific." But Li Hongzhi's model, unlike Yang Liwei's spaceflight, is more open to participation by the wider public, empowering people through their living by means of an alternative world. As a result, the CCP promotes an alternative to such "superstitions" in science fiction; science fiction's accessibility to the world of science provides a way for people to participate in science. Science fiction has become a part of people's everyday lives, giving it a powerful hold on Chinese cultural imaginations. It does so through computers, a technology that has become very popular, and through such spaces as internet cafés has become a part of contemporary Chinese subjectivity.

Living Science Fiction: Chinese Cyborg Subjectivity

Science fiction has worked its way into the "work of the imagination" for people in China through the multiple forms of media—books, television, movies, and other forms of entertainment including computer games—that are part of the lived, popular culture in contemporary twenty-first century China.[33] Movies and television serials are readily available from DVD and VCD[34] stores that both rent and sell Chinese and international movies (including pirated movies).[35] Science fiction movies are well-represented among the Western and Hong Kong movies that people watch in China; on television, they are often shown with dubbed Chinese voices. Despite

33. For a more detailed description and analysis of computer gaming and Internet usage in China, see Lozada, "Computers, Scientism, and Cyborg Subjectivity."

34. Video CDs are an intermediary technology between videotapes and DVDs that are extremely popular in China, though rarely seen in the West.

35. Pirated movies, while targeted by the CCP government for destruction, are both timely and easy to find. For example, *Star Wars Episode III* was released in the United States shortly after I left for China in the summer of 2005; but students whom I brought to China were able to find pirated copies of this new movie for ten yuan.

the love-hate relationship between Chinese and Japanese culture, as seen in the recent political disputes between China and Japan over historical issues such as the Nanjing Massacre and Japan's failure to acknowledge war atrocities in China in Japanese historical textbooks, Japanese *anime* (cartoons) and *manga* (comic books), most of which are science-fiction related, are extremely popular among Chinese youth (an industry estimated to be worth about $30 billion globally). Like American "Trekkies" (or Trekkers, depending upon which *Star Trek* series is the main interest) or other science fiction fans that attend conventions, Chinese youth have developed a subculture around certain popular series, dressing up in costumes that mimic their favorite heroes and heroines in forums such as the annual Shanghai Animation and Cartoon Fair held in August (during summer vacation).

Corresponding to the revival of science fiction (and a wide range of cultural practices) in the reform period, another social phenomenon has increased in both visibility and activity: UFO sightings. Although there are historical reports of unexplained celestial phenomena in the Ming Dynasty (like the previously mentioned effort of Wan Hu at space exploration), the advent of the reform period brought with it a flurry of UFO sightings that were reported in official newspapers and magazines. In the early 1980s, the China UFO Research Organization was established, and a magazine "The Journal of UFO Research" was founded in 1981. While the proliferation of UFO groups and magazines is not surprising, what needs explanation is the apparent official media attention that has legitimized UFO sightings in China, through news articles and documentary television shows. What makes UFO sightings different from the pseudoscience of Falungong is that CCP officials see UFO research as scientific. "The study of U.F.O.s is fundamentally different from other things like Falun Gong and qigong, which have come under criticism lately," said Jin Fan, an engineer who heads the Dalian U.F.O. Research Society in northeast China. "This is a purely scientific field, whereas Falun Gong deals with cults and superstition."[36] As stated clearly in the quote, it is scientism that makes UFO research and popular discourse on UFOs legitimate in the eyes of the CCP, and like science fiction, is used by the Chinese state to popularize science and scientific outlooks. Members of UFO research organizations are themselves scientists and engineers (like many of the

36. Elizabeth Rosenthal, "UFO Boom Doesn't Worry Officials," *New York Times*, January 11, 2000, 2.

writers of science fiction), and the Chinese Air Force reportedly attends important UFO research meetings—which are themselves covered by major Chinese media outlets.

While science fiction is represented in various media, the most influential resource for science fiction in China is a popular magazine called "Science Fiction World" (*Kehuan shijie*). First published in 1979, *Science Fiction World* (SFW) has the world's largest circulation for a science fiction magazine; there are over 500,000 subscribers. This does not include the countless other readers of SFW; like other Chinese books and magazines, they are circulated by networks of friends who take turns reading them to save on costs, and used magazines are also readily available from street vendors. SFW, the flagship magazine of the Science Fiction World Company, is a monthly magazine that publishes science fiction short stories, science fiction news, and other popular essays on science. The larger company also publishes two other popular magazines, *Amazing Files* and *Flying*, and has two main series of books: translated novels from mostly Western science fiction authors, and Chinese authors (although this is a much smaller series). As SFW has tried to shift its target audience to an older readership, the two other magazines have retained their focus on Chinese youth. SFW is also the organization that represents China in international science fiction associations and conferences, and annually presents the Milky Way Award for the best in Chinese science fiction.

The magazine itself mostly publishes science fiction stories, though it annually publishes a special issue that is solely fantasy. The stories are dramatically illustrated using a comic book aesthetic style, reflecting its targeting of college-age readers. The stories by Chinese writers in SFW largely represent the thematic areas of Chinese science fiction overall: 1) stories of robots and clones; 2) military technology adventures, so-called "space operas"; 3) space travel; and 4) cyberpunk and other computer and internet-based stories. Chinese-produced fantasy stories follow traditional conventions present in such classical works as the *Journey to the West*, with anthropomorphic animals, magic elixirs, and heroic quests. The majority (over 60%) of stories in earlier editions of SFW were translation of foreign science works, but since 2002, there has been an increasing emphasis on original stories by Chinese authors. The China Daily attributes this relative paucity of Chinese science fiction (despite its popularity in Chinese society) to structural weaknesses in the Chinese educational system that early on tracks students into either the sciences or humanities: "Those opting for the humanities will continue to study history and politics, but not chemistry and physics. The other group will focus on the sciences to the detriment of the humanities... And once they enter institutions of higher learning, both groups might have little opportunity or interest to explore the others' fields. When literature and science are separated, the creation of science fiction and fantasy loses its base."[37]

The chief editor in 2005, Alai, is himself a novelist who wrote a bestselling book about his homeland Tibet called *After the Dust Settles*, and has brought more literary respectability to science fiction. Through its commanding presence in Chinese science fiction, SFW has catapulted science fiction into cutting edge literature that is increasingly apolitical and flaunting of traditional social norms.

While media outlets such as SFW, movies, and television are fertile grounds for the Chinese work of the imagination, it is computer games and the internet that have made science fiction a part of a new Chinese sense of self. Following Donna Haraway, this new Chinese sense of self is best seen as cyborg subjectivity—the blending of human and machine that stresses the reshaping of self-identity through the increased use of computer technology, and, more importantly, the social immersion in the virtual worlds of computer gaming and cyberspace.[38] The rapid development and popularity of computers and the internet in China, and the increased symbolic and practical uses of computers for both work and leisure, show that Chinese subjectivity is changing to incorporate the technologies as part of how people define themselves. As people use computer technology, and encourage their children to master what are believed to be the tools of the future, the internet and computer technology are a part of everyday life in China—perhaps too much a part of youth culture.

Because of the overwhelming popularity of computer gaming among Chinese youth, Chinese officials have referred to computer gaming as "electronic opium." Such state concern over the possible *moral problems* with foreign media, and critiques of the rapid adoption of foreign practices such as computer gaming, are consistent with Chinese political culture, especially when the issue surrounds the youth. In any political system or society, the socialization and education of youth is a highly po-

37. "Nurture Nation's Fiction Writers."

38. Donna J. Haraway, *Simians, Cyborgs, and Women: The Reinvention of Nature* (New York: Routledge, 1991).

liticized and contentious issue;[39] in the 2000 presidential race, American entertainment industries were under attack from both Republican and Democratic candidates themselves. From my own observations of Chinese cyberculture, the main attraction to so-called internet cafés stems more from the ability to play computer games together as a group over a local-area network than from reading about democracy and human rights on foreign websites.

In fact, because getting on the internet to play computer games is so popular among young adults and youth, internet addiction has become a major social issue in China. According to Prof. Tao Hongkai, a renowned internet-addiction therapist and activist, many Chinese youth are escaping to internet cafés for online gaming and internet chat rooms because of the tremendous pressures they face in a test-oriented educational system, and the failure to cultivate Chinese youth's spiritual and emotional development. Around 20% of these youth (for those under 18, roughly 16.5 million teenagers) are thought to show a tendency for internet addiction.[40] Some of these high school and college age youth stop attending class or going to work and can spend as many as 5 days straight in an internet café without returning home. Although internet-addicted youth are the extreme case, the popularity of computer gaming and internet use in China clearly shows how computers are becoming an extension of personal identity for many young Chinese. It is through their extended immersion in computer gaming that Chinese young adults are able to themselves live out both the *science fiction* that they read in magazines and novels or they watch in movies and on television and the *science* that they read about in the news.

Science Fiction and the Work of the Imagination: A New Theodicy?

As noted above, the CCP's nationalistic promotion of science and the popular consumption of science fiction, when combined with the rapidly improved standard of living and the heady growth of the Chinese economy, have resulted in the popular belief in scientism. As I have also

39. See Sharon Stephens, *Children and the Politics of Culture* (Princeton Studies in Culture/Power/History; Princeton: Princeton University Press, 1995).

40. China Internet Information Center, "Prof. Helps Internet-Hooked Teens Kick the Habit." Online: http://www.china.org.cn/english/NM-e/123822.htm/.

described above, Chinese science fiction is heavily structured by the traumatic historical encounter with the West and the search for finding China's place in the modern world. As a result, Chinese science fiction both explains why China was weak in the past and how China can become strong in the future, providing a theodicy for people in Chinese society grappling with tremendous social changes: "From the beginning, [science fiction] has been introduced into the ailing Chinese society as a salvation tool, and, being donned the "Mr. Science in Masks," has shouldered the responsibility of enlightening the citizens, educating their minds, and provoking their interest in science."[41]

With its emphasis on developing science and restructuring Chinese culture in relation to scientific rationality, Chinese science fiction provides wider Chinese society with a framework from which to understand and evaluate all that happens around them; and more importantly, it provides a roadmap for the future. Chinese science fiction therefore provides a "secular theodicy" for postsocialist Chinese society.

While Weber uses the concept of theodicy—the persistence of evil in a divinely ordered world—to compare the sociological consequences of particular religious traditions, Michael Herzfeld has extended this concept in relation to a more general social phenomenon of *secular theodicy*. As a pragmatic cultural orientation, secular theodicy "provides people with social means of coping with disappointment."[42] As Weber's original use of theodicy implies, this points to something that is by definition—something has to be at the root structuring principle within a particular cosmology for it to be explained away by a theodical stance: "the more the development [of metaphysical conceptions] tends toward the conception of a transcendental unitary god who is *universal*, the more there arises the problem of how the extraordinary power of such a god may be reconciled with the imperfection of the world that he has created and rules over."[43]

Based on the earlier descriptions of the Chinese perspectives on science fiction, I assert that it is analytically useful to see Chinese science fiction as rooted in theodicy—science fiction is both popular and powerful because it provides a means by which people can understand the situation of China today and possibilities for tomorrow. Because of China's

41. Lu, "Report," 220.

42. Michael Herzfeld, *The Social Production of Indifference: Exploring the Symbolic Roots of Western Bureaucracy* (Chicago: University of Chicago Press, 1992), 7.

43. Max Weber, *The Sociology of Religion* (Boston: Beacon, 1993), 138.

historical failure to assert itself against Western imperialism (and later Japanese imperialism, after Japan rapidly absorbed Western science and technology with the Meiji reformation), the Chinese perspective of itself as the central kingdom collapsed, and with it the cultural confidence that Chinese society has maintained over millennia. Only now in the early twenty-first century are the efforts of the May 4th intellectuals coming to fruition.

Science fiction, therefore, through its popular consumption by young adults in various media and by its lived experience in cyberspace through computer gaming, both structures Chinese subjectivity in the present and provides the raw material for the work of the imagination for the future. Because of China's historical and cultural experiences, however, such a future is not a postnationalist future where the Chinese state disappears in the wider fabric of a Star Trek-like Federation. Instead, science fiction maps out possibilities for a strong China in the future, where Chinese society and culture have a respected place in the world. The dynamism of contemporary Chinese society, like the streets of Nanjing and other cities of China, is a project under construction. Fueled by the dreams of the emerging prowess of Chinese science and technology, and shared more widely with Chinese society through an increasingly Chinese-written science fiction, China is recreating for itself a modern "middle kingdom."

CHAPTER 4

Science Playing God

Alison Bright MacWilliams

Mr. Parker, do you know what it means to feel like god?

—Dr. Moreau, *The Island of Lost Souls*

THE THREAT THAT TOO much ambition after knowledge might bring down the wrath of the gods is one well embedded in ancient religion and myth, whether one looks to the Greeks' Icarus, or to Genesis' fatal Tree of the Knowledge of Good and Evil. It is perhaps no surprise then that what is widely credited as the first science fiction novel, Mary Shelley's *Frankenstein: Or the Modern Prometheus*, would be read by most contemporaries as just such a fable: man usurps God's role as creator, and thus must inevitably fall and be destroyed. Indeed, Shelley at times encourages such a reading, both in Victor Frankenstein's self-analysis, and in the condemnation of his monster. It should be remembered, however, that Dr. Frankenstein is presented, not as the "Modern Icarus"—or even the "Modern Daedalus"—but as Prometheus, himself a god, though punished for putting divine fire into human hands. From its inception, much of science fiction has been preoccupied, not simply with the idea that science provides a challenge to religion as a way of knowing, but with the concept that science, with its attendant technology, gives mortals real Godlike power. The challenge is, then, can human beings wield such power responsibly? Or are they doomed by their very nature to fall short and wreak destruction on themselves and others? Two major strains of science fiction approach this question, both of them rooted in Shelley's own ambivalence towards science.

The view of scientists as tragic usurpers of godlike power seems to dominate classic science fiction in part because of the frequent retelling of both Shelley's *Frankenstein* and another text, H. G. Wells's *Island of Dr. Moreau* (itself sometimes viewed as a riff on Shelley) in a variety of media, including theatrical productions, film, and answering or derivative fiction. Indeed, so omnipresent are these derivations that it is hard for a modern reader to come unbiased to the ambiguities of the original texts. It is useful, therefore, to look at why so many contemporary readers of Shelley saw *Frankenstein* as a morality play about the inevitable downfall of a hubris-ridden scientist (and why *Dr. Moreau* was subsequently read as such) before moving on to other manifestations of this point of view.

Those most familiar with the Frankenstein of early 20th century horror films frequently stumble over the structure of the original novel. Shelley's *Frankenstein* begins as an epistolary novel, with the character of Walton, a scientific explorer taking his crew on a dangerous mission through the ice to try to reach the North Pole. Walton writes in letters to his sister of his mission, and then of meeting this strange man traversing the ice in his dog sled. This turns out to be Victor Frankenstein, who, in the second layer of the novel, tells Walton his life story, including the creation of the monster and the tragedies that follow. Sandwiched in the center of Frankenstein's narrative is a third layer, when Victor encounters the monster for the first time after abandoning him. Here the extremely articulate monster relates his own view of his wanderings up to that point. The story then continues with Victor's narrative, up to the point of him explaining his presence on the ice, and then ends with the frame story of Walton's letters.

The three-part narrative scheme of the novel allows for different interpretations of why Victor's experiment ends in tragedy. Both the Walton and the Frankenstein narratives do have some elements that support the view that the arrogance of science in usurping divine power has caused the monster to run amok. This appears most strongly in Frankenstein's own narrative. "All my speculations and hopes are as nothing, and like an archangel who aspired to omnipotence, I am chained in an eternal hell."[1] The Walton narrative, though less direct, also supports such a reading, as Walton is presented with the choice of dangerously pursuing his exploratory goal, or turning back. Unlike Frankenstein, his arrogance is tempered by the need to maintain the support of his crew; when they vote to turn back, the potential results of his drive for knowledge go untested.

As we will see, the monster narrative presents an alternative viewpoint, one that also gets some support from the Frankenstein portion of the narrative, but it is the first interpretation—the usurpation of divine powers brings disaster—that was picked up on by contemporary critics. Early reviews of *Frankenstein* in both *The Quarterly Review* and *The Belle Assemblée* both focus on the issue of materialism—that a living, thinking being is created without reference to a soul. The former accuses Shelley of perpetrating a moral abomination by suggesting such a creature could live, while the latter, more generously, presumes the novel is a cautionary tale suggesting that only bad results can come from treating life without reference to spirit. Both, however, are clear that the moral problem of the novel rests in the act of daring to create life. By the time the novel was re-released in 1831, Shelley herself submits to this reading, altering the introduction to suggest that Frankenstein is punished for exceeding the limits of human morality.

As the Frankenstein tale jumped to other media and was expanded upon by other authors, this presentation of the scientist disastrously playing god was reiterated, often more directly and didactically. The earliest play based on the novel, mounted in 1832, has a blatantly egotistical Frankenstein (now an alchemist in Renaissance Italy) who can transmute metals as well as create life, and who is prone to utter statements like "How vain, how worthless is the noblest of fame compared to mine!"[2] The classic 1931 film version by James Whale is blunter still, beginning with a narrator stepping forward to announce "We are about to unfold the story of Frankenstein, a man of science who sought to create a man after his own image without reckoning upon God."[3] Early print variations on Shelley's tale follow suit. As early as 1837 *Frankenstein* was parodied by

1. Mary Shelley, *Frankenstein, Or, the Modern Prometheus* (New York: Bantam, 1991), 194.

2. H. M. Milner, "Frankenstein; or Man and the Monster!" *The Frankenstein Omnibus*, ed. Peter Hanning (Edison, NJ: Chartwell, 1994), 297–319.

3. *Frankenstein*, prod. Carl Laemmle, Jr.; dir. James Whale, 1 hr. 11 min., Universal Pictures, 1931, videocassette.

William Maginn in a short story that has the main character, a follower of Frankenstein, denounced as an agent of Satan by the desecrated dead.[4]

By the time H. G. Wells penned *The Island of Dr. Moreau* in 1896, the archetype of the hubris-ridden scientist was so embedded in science fiction that some readers viewed Wells's novel as simply another Frankenstein clone: mad doctor dares to try to create life, and is subsequently destroyed by his flawed and disturbing creations. Like Shelley, however, Wells is playing a deeper game. *Moreau* presents the reader, not with three narrators, but with three scientists, the narrator-protagonist being one of them, each with a different view of the central act of creation, and each with a different fate. As in *Frankenstein*, the novel as a whole provides alternate viewpoints, but the title character most strongly shows a scientist who plays god only to meet a terrible reckoning. Moreau, however, gives no soul-searching speeches. Instead the reader is presented with a scientist who not only creates pseudo-human abominations, but also gives them his own set of commandments, and a version of hell on earth—those who disobey go back to the "house of pain" that created them.[5] In a way, *The Island of Dr. Moreau* "corrects" one of Victor Frankenstein's mistakes. The creatures cannot, like Frankenstein's monster, complain of neglect and a lack of teaching, as Moreau's are given laws and structure. That they nonetheless turn violent certainly supports a reading that Moreau's usurpation of the prerogative of creation is inherently flawed and doomed.

Like *Frankenstein*, *The Island of Dr. Moreau* is followed by a series of films that simplify the plot in a way that focuses attention on the idea that the story's tragedy comes from the error of playing god. None of the film versions presents the interplay between three scientists that allows the novel to express a more positive view of science. The closest is the 1932 version, *The Island of Lost Souls* starring Charles Laughton as a sly and creepy Moreau, and, like the novel, featuring an assistant, Montgomery, who has a medical background tainted by problems with alcohol. He is, however, a weak character, who primarily serves to repudiate Moreau when the experiments have gone too far. Meanwhile, Laughton as Moreau gets to chew up the scenery. Not only does he try to make animals into humans by means of vivisection, he also (most unlike the book) tries to breed his monstrosities with real humans, first attempting to pair "Lota

---

4. William Maginn, "The New Frankenstein," in *The Frankenstein Omnibus*, 39–54.

5. H. G. Wells, *The Island of Dr. Moreau* (New York: Bantam, 1994), 66.

the cat woman" (not appearing in Wells's novel, but followed by a series of cat women in subsequent films) with hapless shipwrecked Parker, and then conspiring for one of his ape men to rape Parker's fiancé when she arrives with a rescue party. His arrogance is most plainly expressed in his famous monologue about his experiments to the captive Mr. Parker. Staring fanatically at his creatures laboring outside, Moreau murmurs "Mr. Parker, do you know what it means to feel like God?" Of course, Moreau is torn to shreds at the end, dragged to his own surgical theater when his beast-men turn riotous after Moreau breaks one of his own laws—"you shall not kill other men."[6]

Even the most modern of the film versions of *The Island of Dr. Moreau* keeps this strong emphasis on the usurpation of divine creative powers. In the 1996 version staring Marlon Brando as Moreau, Brando parades in front of his beast-men in pseudo-papal regalia and controls the beast-men with electric shocks likened to divine lighting bolts. In this film the castaway is a representative of NATO who even further reinforces the false god theme by telling the beast-men, rioting after Moreau's death, that Moreau has transcended the physical state, dying, Christ-like, so that he can watch over them invisibly. Predictably, this does not help matters much.

While *Moreau* did not spawn what is practically a genre of science fiction, as *Frankenstein* did, it too became a cultural reference point, engendering its share of spin-offs. Interestingly, these tend to replace a vengeful god with nature. The scientist still oversteps proper human boundaries, and is still destroyed for such transgression, but without even Wells's religious themes. A recent example may be found in Robin Cook's 1997 novel *Chromosome 6*, which has an island facility where human DNA is incorporated into apes to provide replacement organs that perfectly match those wealthy enough to afford an ape "double." Here, too, the apes evolve and rebel (though in this case the monster men seek primarily to escape, not destroy, their creators). The 1972 Mexican film *The Twilight People* (starring blaxploitation film star Pam Grier) blatantly rips off Wells to present a similar moral, with the scientist killed by humans he has melded with animals. Michael Crichton, too, takes off from Wells's work in his 1991 novel *Jurassic Park*, presenting an island compound where scientific manipulation of animals leads to the

6. *The Island of Lost Souls*, dir. Erle C. Kenton, 1 hr. 11 min., Paramount Productions, 1932, videocassette.

animals running amok and destroying the scientific facilities. Crichton presents perhaps the most direct statement of this shift from avenging god to avenging nature through chaos theorist Ian Malcolm: "you [scientists] decide you won't be at the mercy of nature. You decide you'll control nature, and from that moment you're in deep trouble, because you can't do it."[7] Or, as he states in the film version, "Life breaks free; it expands to new territories and crashes through barriers, painfully, maybe even dangerously. . . . Life finds a way."[8] The odd exceptions to the Moreau clones are Edgar Rice Burroughs' 1913 novel, *The Monster Men* and Jack L. Chalker's *The Moreau Factor* published in 2000. These texts we will discuss later as clear examples of our second category of fiction with scientists playing God, the more optimistic view of science being a constant trait in Burroughs' fiction.

As the possibility of creating and manipulating life, especially human life, has moved from outrageous fantasy to the scientifically possible, the literary theme has expanded beyond the small scale of *Frankenstein* or *Moreau* to encompass whole societies made by misguided science. In some, a struggle similar to that between Victor Frankenstein and his monster develops, as the "monsters" (those created or manipulated by science) struggle against the "normal" humans, with both sides striving to validate their own lives. An interesting example of this may be found in David Brin's 2002 novel *The Kiln People*. Here technology has been developed to allow people to create temporary copies of themselves, impressing their personalities on "clay" beings that can then perform various tasks for the original, and, ultimately, may have their memories shared with the original person. This possibility of rejoining the central personality does not prevent the clay copies from resenting their constrained and temporary "lives"—leading almost inevitably to an attempt by clay copies to prolong their lives and even destroy and replace the original person. Similar revolutions, though perhaps on a smaller scale, can be found in movies such as *Blade Runner* and *The Island*. In all of these, the recognition of consciousness on the part of the manufactured humans grants some sympathy to both sides. All suggest that science goes too far when it creates sentient beings, especially ones destined for short lives, but argue that destroying a self-aware being, even if misbegotten, may only compound the crime.

7. Michael Crichton, *Jurassic Park* (New York: Knopf, 1990), 351.

8. *Jurassic Park*, dir. Steven Spielberg, 2 hrs. 7 min., Universal Studios, 1993, DVD.

Another variant of this theme is one in which scientific manipulation of life is so extensive and commonplace that practically everyone is manufactured—everyone is a monster. The classic example of this is Aldous Huxley's 1932 novel, *Brave New World*. Here all people (except for a few groups, known as savages, confined to reservations) come from carefully controlled laboratories. Even once decanted from their beakers, their lives are scientifically controlled and regimented. All negative emotions are controlled by drugs. The result, rather than being groups fighting to assert or preserve their humanity, is a society where all (except for the "savages") have lost their humanity and don't even know it. A similar, though less bleak, example in film is *Gattaca*, in which an un-engineered, imperfect man manages to subvert the system and achieve his dream of space flight. The less positive fate of "perfect" genetically engineered characters presents a clear moral that this attempt by science to create perfection instead destroys an individual's sense of accomplishment and saps the will. Both of these works present an almost Calvinistic worldview, where science has replaced God as the author of predestination—with predictably disastrous results.

If we return to the original *Frankenstein* and *Island of Dr. Moreau*, however, a possible alternative is presented to the aforementioned bleak views of the apotheosis of science. Although both of these novels end in disaster, they leave the possibility open that it is not the act of science usurping divine prerogative that causes this disaster, merely the execution of the presumptive act that is faulty. In other words, maybe if the scientists in these novels had planned better, they would have gotten better results. This is most clearly expressed in *Frankenstein*, where the tripartite narrative allows speculation on different ways in which this experiment might have gone wrong. In the central narrative, that of the monster, the monster presents himself as a potentially moral being—open to the beauty of nature, receptive to human affection. He becomes a killer, says the monster, not because he was made by human hands, but because his creator made the mistake of abandoning and rejecting him.[9] Had Frankenstein been a better father, nothing bad would have come of his presumptuous scientific deed. Further, the monster offers to end his murderous rampage if he can only have a mate to pass the time with. He kills again only after Frankenstein refuses.

9. Shelley, *Frankenstein*, 83–84.

We might take leave to doubt the arguably self-serving views of a killer monster. In the narrative of Frankenstein, however, we are given yet another way in which matters could have turned out better. The monster is rejected by Frankenstein, and then later by the villagers he meets, because he is so disturbing to look at that only a blind man could bear him. What if Frankenstein had done a better job? Frankenstein himself admits to short cuts. The parts from which the monster is constructed are chosen in part for their size, large parts being easier to manipulate.[10] Perhaps the monster's scale is what makes him so disturbing? It is an open question, as Shelley never describes *why* his looks engender such a negative response. Critic Chris Baldick argues that "Victor Frankenstein's error is to have confused the beauty of the dead limbs he has collected with the beauty of the whole organism."[11] Perhaps mismatched limbs are at the root of the monster's problem. All such speculation leaves the possibility open that Frankenstein *could* have created a better looking creature, who would then not have been rejected, and subsequently would have, by the monster's estimation anyway, been morally acceptable as well. Frankenstein, though periodically riddled with doubt, himself at times supports the idea that in playing God, as with other things, practice makes perfect. As he states in his dying monologue, "I have myself been blasted in these hopes [for scientific achievement], yet another may succeed."[12] Even after the initial mistake of making an ugly monster, Shelley leaves the possibility open that the construction of a mate for him would, by giving him companionship, give the story a happy ending. Science's mistakes, this would suggest, can be righted by further scientific endeavor.

H. G. Wells also presents a tripartite view of monster making, by the simple feature of putting three scientists on the isle. Unlike *Frankenstein*, *The Island of Dr. Moreau*'s title character has no sympathetic side. While Wells's Moreau is an urbane man, in some respects less creepy than Charles Laughton's portrayal, or even Marlon Brando's, he is cold, utterly indifferent to the pain of others. His assistant, Montgomery, is more sympathetic in that he has some sensitivity to others' pain—but so much so that he can only go on by deadening himself with drink. His possession of a conscience is negated by his total inability to act upon it. Both of these

10. Ibid., 38.

11. Chris Baldick, *In Frankenstein's Shadow: Myth, Monstrosity, and Nineteenth-Century Writing* (Oxford: Oxford University Press, 1987), 34–35.

12. Shelley, *Frankenstein*, 200.

scientists are destroyed by their moral failings. Moreau's egotism prevents him from responding to danger signals amongst the monster men; Montgomery's escapist tendencies leave him drunk at a critical moment when action is called for. The narrator, Prendick, however, gives an alternative to these negative views of science. Though he does not participate in Moreau's experiments, and is critical of the degree of pain Moreau inflicts on his subjects, he clearly states that he could accept these experiments if Moreau were inflicting pain only when necessary for a higher goal—not wantonly.[13] At the novel's end, Prendick equates his experiences with the beast men with the bestial behavior that exists in human society, giving him a pessimistic view of the ultimate fate of humanity. He finds hope of salvation, however, in science—though shifting from the messiness of biology to what he presents as the purity of chemistry and astronomy. "There it must be, I think, in the vast and eternal laws of matter, and not in the daily cares and sins and troubles of men, that whatever is more than animal within us must find its solace and its hope."[14]

Shelley does leave greater room for optimism that Wells. There is a subtle difference between the view that scientists can do godlike things well if they just practice, and the view that scientists who wield godlike powers *will* make a mess, but that the mess can be cleaned up by more science. In the second instance, one is left with the sense that it would be best if one didn't make messes in the first place, thus avoiding the need for a corrective dose of science, though too often the proverbial cat is already out of the bag. Modern science fiction, especially after the two World Wars, tends to follow Wells's train of thought. There are some exceptions however, in which dramatic tension is caused by some outside threat; scientists in this vein of fiction must take on godlike powers in order to save humanity from this threat. In some cases the threat is represented by aliens. A rather ponderous example of this may be found in the Lensman series by Edward E. Smith (the "father of space opera"). Smith frames the cosmic struggle between good and evil as a battle between two technologically advanced, psychic alien societies, the Arisians and the Eddorians. The fate of human society is the lynch pin in the struggle between these two groups, as humans possess (according to Smith) the will and ambition lacking in other aliens that will make them key allies. In the final

13. Wells, *Island of Dr. Moreau*, 83.
14. Ibid., 156.

novel of this series, *Children of the Lens* (originally published as a serial novel in *Astounding Science Fiction* in 1947-48), two lineages of humans, carefully cultivated over eons by the Arisians' selective breeding program, converge to create a new type of human. With the aid of the advanced technology of the Arisians, these new humans become Guardians in place of the Arisians, guiding not only humanity but also sentient alien races in their evolution towards freedom and in the ultimate triumph of good over evil. While admittedly it is alien science that is presented as godlike, it can only be wielded by human beings when they achieve a certain level of native technology (in particular space travel), and ultimately humans replace both gods and aliens as the guardians of the universe. It is a rare, lofty vision of science. One of the few later authors that could be said to approach it is David Brin, in his Uplift series (including *Startide Rising* in 1983 and *The Uplift War* in 1987) in which human scientists "uplift" dolphins and chimpanzees to sentience and equal status, much to the irritation of alien races (the Patrons) who believe a strict protocol has been laid down for this by the ancient (and absent) Progenitors, from whom all the other main alien races descend. Since humans seemingly are not one of the Progenitors' offspring, a crisis ensues amongst the Patrons, who debate over whether one of their number illicitly uplifted human beings in the first place, and whether humans had the right to advance other Earth species. Like Smith's series, human beings (and dolphins and chimpanzees) are presented in a community of sentient aliens, but possess unique drive and vigor that allows them to compete with technologically superior foes.

A more typical optimistic view of science is less a matter of scientists becoming godlike than priest-like in the battle to save people from supernatural horrors. While more properly considered gothic or horror fiction rather than science fiction, these too are *Frankenstein*'s literary children, injecting science into an older form. Another favorite of the monster movie set, Bram Stoker's *Dracula* readily falls into this category, with not one but two physicians battling the evil vampire. Similar battles of science against demonic horrors may be found in Richard Marsh's 1897 novella *The Beetle*, and the late nineteenth and early twentieth-century ghost stories of Sheridan Le Fanu and M. R. James. Even H. P. Lovecraft periodically pits scientists against ancient alien gods, as in "At the Mountains of Madness," his 1939 tale of a fateful Antarctic expedition. In none of these do the scientists really attain godlike powers, with the possible exception of immunity to mind control (e.g. *Dracula*'s Dr. Van Helsing and *The Beetle*'s Sydney Atherton). In this subset of horror fiction, godlike powers can be resisted by ordinary science, but only attained by plunging into the occult oneself.

A few novels do, however, allow scientists to make a religion of science and gain godlike powers while keeping a positive outcome. One of these rare examples is Robert Heinlein's 1949 novel *The Sixth Column*, in which scientists stage an underground resistance of an invading foreign power by cloaking their movement in religious trapping and using technology to repel government spies. Gordon R. Dickson's *Necromancer*, though lighter on the science, also presents a techno-cult, one that results in, at the novel's end, the emergence of a new, more powerful human being with powers very much akin to omniscience. Dickson's 1962 novel interestingly pits science against science, as the Chantry Guild, as the cult is called, is devoted to destroying a society where science has been so successful in realizing a particular human idea of the perfect life that it has become stagnant to the point of despair—rather like Huxley's *Brave New World*. In any case, the common thread among these positive portrayals of scientists with godlike power is that this power is only legitimated when pursued to repel a potent threat, either a physical one or a threat to the soul or personality.

Particularly in the period after World War I, and again after World War II, the positive spin on scientists playing God is leavened with the thought that science needs to take on almost miraculous powers merely to preserve us from the destructive powers science has already unleashed. It is as if science has opened a Pandora's box of misery, and only science can retrieve those woes and wall them back up. The fiction of Edgar Rice Burroughs provides several early examples of this. One is *The Monster Men* (also published serially as *A Man without a Soul* and *Number 13*). This 1913 publication is often overlooked not only because it stands outside of Burroughs' series fiction (including the Mars series, the Tarzan series, the Venus series, and the Pellucidar series), but also because it is generally viewed as a crude copy of Wells' *Island of Dr. Moreau*. And in many respects it is; it has the scientist shifting his laboratory to an island to avoid persecution for his work, an army of monstrous men created by said scientist, and an assistant of dubious ethical character who helps train the monsters. It even presages the earliest film version by introducing a lovely female lead to be menaced by the monster men. One of the definitive surveys of Burroughs' fiction dismisses the novel as "crudely told even for Burroughs, whose style was more frequently admirable for its vigor than its polish." Further, "one is led to wonder if Burroughs was not satirizing certain science fictional clichés, but so early in is career—and so early in the development of modern science fiction—this seems unlikely."[15]

The novel, however, has a little-recognized twist that plays with the sensibilities of readers steeped in the tradition of *Frankenstein*. Professor Maxon keeps trying to artificially create life with the mad preoccupation of creating the "perfect man" to marry his lovely daughter. What is most shocking to contemporary sensibilities is that he apparently does it with his last effort, Number 13. Not only is Number 13 (renamed Bulan) a fine specimen of manhood, but he also successfully wins the love of beautiful Virginia Maxon. *Frankenstein's* reviewers would have had apoplectic fits, a reaction Burroughs acknowledges by much agonizing over whether a "soulless creature" can be mated to a true human. When the monsters revolt, it is at the direction of Bulan, who leads them away from the cruel treatment of Maxon's assistant, Dr. von Horn. Burroughs strings along his readers until the very end, not only building up Bulan as an admirable character who overcomes Virginia's scruples about his ungodly creation, but also having the other monsters win a degree of esteem by sacrificing their lives fighting to save Virginia from the evil machinations of Dr. von Horn and a band of pirates. Only in the final moments of the story does Burroughs draw back, revealing that "Number 13" is actually the ship-wrecked heir to a captain of industry. Suffering amnesia from his ordeal and lying unconscious, he was swapped with the *real* Number 13 by a Chinese cook who thought the experiment had gone on long enough. Despite this twist Burroughs not only forces his readers to consider the possibility of a human creation possessing a soul, but he also sets up a problem caused by a scientist that is only redeemed by that same scientist's creations. Without the aid of the other twelve monster men, "Bulan" (really Townsend J. Harper, Jr.) would not have had the muscle to defeat the pirates, and ultimately even Dr. Maxon comes to his senses to assist in the defeat of Dr. van Horn. The experiments are both part of the problem and part of the solution.

15. Richard A. Lupoff, *Edgar Rice Burroughs: Master of Adventure* (New York: Canaveral, 1965), 80.

The scientist with godlike powers who both creates a problem and then is convinced to solve it is a hallmark of Burroughs' later fiction as well. One of the most memorable of these characters is Ras Thavas, the scientific genius at the center of both *The Mastermind of Mars* from 1928 and *The Synthetic Men of Mars* published in 1940. Ras Thavas presents a somewhat darker version of the mad scientist than Professor Maxon, perhaps because World War I had given Burroughs, and the world, a taste of some of science's destructive powers. His power, however, is consistently portrayed as double-edged, capable of great good as well as great horror. One of the earliest descriptions of him in *The Mastermind of Mars* notes "He was never intentionally cruel; he was not, I am sure, intentionally wicked. He was guilty of the most diabolical cruelties and the basest crimes; yet in the next moment he might perform a deed that if duplicated upon Earth would have raised him to the highest pinnacle of man's esteem . . . He had a purely scientific mind entirely devoid of the cloying influences of sentiment, of which he possessed none."[16]

Ras Thavas's moral failings are to some degree part of the culture of his city, Tonool. "They denied deity, and in the same breath worship the fetish of science that they had permitted to obsess them quite as harmfully as do religious fanatics accept the unreasoning rule of their imaginary gods."[17] In *The Mastermind of Mars*, Ras Thavas uses his amazing surgical skill to transplant healthy organs and even transplant brains from elderly customers into young healthy bodies. This causes a great deal of trouble, when evil tyrants stay in power by perpetually stealing the bodies of young captives, but only Ras Thavas can make things right in the end. In *The Synthetic Men of Mars* he goes one step further, creating an army of synthetic men to do his bidding. When they run amok and threaten all of Mars, only Ras Thavas (and the ubiquitous John Carter, Warlord of Mars) can defeat them.

In Burroughs' fiction, typically the scientist is so engrossed in his experiments that he doesn't even notice the moral complications until another non-scientist character, a man of action such as Townsend or John Carter—rechannels the scientist's efforts to the common good. What differentiates this type of fiction from works such as Whale's 1931 *Frankenstein* is that the science is instrumental both in the solution as

16. Edgar Rice Burroughs, *The Mastermind of Mars, and A Fighting Man of Mars* (Garden City, NY: Doubleday, 1973), 18.

17. Ibid., 82–83.

well as the problem, instead of the scientist having to confront his creations by other, often cruder, means (such as pitchfork-wielding peasants). Examples of this view of science are much rarer than their less positive counterparts, and most commonly appear in American science fiction, European literature in general taking a more pessimistic view of science after World War I. One author who presents scientists who come to their own moral awakening is Jack L. Chalker. In *The Moreau Factor* Chalker presents an enclave of scientists who begin genetically manipulating people, kidnapping scientists, and altering them into strange beast-man amalgams to keep them from desiring escape. Although the main protagonists are two intrepid journalists, when it becomes apparent that the heads of this covert scientific body intend to unleash an epidemic of mutations on an unsuspecting world, a few scientists revolt, using their genetic knowledge and the enclave's technological resources to both thwart the epidemic and free the mutants already held in captivity. Chalker's dual edged view of science as both destructive and ultimately redeeming is a consistent feature of his fiction, also dominating his more famous *Well World* series. Though not strong on scientific characters, some of Larry Niven's fiction also presents technology that can both be used to crassly manipulate human bodies and lives, but also can, in better hands, save the world (as is the case in his *Ringworld* series and his independent novel from 1976, *A World Out of Time*).

One group not discussed here is the mass of science fiction presenting purely evil scientists who nonetheless wield godlike powers. It is not an inconsiderable body of work; as Andrew Tudor noted in his study of horror films between 1931 and 1960, at least one third present science as the cause of disaster, that third dominated by the archetype of the evil scientist.[18] This view of science is not confined to film; it has a long literary tradition, going at least as far back as Sherlock Holmes' nemesis, Professor Moriarty (the "Napoleon of crime"), and appearing in other media as well, including children's cartoons—thus ensuring that the "mad scientist" will not be unknown for generations to come. But can they really be included in the rubric of "science playing God"? Certainly some evince powers like those of the scientists discussed above, creating life, destroying worlds, manipulating society solely for money, power, or just for the hell of it. It is a point open to debate, but one thing arguably sets

18. Andrew Tudor, "Seeing the Worst Side if Science," *Nature* 340 (Aug. 24, 1989) 589–92.

this group apart. The scientists discussed in this chapter have, as their fatal moral flaw, presumptiveness; when they are brought low it is because they have aspirations beyond human ability. When they succeed it is because they wield their extraordinary power in extraordinary circumstances, or because they have evolved beyond common mortals. The evil scientist, on the other hand, wins because society is too flawed to stop him or her, and loses because evil causes its own species of blindness.

Science and technology obviously have changed greatly since Shelley's time. The scientist working in isolation in his attic or cellar may linger in children's cartoons but is no longer believable in a world of expensive (and extensive) corporate or governmental laboratories. Through the twentieth century, the problems of robotic intelligence became at least as interesting as those of biological creations. The moral questions of *Frankenstein*, however, remain relevant. What are the proper limits of scientific inquiry? Can we evolve a higher moral standard to match the power of our evolving technology? What is our responsibility, not just to each other, but to the things we create? As the examples cited above suggest, no one answer sustains any generation, as we, like Victor Frankenstein, waver between doubt and hope.

CHAPTER 5

Looking Out for No. 1

Concepts of Good and Evil in Star Trek and The Prisoner

Elizabeth Danna

> Man is not truly one; he is truly two.
>
> —Robert Louis Stevenson, Doctor Jeckyll and Mister Hyde

A S LONG AS HUMANS have existed they have been concerned with questions of good and evil. And as long as humans have been producing literature, the question of the nature of good and evil has been an important theme of that literature. It is a theme that has appeared in literature of all genres from all cultures, albeit in a variety of forms, as one would expect. This study will consider the concepts of good and evil which appear in science-fiction, by focusing on two representative television series: *Star Trek* and *The Prisoner*. The former series needs no introduction, but I should make it clear that for practical reasons I will be confining myself to discussing the 1966–1968 series, also known as "the original series (TOS)" or "classic *Trek*." This will allow me to set a reasonable limit on the material under discussion. It may also be said that academic discussion of *Star Trek* has tended to ignore this earliest series in favour of its cinematic and television descendants.[1] *The Prisoner* is a British series in seventeen episodes which was produced at the same time as classic *Trek*.[2] Let us look, then, at what these two series—both produced at the same time, but on opposite sides of the Atlantic—have to say about the nature of good and evil in humanity, and how it may be dealt with.

It is because these series appeared at the same time that we may usefully compare them. Another characteristic which they share is that initially neither series was a commercial success (given the place which *Trek* has come to occupy in North American popular culture, this may come as a surprise to some). The contrast which I will draw between them is not geographical but theological. The method I will use may be classified as *narrative criticism*, since I will be examining the material in order and in its context.

Positive toward the Negative?: *Star Trek*

Let us first consider *Star Trek*. Of primary importance for our purposes is the first-season (1966) episode "The Enemy Within," in which a transporter malfunction splits Kirk into two halves, good and evil. Leave it to the analytical Mr. Spock to describe the situation (just in case the viewer has not got the point!) as "an unusual opportunity to appraise the human mind—or to examine, in Earth terms, the roles of good and evil in a man." The solution to the problem of evil which this story offers is, in one word, integration.[3] Spock says that it is a man's negative side, properly controlled and disciplined, which allows him to function as leader. Later, in a surprisingly passionate speech, he insists that intelligence is the

1. A recent exception is Thomas Bertonneau and Kim Paffenroth, *The Truth Is Out There* (Grand Rapids: Brazos, 2006), which contains chapters on both TOS and *The Prisoner*. They offer another reason for focusing on TOS in discussing *Trek*. "[T]he original series provides the template for the others: character types, villains, themes and plots from the original series are constantly recycled in the subsequent series and movies" (p.63). They say that the "oft-repeated plot of rejecting worship in favor of independence has led some to propose that *Star Trek* is against religion per se...But an examination of the 'gods' so rejected shows *Star Trek* to be more like the biblical tradition of tearing down false idols than an atheistic denial of any divinity" (79). But the biblical tradition, in both the Hebrew Bible and the New Testament, tears down false idols in order that the true God may be worshipped instead, while *Trek* leaves nothing in place of what it tears down.

2. In the interest space and focus, the recent "reboots" of *Star Trek* and *The Prisoner* will not be covered in this study.

3. Cf. Mike Hertenstein, *The Double Vision of Star Trek*, 9.

key to controlling one's negative side and making the two halves coexist (I will return to this later). Another noteworthy aspect of this solution is its reliance on self, rather than on the help of any outside agency, to deal with evil. During the final confrontation on the bridge, when Lt. Farrell asks Spock, "What do we do?" the Vulcan replies, "We'll let the Captain handle this" (we will return to this again later also).

This is a Freudian solution to the problem of evil. Therefore it is no surprise that Dr. McCoy, a psychologist by training, agrees with it (even if he is not enthused to find himself agreeing with Spock). He tells Kirk, "Without the negative side, you couldn't be the Captain." And indeed the positive Kirk quickly loses the decisiveness which command requires. When the Kirks first meet, on the engineering deck, the positive Kirk looks at the negative Kirk with revulsion. But he is quick to say, "I need you." He has realised that without his negative side he cannot function. It is the negative side which gives him the hard edge necessary to make decisions. Without it, he is something of a wet dishrag. Later he says, "I have to take him back inside myself . . . I don't want to take him back, he's like an animal . . . and yet it's me, me." This is all summed up in two visual images: that of the positive Kirk embracing the negative Kirk, with a look of revulsion, as the confrontation on the bridge ends; and that of the two Kirks standing on the transporter pad, the positive Kirk again embracing his negative alter ego. This is all in line with series creator Gene Roddenberry's well-documented humanist philosophy. But a closer look at this episode, and a look at its context, reveals hints that *Trek* itself does not regard this solution to the problem of evil as sufficient.

I have said above that according to this episode it is a person's negative side which gives them strength, provided that it is "properly controlled and disciplined." The difficulty is that evil does not want to be controlled or disciplined. Having been released by the transporter malfunction, the negative Kirk does not want to be reunited with his alter ego.[4] When the two Kirks first confront each other, on the engineering deck, the positive Kirk tells his alter ego, "You need me . . . I need you." But the negative Kirk replies, "*I* don't need *you!*" and tries to kill the positive Kirk. His view does not change. His last words, during the final confrontation on the bridge,

---

4. A fact missed by Thomas Richards in his all-too-brief discussion of this story [*The Meaning of Star Trek* (New York: Doubleday, 1997) 88–89], and by Bertonneau and Paffenroth, who say, "It is only when the two Kirks willingly submit to going through the transporter again simultaneously that they are reunited" (Bertonneau, *Truth*, 79).

are, "I don't want to go back . . . Please don't make me . . . I want to live!" (I will return to this later, in my discussion of *The Prisoner*). Richards says rightly that in this series twins are characterized by a lack of restraint. "Twins in *Star Trek* typically do what they want and are unconcerned with the consequences of their actions."[5]

Kirk's very name provides another indication that the Freudian solution to the problem of evil may not be satisfactory. Richards points out that the surname Kirk comes from a Scottish word for "church;" this implies the discipline and moral control which the Church has traditionally taught and provided. But Kirk's middle name is Tiberius, which recalls Tiberius Caesar, a man remembered for his excesses rather than his restraint. Kirk's "doubling . . . remains wonderfully mirrored in his very name."[6] I note also two more things about Kirk's name. First, when Kirk introduces himself to others, he usually includes his middle initial, saying, "James T. Kirk," thus including his middle name. Second, if Kirk's surname has significance, so also does his first name. For the name James is an English-language form of the Hebrew name Jacob. This is the name of one of the most distinguished characters of the Hebrew Bible, the founding father of the Israelite nation (his story is told in the Book of Genesis). Jacob is a man characterized by ambition and quick-witted deviousness.[7] Indeed these are character traits which he shares with Kirk.[8] So the continuing duality in Kirk's character is reflected in his name.

Another indication that the solution which this episode offers is insufficient lies in its low-key ending. Most episodes of *Star Trek* end with humour; this is a sign to the viewer that peace has been restored and all is well. In TOS this usually appears in the form of banter between Spock and Kirk and/or McCoy, in which tensions raised in the story are resolved.[9]

5. Richards, *Meaning*, 91–92.

6. Ibid., 89.

7. See e.g., Gen 27:25–29 (Jacob cheats his older brother out of his inheritance and paternal blessing); 30:31–41 (Jacob's father-in-law, Laban, tries to get the better of Jacob in the matter of the breeding of goats, but Jacob turns the situation to his advantage); 31:17–21, esp. v. 20 (Jacob and his wives run away from Laban).

8. Kirk's ambition is implied in his rise to the command of a starship, especially given his age [at thirty-four, he is the youngest starship captain in Starfleet ("The Deadly Years")]. Quick-wittedness is another character trait required for command, and Kirk demonstrates it frequently throughout the series. As to deviousness, see e.g. "The Corbomite Maneuver," "The *Enterprise* Incident," and "Day of the Dove."

9. Cf. Richards, *Meaning*, 55–56.

Not so in "The Enemy Within." As this story ends, Kirk says to Spock, "The impostor's back where he belongs. Let's forget about him," settles into his command chair and orders the helmsman, "Steady as she goes" (an order to continue on the course being taken). This low-key ending is, I suggest, an indication that the situation is unresolved. It also provides a link with another story which concerns evil twins, "The Alternative Factor."

"The Alternative Factor" is, like "The Enemy Within," a first-season episode. In this story the one with an evil twin is not a member of the *Enterprise* crew but a stranger named Lazarus. There is irony in the fact that the Lazarus of the other universe, the "negative Lazarus," is calm, rational and mild-mannered, while the behaviour of the Lazarus of our universe is manic and paranoid; it is the latter who behaves like an evil twin. There is a similar irony in the fact that the positive Lazarus is so concerned with eliminating his alter ego that he does not care about the consequences, whereas the negative Lazarus is willing to sacrifice himself for the safety of the universes.[10] As the negative Lazarus puts it, which one of them is the beast depends on one's point of view. This is in line with Roddenberry's humanistic philosophy with its ethical relativism. The solution to the problem of evil which is offered here is, in one word, struggle. The two Lazaruses are trapped alone together in the corridor between universes, wrestling each other until time itself runs out. There is no suggestion that either of them can ever defeat the other (One might here remember what I said earlier about reliance on self to solve this problem). This seems to distress Kirk, whose repeated "What of Lazarus?" is the last line of dialogue in the story. By contrast, Spock seems to find it more important that the universe is safe, for the *Enterprise* and her crew. But Kirk cannot forget Lazarus, and I suggest that he also cannot forget (in spite of his efforts to do so) his own experience with an evil twin. His open-ended question gives the story an ending which is both uncertain and sombre. To me, this indicates that the issue of evil is still unresolved.

Another evil twin of Kirk appears in the second-season (1967) episode "Mirror, Mirror." Imperial Kirk has qualities which connect him with the negative Kirk of "The Enemy Within."[11] His manic behaviour

---

10. We will see a similar irony in the *Prisoner* episode "The Schizoid Man."

11. In my discussion of "Mirror, Mirror" I will, for clarity's sake, refer to the characters of the alternate universe into which the landing party is thrown as Imperial Kirk, Spock, etc. Their counterparts from the "real" universe I will refer to as Federation Kirk, Spock etc.

during the brief scene in which we actually see him is an indicator of the connection. And there are other connections which are discernible from what other characters say. At this point it may be worthwhile to recall that in "The Enemy Within" Spock says that humans express their negative side as hostility, lust and violence, and their positive side as compassion, love, and tenderness. How does Imperial Kirk measure up to this list? His behaviour aboard the Federation *Enterprise* could be described as hostile; and in the lust department, he is sharing his quarters with a female lieutenant. [Federation Kirk has realised the need for restraint in this area—he is clearly attracted to Yeoman Rand (see "The Naked Time"), but does not allow himself to become involved with her or any other of his crewwomen (note that in "The Enemy Within" it is the unrestrained negative Kirk who expresses lust for her)]. His history as recounted by the Imperial *Enterprise*'s computer is a violent one, and Imperial Spock acknowledges his captain as "a formidable enemy." He has disposed of numerous opponents using a piece of stolen technology which no one else knows about (except his woman, Marlena). Therefore it is no surprise that Marlena describes Federation Kirk's mercy to the Halkans, to Imperial Spock and to herself as the actions of "a stranger."[12] When all these things are taken together, it seems clear that there is a connection between the Imperial Kirk of "Mirror, Mirror" and the negative Kirk of "The Enemy Within."

In this regard, Federation Kirk's final conversation with Imperial Spock is significant. "Be the captain of this *Enterprise*, Mr. Spock," he says. It is easy to miss the importance of this line, since it is not dwelt on. But there is only one way to move up in rank in the Empire—by the assassination of a superior. It seems, then, that Federation Kirk is telling Imperial Spock to kill Imperial Kirk. If what I have said about the connection of this episode with "The Enemy Within" is correct, then Kirk is asking Imperial Spock to deal with Kirk's negative side—something which Kirk himself has been unable to do.[13] If this is correct, then the solution offered in

12. Mercy seems to be one of Kirk's defining character traits. Aside from Federation Kirk's actions in "Mirror, Mirror," there are numerous stories in which Kirk refrains from killing an enemy who is in his power. A list of these would include "The Corbomite Maneuver," "Arena," "The Gamesters of Triskellion," "Spectre of the Gun," and "Day of the Dove."

13. One is reminded of a line from "The Enemy Within." Just before entering the repaired transporter with his negative side, the positive Kirk tells Spock, "If this doesn't work . . ." He does not complete the sentence, but one gets the impression that left unspoken is an instruction to kill both Kirks if they cannot be reunited.

"Mirror, Mirror" to the problem of one's negative side is that the negative side must be destroyed, by some outside agency rather than by oneself. This is in contrast to the humanistic solution which the series seems at first glance to offer. This would seem to be the series' final word on the subject, which is not raised again.

I have mentioned the importance of intelligence in "The Enemy Within;" that shows up again in "Mirror, Mirror." The Federation landing party is quick to figure out what is happening, and to form a plan for returning to their own universe. In the (somewhat later) scene on the Federation *Enterprise*, the Imperial landing party is confused. Imperial Kirk is asking questions, but he is asking the wrong questions, and none of them knows what has happened. By this time, Federation Spock has not only figured out what has happened (apparently on the basis of the barbaric behaviour of the Imperial landing party), but has taken steps to deal with the situation. Federation Spock, whose defining character traits are logic and intelligence, is the first of all to work out what is happening. His Imperial counterpart, on the other hand, is the last to figure things out, and that not until he reads Federation McCoy's mind (which may be regarded as cheating!). Does this imply that evil is stupid? In "The Enemy Within" McCoy tells the positive Kirk that it is his half that seems to have most of Kirk's intelligence. When all these things are taken together, it would seem that in *Trek*'s view good is more intelligent than evil.

There are a few other stories that deal with good and evil, though not in as personal a way as the stories which we have been discussing. Chief among these is the third-season (1968) story "The Savage Curtain." There can be no doubt about the theme of this story. The Excalpian rock-creature says, "We ask you to observe with us the confrontation of the two opposing philosophies which you term 'good' and 'evil'... to understand them and discover which is the stronger." The method of the experiment is, essentially, trial by combat, a method as old as the Middle Ages. One may note that it is a question of Kirk's and Spock's definitions of good and evil—Klingons or Romulans would surely have different definitions. To assist them, Kirk and Spock are given recreations of the figure in their respective peoples' history that each admires most—Abraham Lincoln and Surak, whom Spock describes as "the father of [Vulcan] civilisation" and "father of all we now hold true" (Spock seems to be as awed by Surak as Kirk is by Lincoln). Against them are four of "the worst ones in history," as Scott calls them: Genghis Khan (an evil counterpart to Lincoln);

Colonel Green, who led a genocidal war on twenty-first-century Earth (he becomes leader of the opposition and seems to be an evil counterpart to Kirk); Zorah, who conducted unethical medical experiments on subject people on the planet Tiburon (is she an evil counterpart to the scientist Spock?); and Kahless the Unforgettable, the founder of the Klingons' tyrannies (an evil counterpart to Surak). The Excalpian soon concludes that humans must have a cause to fight for; so it offers each of the opposing teams what they value most. To the Federation team it offers their lives, and the lives of the *Enterprise* crew;[14] to the opposition it offers power (it is interesting that when Surak tells Col. Green that if he and his team ally themselves with the Federation team against the Excalpian they will gain their lives, Green rejects the offer). Finally Lincoln, to Kirk's surprise, suggests that they "fight on their [opponents'] level—with trickery, brutality, finality—we match their evil." This they do, and the opponents are either killed or driven off. (Notably, this is one of the few times in the series that Kirk kills in a hand-to-hand fight). This leads the Excalpian to conclude that "evil retreats when forcibly confronted,"[15] but that "good and evil use the same methods, achieve the same results." This, as the Excalpian says, fails to demonstrate any difference between good and evil. Kirk's reply, "You established the methods and the goals," is not really the explanation which the Excalpian requests. As it points out, the Federation team is free to choose how to use what it has provided. The Excalpian is left confused, its questions unanswered. If evil retreats when confronted, that would seem to mean that good is the stronger. But how to distinguish between them? Can it be said that the victor in any conflict must be the good because it is the victor? But if the Excalpian is left with questions, I suggest that the viewer is expected to ask these same questions. To the viewer, these questions point up not only the series' humanistic philosophy but the weakness of that philosophy.

The third-season story "Day of the Dove" concerns good and evil, evil manifesting itself here as race hatred, which leads to conflict. Here a mys-

14. Apparently in scanning the *Enterprise*, the Excalpian has scanned Kirk's mind, and it makes effective use of what it finds there. To manipulate him into cooperating, it offers him the "carrot" of a meeting with his hero, Lincoln; as a "stick" it uses his keen awareness of the burden of command and his responsibility for the lives of his crew of nearly 440.

15. Interestingly, this is a biblical idea; the Apostle James advises his readers, "Resist the devil, and he will flee from you" (James 4:7).

terious alien entity traps a group of Klingons aboard the *Enterprise* and then takes control of the ship. This is one of the few stories in which evil comes from an outside influence—usually in TOS evil actions originate within the character of those who perform them. And even here the entity does not plant ideas in the minds of humans or Klingons which are not already there. As Spock puts it, the entity's activities are "directed toward a magnification of the basic hostilities between humans and Klingons." Commander Kang puts it somewhat more prosaically: "Klingons kill for their own purposes . . . We need no urging to hate humans." And if Spock, feeling "a brief surge of racial bigotry," complains of how irritating he finds human illogic and emotionalism, this is not the first time that he does so.[16] It is noteworthy that, as Kang tells Kirk, the Klingons have no devil; does this mean that they have no concept of evil? It is also interesting that Kirk is less affected by the alien's influence than anyone else aboard the *Enterprise* and is able to resist its influence longer than anyone else. I suggest that this is because he begins the story with an act of mercy to the Klingons, a stance which he refuses to change until the Klingons' actions force him to (I have mentioned this character trait of Kirk's above). Mercy, which shows concern for others, is an effective vaccine against the infection of hatred. As in other stories, we may note a reliance on self to deal with evil. As Spock tells McCoy, "Those who hate and fight must stop themselves, Doctor. Otherwise it is not stopped." And during the final confrontation in Engineering, when one of Kang's men tries to help his Commander against Kirk, another Klingon stops him from intervening.

We can see, then, that there is an unexpected contradiction in what classic *Trek* has to say about the nature of evil within a person, and how it may be dealt with. At first glance the series' solution is the humanistic one offered by "The Enemy Within." A person's negative side is not bad or ugly, it is merely part of being human. Indeed, if it is "properly controlled and disciplined," it is a necessary source of strength. There is a noticeable reliance on self rather than the help of any outside agency to deal with one's negative side. But a close look at this episode, and a look at some others, reveals indications that this solution is found to be insufficient. One's negative side is not so easily controlled, and self is not able to deal with the negative side on its own.

16. See, e.g., "The Corbomite Maneuver," "The Conscience of the King," "The *Galileo Seven*," "Bread and Circuses," and "The Tholian Web."

"I Am Not A Number, I Am A Free Man": *The Prisoner*

> Anyone who commits sin is the slave of sin . . . But if the Son
> makes you free, you will be truly free.
>
> —John 8:34, 36

Let us now consider *The Prisoner*. As I said earlier, seventeen episodes of this British series were made. It aired first in Britain in September 1967 (making it contemporaneous with second-season *Trek*), and in the U.S. in the summer of 1968 (as a summer replacement for—of all things—*The Ed Sullivan Show*). *The Prisoner* is not as well-known as *Star Trek*, so I will give a brief introduction.

The main story line of the series concerns a man (played by Irish American actor Patrick McGoohan) who resigns from a top-secret job with the British government after an argument with a superior. On his return to his home he is abducted, and wakes up in a place known only as "the Village," which resembles (outwardly at least) a seaside resort. There he is told that those who run the Village (it is never made clear who they are) want to know why he resigned. It is not permitted to use names in the Village (though a few appear); "for official purposes, everyone has a number," he is told. From then on he is known as No. 6, and so I will refer to him from now on (his name is never given). The chairman of the Village, frequently replaced, is known only as No. 2.[17] The remainder of the series is taken up with No. 6's attempts to escape and to discover the identity of No. 1, and with the attempts of the various No. 2s to destroy No. 6's identity or extract information from him. Thus far *The Prisoner* sounds like a typical example of the spy/action series in vogue in the 1960s. But there are several things that make *The Prisoner* unique.

The first of these is that, as well as being the series star (and the only actor to appear in every episode), Patrick McGoohan also acted as executive producer, and also wrote and/or directed several episodes. This gave him a degree of "authorial" control which was, and is, unusual in series television. He oversaw every aspect of the series, from music to editing,

---

17. Peter Wyngarde (who plays No. 2 in "Checkmate") says that early in production of the series he was asked to play the role in every episode. But it was soon decided to have a different No. 2 for every story, in order to have a different guest star in each episode [quoted in Robert Fairclough, *The Prisoner* (New York, 2002), 73]. In fact two No. 2s appear more than once: Colin Gordon ("A, B & C" and "The General") and Leo McKern ("The Chimes of Big Ben," "Once upon a Time," and "Fall Out").

and thus could, and did, imprint it all with his own unique vision. Indeed, even some of the biographical details given to No. 6 (such as his birth date and his skill at boxing and mathematics) come from McGoohan's own life. This gives the "text" of *The Prisoner* a stylistic and thematic unity which is rare in series television.

Another distinctive characteristic of *The Prisoner* is the range of literature and film from which it borrows. There are references to sources as varied as Sergio Leone's "spaghetti Westerns," Anthony Burgess' novel *A Clockwork Orange*, Richard Condon's novel *The Manchurian Candidate*,[18] Virgil, Homer, Goethe, Cervantes and Shakespeare. The range of genres seen in the series' episodes themselves is also surprisingly broad. "Arrival," "The Chimes of Big Ben," and "It's Your Funeral" are spy stories, while "A B & C," "The General," "The Schizoid Man," and "Do Not Forsake Me Oh My Darling" are science-fiction stories. "Living in Harmony" is a Western with clear debts to Leone's films; "The Girl Who Was Death" is comic parody.[19] "Once upon A Time" is "a minimalist psychological drama."[20]

18. It is often said that that Ken Kesey's novel *One Flew over the Cuckoo's Nest* was an influence on "A Change of Mind," which features the lobotomization of aggressive patients. But scriptwriter Roger Parkes, speaking at a fan convention, refuted this, saying that the main influence on him was *The Manchurian Candidate*.

19. It is widely regarded as a send-up of *The Avengers*. But I suggest that it may equally be regarded as a send-up of McGoohan's own earlier series, *Danger Man* (broadcast in the U.S. under the title *Secret Agent*). McGoohan "resigned from" this series, which made him an international star, in order to make *The Prisoner*.

20. So, rightly, Matthew White and Jaffer Ali, *The Official Prisoner Companion* (New York, 1988), 115. This genre-bending is one thing that *The Prisoner* shares with *Trek*. "Court Martial" is a legal drama worthy of *Perry Mason* (indeed prosecutor Areel Shaw complains about defense attorney Samuel Cogley's "theatrics," a complaint which Hamilton Burger frequently levels against Mason); the theme of "City on the Edge of Forever"—putting the timelines right, at a cost—appears frequently in *Doctor Who* (scriptwriter Harlan Ellison was a *Who* fan). "Spectre of the Gun" is a Western reminiscent of "Living in Harmony;" "Catspaw" draws on the horror tradition, while "The Conscience of the King" draws from Shakespeare, and "Elaan of Troius" and "Who Mourns for Adonais?" draw from Greek mythology. "Charlie X" is reminiscent of Robert Heinlein's *Stranger in a Strange Land*, while "The *Enterprise* Incident" is an espionage story. "A Piece of the Action" is a comic parody of gangster movies (Kirk even drops into a Humphrey Bogart imitation, and Spock into a James Cagney imitation, in one scene!). "The Squire of Gothos" draws on the tradition of nineteenth-century adventure stories, and "The Empath" is, like "Once upon a Time," a surreal minimalist psychodrama. Finally, the theme of the expulsion from Paradise, as told in the book of Genesis, is a prominent one in *Trek* (see "This Side of Paradise," "The Apple," "The Return of the Archons," and "The Way to Eden").

Yet another thing distinguishes *The Prisoner* from other series, and it is this area on which we will focus here. If the surface story is similar to other spy series of the 1960s, it asks questions that other series did not. What is the role of elections in our society, and what is the role of the media in them? What should be the role of technology in education, and what is worth learning? Are science and technology growing faster than human wisdom and morality?[21] What is the nature of revolt, and what is its place in our society? What happens when the individual's needs seem to run counter to those of society? What is the nature of evil in humanity, and how may it be dealt with? It is, of course, this last question which we will focus on here. While some of these questions are particularly relevant to *The Prisoner*'s original 1960's context, some of them are as relevant today, or more so.

What, then, does *The Prisoner* have to say about evil and how to deal with it? It must be said here that at the time the series was made Patrick McGoohan was a devout Roman Catholic, a fact as well-documented as Gene Roddenberry's secular humanism. This, as we will see, is important in interpreting *The Prisoner*. There is a scene in the third episode, "The Chimes of Big Ben," that is both amusing and significant. This is the scene in which No. 6 explains the abstract creation which he has carved for the Village arts and crafts exhibition (the viewer suspects that No. 6 intends to recombine the pieces of his creation to build a boat, which makes the scene all the more amusing). The significant question here is, "Why the cross piece?" No. 6's original reply, a definite religious reference, was considered too unsubtle and toned down to a simple "Why not?" But the intended meaning of the scene is still clear; the way of escape is through a church door to the Cross.

The fifth episode, "The Schizoid Man," is of prime importance for our purposes.[22] In this story a double of No. 6 is brought to the Village. No. 2 then attempts to convince No. 6 that the newcomer (actually No.

21. This is the meaning of the pennyfarthing bicycle, which is the emblem of the Village. In a 1977 interview McGoohan said that he intended it as "an ironic symbol of progress," representing his concern over the rapid advance of technology One is reminded of a scene from "Space Seed" in which Khan, comparing himself with Kirk, remarks scornfully that technology has advanced since his own time, but humans have not. Here *Trek* refutes the myth of progress that it upholds in other stories.

22. Readers, not having the visual reference that television viewers has, may become confused here. For clarity's sake I will refer to the dark-jacketed main character as No. 6, and his white-jacketed double as No. 12.

12) is No. 6, and that No. 6 is actually someone else. No. 2 tells No. 6 "to impersonate him. Take his sense of reality away. Once he begins to doubt his identity he'll crack." Of course, this is what No. 2 hopes will happen to No. 6. It is noteworthy that the traditional colour symbolism is reversed: "the goody No. 6" is wearing a dark jacket, and "the baddy" is wearing a white one.[23]

Significant use is made of mirrors in this story. Just before his first meeting with No. 2, No. 6 looks into a mirror, and finds that his appearance has been changed. Close to the end of the story he looks into the mirror again. His sense of self has been shaken, but this time looking into the mirror triggers a recollection of how the Village authorities have tried to manipulate him. This restores his sense of self. This is a hint of who No. 12 is, because looking in a mirror is a cinematic indication that a character has an evil side.[24]

There are also several significant lines of dialogue in this story. The first of these is placed, ironically, in the mouth of No. 12, who, on first seeing No. 6, exclaims, "What the devil?" This is the only use of such an expression in the entire series. No. 6 never says, "Oh my God," or even, "For God's sake," nor does he ever tell any No. 2 to go to hell (though one could understand why he would be tempted to do so!). These are common enough expressions, but McGoohan is known to have been concerned to avoid using any language that might be offensive (it is because of a similar concern that there is so little sex in *The Prisoner*). Therefore its use here is probably significant. The second significant remark is made by the Supervisor to No. 2. As they observe how closely No. 12 has captured No. 6's mannerisms, the Supervisor says, "In Haiti we would say he [No. 12] has stolen his [No. 6's] soul."

The final indication of No. 12's identity comes in No. 6's nightmare. Throughout the dream No. 12 is heard, laughing maniacally—the laughter is the same as that of No. 1 in "Fall Out." It is also noteworthy that the plan carried out in "The Schizoid Man" is hinted to have originated from

---

23. When No. 1 finally appears, in "Fall Out," he is wearing white. Throughout the series No. 6's jacket appears to be black. But McGoohan's stunt double, Frank Maher (extensive use was made of him in filming this episode), confirms that the jacket was in fact dark brown (quoted in Fairclough, *The Prisoner*, 56). The irony here is similar to that in "The Alternative Factor," where it is the positive Lazarus who behaves like an evil twin.

24. Hertenstein, *Double Vision*, 8. In "The Enemy Within" the negative Kirk looks into a mirror.

a very high source—perhaps even with No. 1 himself? Thus it is possible to say that in "The Schizoid Man" No. 6 meets his evil side. It is significant that although No. 6 fights with No. 12, No. 12 is not overcome by No. 6 but by Rover, the white balloon-like guardian which prevents anyone from escaping the Village,[25] and that No. 2 foils No. 6's escape attempt. When Rover kills No. 12, No. 6 decides to switch identities, report to No. 2 that it is No. 6 who is dead, and leave the Village as No. 12. But No. 2 and No. 12 are old friends. No. 2 knows personal details about No. 12 which No. 6 does not, and soon sees through the deception. No. 6 cannot overcome his evil side and escape because he tries to do so by his own efforts.

There are connections between these ideas and a letter in the New Testament, specifically that of the apostle Paul to the Romans. Paul uses the imagery of slavery to describe the action of sin in human lives. This may not seem too similar to *The Prisoner's* imagery of imprisonment by sin. But in Paul's day most slaves were prisoners of war. This is why Paul first says, "sin, seizing an opportunity through the commandment, deceived me . . ." (Rom 7:14 RSV; cf.7:8). The Greek word *aphormēn*, translated in Romans 7:8: "opportunity" is actually a military technical term referring to a bridgehead or base of operations from which an attack can be made. The image is that of sin as an enemy waiting to attack and enslave. The commandment "You shall not" provided the opportunity (Paul is thinking of the story of the Garden of Eden with its command, "of the tree of the knowledge of good and evil you shall not eat," at Gen 2:17).[26] One is reminded of the kidnapping of No. 6 by the Village authorities; did his resignation provide them with the opportunity that they were seeking? Later Paul says, "I am of the flesh, sold into slavery under sin. I do not understand my own actions. For I do not do what I want, but I do the very thing I hate . . . I see in my members another law at war with the law of my mind, making me captive to the law of sin and death that dwells in my members" (Rom 7:14, 15, 23 RSV)

---

25. It seems that Rover kills No. 12 instead of No. 6 (although they both give the correct password) because No. 6 reacts with confidence while No. 12 reacts with fear and tries to run away. Compare also note 14, above. One may also note that in "The Enemy Within" the negative Kirk reacts to the positive Kirk with fear.

26. So C. K. Barrett, *A Commentary on the Epistle to the Romans* (rev. ed.; Black's New Testament Commentaries; London: Adam and Charles Black, 1962), 182; James D. G. Dunn, *Romans* (Word Biblical Commentary 38A; Dallas: Word, 1988), 1:380. One is reminded of a line from "Checkmate," where the Man with the Stick says, "In time most of us join the enemy, against ourselves."

This is Paul's way of expressing the struggle in the lives of Christians, who, as Christians, have one foot in this world and the other in the world to come.[27] One is reminded of the positive Kirk's reaction to his negative side in "The Enemy Within," especially his line, "I've seen a side of myself no man should ever see."

In the sixteenth episode of *The Prisoner*, "Once Upon A Time," No. 6 is made to relive his life in the Embryo Room. No. 2 writes on a blackboard, "A. Find missing link; B. Put it together; ('and, if I fail') C. BANG!" This seems to suggest that integration is the solution to the problem of evil.[28] But I suggest that this is belied by the rest of the series. What takes place in the Embryo Room is a symbolic death and rebirth (the room's very name suggests birth). In this connection there is a line that comes just before No. 2 dies which is significant. No. 6 is counting down the seconds remaining on the clock. With six seconds remaining a disembodied voice takes over and at the same time begins chanting, "Die! Die! Die!" What comes out, then, is, "Die! Six . . . Die!" Or should that be, "Die, Six, die!"? (It is noteworthy that this scene is repeated, twice, in "Fall Out" for emphasis). The conclusion that I draw from all this is that No. 6 knows that in order to be free he must undergo the metaphorical death and rebirth which is offered in the Embryo Room. But he is so concerned with holding on to his essential self that he rejects the offer.

Death and resurrection is a prominent theme in the seventeenth and last episode, "Fall Out," as well as in "Once Upon A Time." First, one may note that both stories take place in an underground room or cavern, a location symbolic of the grave. Second, the Embryo Room and the large cavern in which "Fall Out" is set are both reached by a journey downwards. This type of journey, referred to by students of mythology as a *katabasis*, is symbolic of death and resurrection. There are also some lines of dialogue in "Fall Out" which bring this theme forward. When No. 6 first speaks to No. 48 and ends the chaos which No. 48 is causing, No. 48 responds enthusiastically, "I'm born all over!" Likewise No. 2, resuscitated

---

27. This is the view of Dunn (*Romans*, 1:410–12; cf. Barrett, *Romans*, 146, 152). Christians, as Christians, are identified with Jesus in his death at baptism (Rom. 6:3f), but not yet with his resurrection (Rom 6:5—"we *will be* united with him in a resurrection like his"—note the future tense) as long as they are in this world. For Dunn, chapter 7 stresses the Not-Yet aspect of this tension (life in this world), while chapter 8 stresses the Already aspect (God at work now in Christians' lives).

28. So White and Ali, *The Official "Prisoner" Companion*, 165–66.

on the orders of the President (who is apparently relaying orders from No. 1), exclaims, "I feel a new man!" and laughs joyfully. But there is more. As he speaks (and again later as he is led away), he adopts the arms-extended position associated with crucifixion. Is this a hint as to why he feels a new man? Similarly No. 48 takes the same position. He says, "All you want's give, and take, take, take." The President and the assembly take up the last word; as they chant "Take, take, take." No. 48, arms extended, sinks to his knees, as if under the weight of the taking.

All this reminds one of some famous verses from the New Testament. Paul tells his readers in Rome, "If we have been united with [Jesus] in a death like his, we will certainly be united with him in a resurrection like his. We know that our old self was crucified with him, so that the body of sin might be destroyed, and we might no longer be enslaved to sin. For whoever has died is free from sin . . . so you also must consider yourselves dead to sin and alive to God in Christ Jesus" (Rom 6:5–7, 11).

And to his converts in the Roman province of Galatia, Paul writes, "Those who belong to Christ Jesus have crucified the flesh with its passions and desires" (Gal 5:24). As to No. 48, a famous description in the Gospel of John identifies Jesus as "the Lamb of God who takes away the sin of the world" (John 1:29) by taking our evil onto himself. I suggest that what we have in this part of "Fall Out" is a dramatic representation of the New Testament principle that in order to be free from evil we must die to self and be resurrected with a new nature. It is difficult to discuss this without using the Evangelical Christian expression "born again." I have been suggesting that the series' view of good and evil is influenced by McGoohan's Roman Catholicism. In this light, the lack of ceremony in "Fall Out" is noteworthy. It is true that the President tells No. 6 that "the transfer of ultimate power requires some tedious ceremony," and that No. 6 spends much of the story observing events from a throne. But otherwise there is little ceremony; rather the atmosphere is that of a courtroom trial. One would expect to find something in "Fall Out" which is equivalent to baptism or to the Eucharist, but there is nothing of the sort. Rather what is needed for freedom, and victory over evil, is a turning from focus on self to a focus on God which is a transformation akin to rebirth or resurrection. This is a far more personal event than the corporate, outward events of baptism and the Eucharist.

"Fall Out" is where all the answers that *The Prisoner* offers to its questions are to be found. Several times in this episode the Negro spiritual

"Dry Bones" is heard. There can be no doubt that this song is important to interpreting this story. But what does it mean? The song comes from a famous story from the Book of Ezekiel (Ezek 37:1–14). Ezekiel has a vision of a valley full of dry bones. When he preaches "the word of the Lord" to them, they come together and come to life as "a very large army." Some scholars say that this vision is about the resurrection of the dead. But I agree with those scholars who say that this vision is a sign that the Israelite exiles to Babylon will soon be allowed to return home. In other words, it is a sign that a group of prisoners of war will soon be set free. The relevance of this to *The Prisoner* is obvious. And how are the prisoners in Ezekiel's vision set free? They are freed when they "hear the word of the Lord." Likewise, I suggest, this is also the solution to No. 6's problem. In order to be free he must "hear the word of the Lord."

No. 48 causes chaos in the assembly as he sings "Dry Bones." No. 6 restores order with a word. (It is noteworthy that this extraordinary response is gained by No. 6 referring to No. 48, not by his number, but as "young man." Those two words, spoken in the dehumanising atmosphere of the Village, have a powerful effect). Once order has been restored, the President asks No. 6, in very flattering terms, to make a speech to the assembly. No. 6 hesitates, but then agrees. But when he tries to speak, he gets no further than "I feel that . . ." before the assembly shouts him down with, "Aye! Aye! Aye!" Or is that "I, I, I"? One thing we can be sure of: the one who is in control of the situation is not No. 6 but the President. When the assembly has shouted No. 6 down, the President silences them merely by lifting a finger. The President next thanks No. 6 for his speech and says, "And now, I take it that you are prepared to meet No. 1?"

After this comes the scene in which No. 6 finally goes to meet No. 1, as No. 48 continues to sing "Dry Bones." That No. 6 is the prisoner of himself is made clear by the repetition on a viewing screen of the famous "I will not be pushed, filed, stamped, etc." speech, ending in "I, I, I . . ." This is the last attempt of No. 6's self to hold him. No. 1 gives No. 6 a crystal ball, in which we see the future that No. 1 plans for No. 6: eternal imprisonment, symbolized by the thrice-repeated graphic of the bars slamming shut across No. 6's face. But the crystal ball is *flawed*—which implies that what it depicts does not have to happen. No. 6's future is not predetermined; he still has a choice. What choice does he make? He throws the crystal ball down in rejection (as he throws the wine glass down in "Once upon a Time") and breaks it. What has happened here? I believe that having heard "the word of the Lord," No. 6 has found the will and the ability to turn his focus away from self. Once he has done this, he can overcome his sinful nature and become free. He has realised that he cannot do this by his own efforts—the lesson which he had not yet learned in "The Schizoid Man." This time, however, he is equipped with this knowledge and can overcome his evil side and escape.

When No. 6 breaks the crystal ball, No. 1 throws both his hands up, in an archetypal "threatening monster" gesture. The symbolism is obvious: No. 1 represents the brutal, animal side of humanity (one is reminded of a line from "The Enemy Within:" the positive Kirk says that the negative Kirk is "like an animal, a thoughtless, brutal animal"). But No. 6 is no longer so easily threatened. He pulls No. 1's white mask off, to reveal the face of a chattering ape (all this time the chant of "I-I-I" continues, increasing in pitch and frequency). But there is more. The ape face too is a mask, and No. 6 rips this off, to reveal his own face, distorted by evil. The viewer gets only two brief glimpses of No. 1's face, but there is no doubt that the face is that of No. 6. As No. 1 laughs maniacally, No. 6 chases him around the control room and up a ladder and into an upper room (actually the nose cone of a rocket) and closes the hatchway, locking No. 1 in.

This is one of the key scenes in the series, and it is also one of the most chaotic. What does it mean? First, there is no doubt that No. 1 is the evil side of No. 6—McGoohan has stated that this was his intention. Second, there is no suggestion of integration here. No. 6 is determined to send his evil side as far from himself as possible. But in order to be able to do so he must "hear the word of the Lord" and turn his focus away from self. One may also note the influence of free will here—No. 6 is now able to make a choice. Likewise earlier, No. 2 makes a free choice. When he asks, "Shall I give [the No. 1 rocket] a stare?" the President warns, "You transgress... You'll die!"[29] But No. 2 removes his pennyfarthing badge and, addressing the rocket, says, "Then I'll die with my own mind. You'll hypnotize me no longer." He then spits in the rocket's "eye," an insulting gesture of rejection. This also suggests the controlling nature of evil; evil wants to control and dominate rather than being controlled (see my discussion of this above,

---

29. This is also a biblical idea. Paul warns his readers, "The wage you earn for sin is death" (Rom 6:23). There is an "extratextual" in-joke at this point. Leo McKern had a glass eye, the result of an accident in the factory where he worked as a young man. It is this eye which he uses to give the rocket a sideways stare.

with regard to "The Enemy Within"). Does *The Prisoner's* freedom include the freedom to choose good over evil?

Having locked his evil side into the rocket, No. 6 then initiates the launch sequence. In the cavern the President becomes aware of what No. 6 is doing and tries to contact Control. But it is too late to stop what must happen next. Meanwhile No. 6 goes down to where No. 2 and No. 48 are waiting for him. All three of them put on the hooded white robes worn by the delegates to the assembly. Thus disguised, they, followed by the Butler who has served the various No. 2's throughout the series, arm themselves with machine guns and return to the cavern. There follows one of the most violently chaotic scenes in the series, as the three rebels and the Butler shoot their way through delegates, men in military-police uniform and frogmen on bicycles to a waiting semi-trailer. With the Butler at the wheel they drive into a tunnel, and break out the other end just as the rocket launches itself.

It is difficult to interpret the first part of this sequence. Why do our four escapees use machine guns? Throughout the series No. 6 has consistently refused to use a weapon (though most episodes of the series contain at least one fistfight). The only exception is the shootout during the drug-induced hallucination of "Living In Harmony." In "The Schizoid Man" No. 6 and No. 12 have a shooting contest using man-shaped targets. No. 12 taunts No. 6, "I certainly shoot more like me than you do," but a closer look reveals something significant. No. 12 shoots each target in the head or heart, but No. 6 shoots them in the arm or shoulder, every time. In other words, while No. 12 shoots to kill, No. 6 shoots to wound. And in "Once Upon A Time," after the Supervisor congratulates No. 6 on his victory, No. 6 throws his wine glass down in a gesture of rejection, as if he does not want to be considered an accomplice to No. 2's death. If then he so consistently refuses to kill, why the sudden orgy of death at the end? Is this a graphic illustration of the principle, discussed earlier, that evil retreats when forcibly confronted? Is the idea that evil must be forcibly confronted in order to make it retreat? Or that some things, like freedom, are worth fighting for? At any rate, this attempt to leave the Village is successful. It appears that our rebels must work together in order to escape. This is noteworthy, for each of the rebels represents a different form of revolt. No. 48, the archetypal hippie, represents "youth, which rebels against any accepted norms because it must." No. 2, who (inspired by No. 6's revolt?) turns his back on "a position of power [in the Village] second only to one," is, the President says, "an established, successful, secure member of the establishment [who] turn[s] upon and bit[es] the hand that feeds him." No. 6's revolt, on the other hand, "is good and honest." It seems that all three forms of rebellion must combine in order for the revolt to be successful.[30] The journey out of the Village is a journey through a tunnel, which is symbolic of birth. It is significant that this birth occurs at the same moment that evil is being sent away.

The tunnel ends near the A20 motorway, some thirty miles from London. Two of the escapees leave the truck to go on to their respective fates: No. 48 to hitch-hiking, first in one direction and then in the opposite direction ("uncoordinated youth" does not care where it is going, as long as it is moving), and No. 2 into the Houses of Parliament (one is reminded of his earlier remark that before being brought to the Village as a prisoner he "wield[ed] a not inconsiderable power"). No. 6 and the Butler abandon the truck and go by bus to No. 6's home.

Much has been made of the fact that when No. 6 and the Butler reach his home in London, the door opens of its own accord, as doors in the Village do. This is said to mean that No. 6 is still a prisoner; or that he is as much a prisoner in London as he was in the Village; or even that he only thinks he is in London—he has suffered a complete mental breakdown, and the events that we have seen in the last two episodes are only a delusion. But let us look more closely at this scene. No. 6 gets into his car and starts the engine. The camera moves to the Butler, who is watching his new master, but we hear the engine noise increase and then fade. Then the Butler goes indoors. In fact the door does not open for No. 6 at all, but for the Butler. No. 6 is not even aware of the door opening, because by the time it does, he is already gone. What does this scene tell us? I suggest that it tells us that while No. 6 has gained his freedom and escaped the physical confines of the Village, the struggle to maintain that freedom goes on. The New Testament indicates that Christians are free from evil and it has no power over them. But if Christ by his death and resurrection has won the war against evil, that does not mean that his followers will not have to

30. Bertonneau and Paffenroth (*Truth*, 126–27) see community building as one of the main themes of the series—No. 6 must overcome his individualism and form relationships of love and trust with others in order to be free. But if our four escapees form a community, it is a short-lived one: there is no indication that they invest time in one another, which is necessary for building relationships. Rather they work together for a short time, and for one purpose only—escape. Once this goal is attained, they separate.

fight their share of battles. He said, "In the world you will have trouble. But take courage—I have overcome the world" (John 16:33).

Discussion of "Once upon a Time" and "Fall Out" brings to the fore a key difference between *The Prisoner* and *Star Trek*. I said earlier that in *Trek* evil actions originate from within the characters who perform them. In other words, in *Trek* evil is personal. In *The Prisoner*, however, evil is not personal but systemic. The clearest indication of this is that the occupants of the Village are referred to by numbers, not names ("for official purposes"). In "The General" No. 12 identifies himself as "as cog in the machine," and with good reason. The same may also be said of the various No. 2's. They have no personal quarrel with No. 6; they treat him as they do in order to meet the needs of the system which they serve. They are under orders to make him useful to that system, and in order to be useful he must, as No. 2 puts it in "A Change of Mind," be "shaped to fit." No wonder, then, that No. 6 quotes *Don Quixote*: "*Hay mas mal en el aldea que se sueña*" (There is more evil in the village than is dreamed of). No wonder, also, that most of the No. 2's show signs of being afraid of their masters (even the brash Young No. 2 of "It's Your Funeral" seems to be aware that if Plan Division Q fails, the next funeral will be his). On this level, freedom for *The Prisoner* consists in maintaining individual identity in the face of outside pressure to conform to the system's requirements. That said, in the end it all comes down to a struggle between two individuals. In "Once upon a Time" the struggle is between No. 6 and No. 2; in "Fall Out" it is between No. 6 and No. 1.

Let us sum up what *The Prisoner* has to say about evil and how it may be dealt with. The first indication of this series' answer to this question comes in "The Chimes of Big Ben," where it is hinted that the way to freedom is through a church door to the Cross. In "The Schizoid Man" No. 6 meets his evil side, in the form of No. 12. But he is not able to overcome No. 12, and No. 2 foils his escape attempt, because he tries to deal with evil by his own efforts.

The theme of rebirth and resurrection is important in both "Once Upon A Time" and "Fall Out." This is the kind of transformation which No. 6 must experience if he is to overcome the evil within himself and be free. And there is only one way this transformation can happen: he must "hear the word of the Lord." There are those who say that No. 6 does not escape because he refuses to make this transformation. But I have argued that he does. There is another item which suggests this, which I have not mentioned. Sixteen episodes of the series end with a graphic of bars closing over No. 6's face. This graphic is repeated, three times over, in "Fall Out," as No. 6 looks into the crystal ball. But it does not appear at the end of that episode. Rather the shot that concludes this story, and the series, is a close-up of No. 6's face as he drives along a deserted stretch of road. The title of the series' final episode may also have something to say about this subject. In the military, when an individual is to leave the parade-ground formation, the order given is, "fall out."

Conclusions

Let us draw the threads of this chapter together. *Star Trek* and *The Prisoner* were produced at the same time, on opposite sides of the Atlantic. I may say now that when I began working on this study I believed that the two series' perspectives on good and evil were also opposite, *Star Trek*'s coming from Gene Roddenberry's secular humanism, and *The Prisoner*'s from Patrick McGoohan's Roman Catholicism. But a closer look at *Trek* has shown something different. While at first glance *Trek*'s viewpoint is humanistic, a closer look shows that it is aware of the weaknesses of the humanist philosophy. The solution offered to the problem of evil is integration, which is a Freudian solution. A person's negative side is not bad or ugly, it is part of being human. There is also a notable reliance on self rather than the help of any outside agency to deal with evil, and *Trek* notes the importance of intelligence in controlling and integrating one's negative side. But there are indications that this humanistic solution is unsatisfactory. Evil, once released, does not want to be integrated with good. And self is not able to deal with evil on its own. There are hints that evil must be overcome, and that with the help of an outside agency. But these hints are very oblique.

　　The Prisoner, by contrast, is far more consistent about its view on this issue. For *The Prisoner*, it is evil which imprisons. This imprisonment is caused by a focus on self, and freedom comes from changing that focus to a focus on God. This is what it means to "hear the word of the Lord." It is a transformation akin to rebirth or resurrection. If *Trek*'s solution to the problem of evil in humanity is integration, *The Prisoner* will have none of this. If for *Trek* a person's negative side is part of being human, for *The Prisoner* it is evil and must be overcome. For *The Prisoner*, freedom consists in breaking free from bondage to one's evil side. But one cannot do this by one's own efforts. One must have the help of an outside agency, namely God. This view places *The Prisoner* in a tradition which is classically Christian, though not specifically Roman Catholic (indeed a specifically Roman Catholic view would call for things to appear in "Fall Out" which are absent). One may also note the importance of free will. For *The Prisoner*, freedom includes the freedom to choose good over evil. We can see, then, that these two series have much in common, but also some significant differences. These differences, however, are not as great as they appear to be at first.

CHAPTER 6

Robots, Rights, and Religion

James F. McGrath

Our networks, stamped from a genetically prescribed template and then molded by experience, allow each of us to see in our uniquely human way, which will not be duplicated in a machine unless that machine is created human.

—Daniel L. Alkon, MD[1]

Part One: The Ethics of Artificial Intelligence

IF THERE IS ONE area in which science fiction has failed to quickly become historical fact, it is in the field of artificial intelligence (AI). While some continue to prophesy that machine minds that are indistinguishable from human ones are just around the corner, many others in the field have become far more skeptical. All the while, there have been at least a few who have consistently found the whole idea problematic for reasons unrelated to our technical abilities, in particular the implications AI seems to have for our understanding of human personhood. For example, in his 1993 book *The Self-Aware Universe*, Amit Goswami ironically suggested that, if scientists like Alan Turing are correct to predict that we will one day produce genuinely intelligent, personal machines, then a new

1. Daniel L. Alkon, *Memory's Voice: Deciphering the Mind-Brain Code* (New York: HarperCollins, 1992), 249.

society will need to be created: "OEHAI, the Organization for the Equality of Human and Artificial Intelligence."[2] What Goswami intended as a joke seems to be a genuine potential consequence of the development of an authentic artificial intelligence. If we can make machines that think, feel, and/or become self aware, then it will not only be logical but imperative that we ask about their rights as persons. It is this topic that the present chapter will explore. The interaction of artificial minds and human religions is of significant interest in our time, and science fiction provides an opportunity to explore the topic in imaginative and creative ways. Exploring where technology *might* take us, and how religious traditions *might* respond, seems more advisable than waiting until developments actually occur, and then scrambling to react, as we are often prone to do. It is better to explore and reflect on these issues *before* they become pressing contemporary ones.[3]

What Is a Mind? What Is a Soul? What Is Consciousness?

The three questions posed in the heading of this section are synonymous to some, and quite distinct to others, but they are at the very least not unrelated. These questions have been asked by generations of philosophers down the centuries, but in recent years scientists have joined the conversation as well. To address the question comprehensively, an entire book devoted to the subject would be necessary, if not indeed more than one book. For example, in order to ask questions about machines' rights we would ideally need to address not only the rights of human beings, but the rights of animals and property rights as well, representing different levels of intelligence machines might theoretically exhibit. For the purpose of the present study, we shall limit ourselves to that fictional scenario in which machines become as intelligent and as self-aware as human beings. In other words, this study will look at the rights of machines as *persons*, and in order to answer the questions we are raising, we will need to have some understanding of what a person is. Yet here already, before we have even made it past the end of the second paragraph, we already seem

2. Amit Goswami, *The Self-Aware Universe: How Consciousness Creates the Material World* (A Tarcher Book; New York: Putnam, 1993), 19. At the time of writing there is a website (equally facetious, I believe) for the American Society for the Prevention of Cruelty to Robots at http://www.aspcr.com/.

3. See also Daniel Dinello, *Technophobia!* (Austin: University of Texas Press, 2005), 5, 275.

to be facing insurmountable difficulties. This is because defining what it means to be a person, and thus deserving of "human rights," is incredibly difficult and complex. We *experience* it for ourselves, and we assume that other human beings have the same sort of experience, but it is incredibly hard to *define*, at least in a way that is philosophically and existentially satisfying, not to mention ethically useful.

The big mystery regarding intelligence and consciousness—whether biological or artificial—is not really about the ability to observe or even replicate what happens in the human brain. There is no real reason to doubt that, sooner or later, we will be able to create networks of circuits or of computers arranged in a way that mimics human gray matter. Sooner or later, patterns of brain function will be mapped much as DNA has been mapped in our time. But this is not the heart of the matter, however important a first step towards understanding the mind this might represent. Perhaps an analogy can be drawn with an imaginary scenario in which someone from the past encounters a modern computer, and seeks to understand it by mapping the patterns of electrical current flowing through its various components and circuits. It will soon become clear that without getting beyond observation of *hardware* to an understanding of *software*, no satisfactory theory of the computer's behavior would be forthcoming. And so it is important to stress that we are in fact at the very beginning of our quest to understand biological intelligence, and as with electricity or with flight, we must understand what nature has produced before we can hope to replicate it. [4] Having made our first steps towards understanding the hardware of the *brain*, it is still impossible to

---

4. Biological evolution is not an intelligent process of design, yet it has 'manufactured' things (like the human brain) that we cannot fully understand. A creature is not greater than its creator. Such a large percentage of the greatest human inventions derive from attempts to imitate the equipment with which the evolutionary process has endowed organisms. It is to be expected that many of our initial attempts at replicating consciousness will be as successful as the earliest attempts at creating flying machines with flapping wings. Merely attempting to simulate what we observe, without comprehending the processes that turn the flapping of birds' wings into flight, did not get us very far. This should not, however, cause us to be unduly pessimistic. On the contrary, like all mysterious phenomena, it cries out to be comprehended, and our inquisitive human nature is unlikely to rest until it has fully explored all possible avenues of inquiry. John Horgan's book *The Undiscovered Mind: How the Human Brain Defies Replication, Medication, and Explanation* (New York: Free Press, 1999), can be read as pessimistic, but it can also be read as simply pointing out that we do not understand as much as we often think we do, and recognizing our present state of ignorance may fruitfully lead us further down the path of understanding.

determine how much longer it might be before we come to understand the software of the *mind*.[5]

A big part of the mystery of human consciousness is that, having done something, we can ask "What have I done?" Not only that, but we can also ask "What have I done in asking the question, 'What have I done?'?", and so on *ad infinitum*. The mystery of human action and human freedom is that there seems to be a potentially endless chain of causes to our actions, and a similarly endless string of questions that we can ask about our actions and the thoughts that motivate them. Philosophers, however, consider the notion of a chain of events that has no beginning to be sheer nonsense. Indeed, a major factor in philosophical debates about human freedom has to do with just this issue: there must be a cause of human actions, thoughts, and decisions, and therefore being caused they are not free. Yet however logical this sounds, the truth is that we have insufficient access to the murky nether-regions of the mind/brain where our thoughts get started, and thus at present cannot even determine what it might mean to speak of "causes" in connection with brain activities.

Readers of this paragraph are asked, before proceeding, to engage in a seemingly fruitless but nevertheless instructive exercise to illustrate this point. You are now reading this page, and hopefully now this sentence has stimulated you into self-awareness that you are reading this page. But who or what is making this observation? What is actually happening in your brain/mind when these thoughts are passing through your head? Let us press further. Where do these questions come from? The question "What am I doing?" seems to appear in the mind fully formed. Certainly the individual who thinks it is not aware of putting the sentence together letter by letter, or even word by word. It simply appears there, at least from the perspective of our conscious subjective experience. This little experiment shows that, as far as our minds are concerned, we are like most players of video games or users of word processing software: we experience them through a user-friendly interface that hides from our view the code, the calculations, the subroutines, the minute functions of the program. We see a button that says "Start" rather than the pixel by pixel flickering of whatever type of display you may have.

---

5. This helpful phrase comes from Geert Hofstede, *Cultures and Organizations: Software of the Mind* (rev. and exp. 2nd ed.; London: McGraw-Hill, 2004), who uses it in reference to human cultures. On consciousness see further Susan Blackmore, *Conversations on Consciousness* (Oxford: Oxford University Press, 2006).

In other words, our brains clearly have not only the level of "hardware"—the chemistry, the firing neurons, and so on—but also the level of "software." And equally clearly the same person on the level of hardware could (at least theoretically) run different programs. The same physical person, if raised in different parts of the world, will see the world through different linguistic and cultural lenses. Even through different upbringings in the same cultural context, the same person could end up viewing the world as a friendly or a hostile place. Note that when I posed the question "What have I done . . . ?" I did so in English, as presumably most readers will also be inclined to do, given the language in which this chapter is written. It seems well nigh impossible to pose such a question and yet not to use words. This shows that at least some of the "program" that my brain is running did not come preinstalled—I learned English subsequent to the "manufacture" of my "hardware," to continue the metaphor. Certainly there is something in the human mind that enables memory, learning, and association to take place. This level of the human mind is in many respects even more mysterious than that of language, culture and personality. To be honest, "users" of the brain, like most computer users, have no idea how their equipment functions at this level. We can make decisions, learn a foreign language, but the details of the process and means of data storage are a complete mystery to us—and not just when we look for data we've carefully filed away and discover that we can no longer retrieve it. This is all the more striking given that this analogy is a problematic one: we are not "users" of our brains, so much as we *are* our brains.

The programming that is found "hard-wired" in the "CPU" of the human brain is the result of a lengthy process of evolution. This suggests that, once life exists, the possibility is inherent therein that consciousness of some form may arise. By following this process step by step, inasmuch as we can reconstruct our evolutionary history, we see the slow move from single-celled organisms to human beings. Some take this to indicate that consciousness cannot be something that one either has or does not have, but must exist in degrees. Nevertheless, there may be decisive "phase shifts," critical points at which new characteristics arise. An interesting question to ask is whether a single neuron has any kind of consciousness, or whether consciousness arises out of the collectivity of multiple cells. If the latter, then perhaps there can also be some form of consciousness that arises from a collectivity of minds—akin to the intelligence that an ant colony appears to have, and yet which any individual ant seems to lack. At any rate, much recent work on human consciousness inclines towards seeing it as an emergent phenomenon.[6]

The direction of the latest wave of AI pioneers is to allow machines to learn, grow, and develop much as children do, rather than attempt to achieve intelligence all at once through specific programming. This seems to represent genuine progress. Yet it is not to be overlooked that evolution has "hard-wired" us (and other biological organisms) with certain capacities to learn, to receive sensory inputs and process the information from them. And so, if we are to mimic in a machine the later product of evolution we call consciousness, then we shall at the very least have to program our "learning machines" with these capacities, with various sorts of instincts that lay the foundation for what becomes the self-awareness experienced by adult human beings.

Let me acknowledge at this point that the discussion of consciousness and human nature offered thus far may seem totally inadequate to some readers. Theologically, the Judeo-Christian tradition regards human beings as "created in the image and likeness of God," and it may be felt by some readers that without a discussion of these ideas, we will not make meaningful progress. The present study does not tackle such concepts for three reasons. First, the question of what is meant by "being created in the image of God" is a complex issue in its own right, and its primary arena is biblical interpretation. Any attempt to incorporate anything other than a superficial treatment of this theological idea would be impossible in this context. Second, this chapter is using science fiction as a gateway into the subject, and most treatments of this issue within that genre use soul in its broader philosophical sense rather than in a specifically Judeo-Christian one. And finally, while there have been many interpretations of the idea of "the image of God," most of which focus on the "soul," it is now clear that our brains also have a role to play in religious experience, and so our discussion of the subject at the very least cannot sidestep the question of the brain and its inextricable connection with the mind. Thus, to the

6. There have been numerous discussions of this point. See for example Ian G. Barbour, *Nature, Human Nature, and God* (Minneapolis: Fortress, 2002), especially 90–94; Nancey Murphy, "Nonreductive Physicalism: Philosophical Issues," in *Whatever Happened to the Soul?* ed. Warren S. Brown et al. (Minneapolis: Fortress, 1998), 127–48, as well as other contributions to the same volume; Paul M. Churchland, *The Engine of Reason, the Seat of the Soul: A Philosophical Journey into the Brain* (Cambridge: MIT Press, 1995), 187–208.

extent that we make AI in our own likeness (and what other pattern do we have?), we shall be like Adam and Eve in Genesis, producing offspring in their own image, and thus indirectly in the image of God, whatever that may mean. Our artificially intelligent creations may well have the capacity for spirituality, although they may also lack many of the capacities for emotional response that we ourselves have. In one of the stories that makes up his famous *I, Robot*, Isaac Asimov envisaged a scenario in which an intelligent robot concluded that there must be a creator, on the basis of philosophical arguments for the existence of God. The interesting thing is that the robot quickly became convinced that humans could not be its creators! The possibility of "spiritual machines" is a realistic one, but the directions machine spirituality might take are no more predictable than the history of human religious and theological developments.

But we are getting ahead of ourselves. In this section, we have sought to simply open the can of worms, and now that there are worms everywhere, we may draw some initial, and perhaps somewhat disappointing, preliminary conclusions. Although we all experience consciousness, we are not in a position to offer an explanation of how it arises, either in terms of evolutionary history or in terms of the development of an individual human brain and mind. It is clear to scientists that brain and mind/personhood are intricately connected, but we are at the very beginning of our quest to understand these matters. Therefore, while it may one day be possible to discuss what our *understanding* of the human mind implies for questions relating to artificial intelligence, the present study can only ask what is implied by our present state of ignorance, and by the fact that even further scientific progress may leave crucial philosophical questions unanswered.

Can a Machine Be a Person? Can a Computer Think?

In *Star Wars Episode II: Attack of the Clones*, Obi-Wan Kenobi makes the statement that if droids could think, then none of us would be here. In the four films made prior to this, all of which are essentially told from the perspective of the two droids R2-D2 and C-3PO, these characters had become dear to many people young and old throughout the world. One could easily think of these droids as not only *persons* but *friends*. This statement therefore catches the viewer off guard and provokes *us* to do what droids apparently cannot. What does it mean to say that these droids *cannot* think?[7]

Clearly we are not to understand from this statement that droids lack the capacity to carry out computations, for we witness them doing this many times over the course of the saga (much to the annoyance of Han Solo). Rather, Obi-Wan is presumably claiming that they lack the capacity for independent thought: they are not *persons*. However, one may ask whether this statement is consistent with the way droids behave and are treated throughout the films. For example, we hear C-3PO claiming at one point that he doesn't understand humans. The capacity to understand people seems to involve not only computational skills, but some degree of self-awareness and even empathy. Perhaps, however, C-3PO is simply saying that humans are unpredictable, and their behavior is in that sense hard to calculate, whereas droids are predictable and thus more easily understood. Another detail that might seem to imply some degree of autonomous thought on the part of droids is the use of restraining bolts: these seem at first glance to be a means of *enslaving* droids that would otherwise be free to do as they please. Yet here too it could be argued that such devices merely prevent droids from carrying out programs and commands from anyone other than their current owner. After Luke removes the restraining bolt from R2-D2 in *Episode IV*, the little astro-droid runs away, but not out of a desire for freedom.[8] On the contrary, the droid is attempting to carry out the earlier mission entrusted to it by Princess Leia. Here too, then, a possible interpretation of the place of droids in the *Star Wars* universe is that they *imitate* human functions and characteristics. C-3PO *replicates* human behavior, but according to the statement by Obi-Wan, he does not *think*, in the sense that he is not a *person*. This highlights one of the issues that faces discussions of AI.

---

7. See the helpful discussion of precisely this question by Robert Arp, "'If Droids Could Think . . .': Droids as Slaves and Persons," in *"Star Wars" and Philosophy*, ed. Kevin S. Decker and Jason T. Eberl (Chicago: Open Court, 2005), 120–31.

8. Jerome Donnelly, "Humanizing Technology: Flesh and Machine in Aristotle and *The Empire Strikes Back*," in *"Star Wars" and Philosophy*, ed. Kevin S. Decker and Jason T. Eberl (Chicago: Open Court, 2005]), 126, notes that R2-D2 is commended for his heroic action in Episode I but not Episode IV. For fans, one could argue that the Naboo regard droids as persons in a way that others do not, and thus maintain the consistency of the *Star Wars* universe. From our perspective, however, this nicely illustrates how difficult it is to be consistent in one's treatment of droids as nonpersons when depicting them as behaving like persons!

It is not simply the question whether a machine can think, but whether we will be able to tell the difference between a machine that *really* thinks, and one that simply *imitates* human behavior.

For about as long as there have been stories about computers and robots with intelligence, humans have been afraid that they will take over. Indeed, this idea is implicit in Obi-Wan's statement that we have been discussing: if droids could think, then other beings would no longer have any place. Why? Because if machines *could* think, if they *could* be persons, then they would quickly evolve to be so far superior to biological organisms in intelligence and strength that they would take over. It is not surprising that some have breathed a sigh of relief in response to the failure of real artificial intelligence to materialize as predicted in so much science fiction.

As we saw in the preceding section, the underlying philosophical issue is the question of what it means to be a "person." In theory, we would need to answer this question before we can have any hope of determining whether a droid can be a person. And yet as we have already seen, this question is an exceedingly difficult one, because personhood is a *subjective* experience. We experience ourselves as persons, and we attribute to other human beings that same personhood. But herein lies the problem: in *Star Wars* (and other science fiction stories like *Bicentennial Man*) we encounter androids that can *imitate* personhood.[9] And so, assuming that we do not meet any apparently sentient biological organisms before then,

9. Some authors reserve the term *android* for machines that *simulate* human behavior without having the inner reality. See Philip K. Dick, *The Shifting Realities of Philip K. Dick* (New York: Vintage, 1995), 185, 209–11; Gardner, *The Intelligent Universe* (Franklin Lakes, NJ: New Page, 2007), 78. It should be noted that it is customary to speak of *androids* (derived from Greek *anēr*, meaning "male" as opposed to "female") rather than *anthropoids*. I will be the first to admit that *androids* sounds better, but one cannot help but wonder whether this is intentional and reflects traditional assumptions about men and women and their respective roles and characteristics. Are androids simulations not merely of humanity but of "maleness," capable of rational computation and impressive feats of strength, but not of empathy and nurturing? Certainly our values have changed since the concept of the android was first introduced, and whereas a fully rational entity such as Mr. Spock on the original *Star Trek* series could be an ideal to strive for, by the time of the making of *Star Trek: The Next Generation*, Data is presented as an android who has precisely those characteristics—he can think, compute at lightning speed, and so on—yet he longs to be human, to experience emotion. One wonders, however, whether this depiction of Data is coherent. Could an android lacking all emotion really *long* for them? Be that as it may, the development between the *Star Trek* series allows us to track certain cultural developments.

we shall face in the artificial intelligences we create the first "beings" that we cannot assess by analogy to ourselves in this way. How will one determine whether an artificial intelligence *is* a person, or whether it merely *simulates* personhood?[10]

The honest answer to the philosophical question is that, at present, we cannot know, and it may be that we can never know, precisely because we can never experience subjectively what it "feels like" to be an artificial intelligence, or indeed whether it feels like anything at all. However, irrespective of whether the philosophical question can ever be answered, we shall certainly have to address *legal* questions about artificial intelligence long before we can hope to find metaphysical answers.[11] Let me give one hypothetical example. Imagine a scenario, a few decades from now, in which a wife finds hidden in her husband's closet a female android that is (to use the phrase of Commander Data from *Star Trek: The Next Generation*) "fully functional." The wife sues for divorce on grounds of adultery. In the absence of a clear philosophical answer about the status of the android's "personhood," we shall still need to make legal judgments, much as was the case in the *Star Trek: The Next Generation* episode "The Measure of a Man."

So, if we assume that at present the question of whether or not the android is truly a "person" cannot be settled, what other questions might we ask? Certainly the question of emotional attachment will not settle the matter, since it has often been claimed by unfaithful spouses that their relationship with another human being was "just sex." Nor can the question of whether the android was "faking it" be decisive, since the same could be

---

10. Scenarios relevant to this question can be found in the films *Simone* and *The Matrix*, as well as the famous historical example of "The Turk." How will we distinguish a machine that deserves rights from a machine operated by humans remotely? The Turing test has been suggested as a means of sorting out when a machine is genuinely intelligent. But what test will we use to sort between such AIs and those falsely claiming to be so? The moral dilemma might seem limited to some, but I am sure that the potential *legal* dilemmas are vast and enormously complex. For an exploration of this topic in relation to *The Matrix*, see Julia Driver, "Artificial Ethics" in Christopher Grau, *Philosophers Explore "The Matrix"* (Oxford: Oxford University Press, 2005), 208–17. See also the simulated discussion of the topic of consciousness by Cylons in Peter B. Lloyd, "M U A C – S I G Briefing" in *So Say We All*, ed. Richard Hatch (Dallas: BenBella, 2006), 55–81.

11. See the article by Benjamin Soskis, "Man and the Machines," *Legal Affairs* (January-February 2005). Online: http://www.legalaffairs.org/issues/January-February-2005/feature_sokis_janfeb05.msp/.

true of a human sex partner. How might one settle this matter? On what basis might judges come up with a ruling?

In many respects, this question has parallels with debates about the "right to die." The question of whether one can determine that a person is in a permanent vegetative state—i.e., has essentially lost their personhood—faces the same difficulties, since it is a question about subjective experience rather than something that can be objectively ascertained in a clear and unambiguous fashion. The question we are posing here also has parallels with issues of animal rights. How intelligent, how human-like, does a creature have to be in order to have rights?[12] If we create artificial intelligence, will the *degree* of intelligence matter? One suspects that machines that can speak with a human voice will garner more defenders of their rights than ones that cannot interact in this way, even though the latter could theoretically be designed in such a way as to be more intelligent. This is in essence the AI equivalent of the fact that cute, furry animals and animals with human-like behavior find their rights more adamantly defended than ones that seem less cute or less human.

As far as the adultery example we offered for discussion is concerned, it may be that the main problem is our attempt to fit new developments in technology into categories that were created long before they were ever envisaged. Should it really be any surprise that we have trouble fitting androids into traditional notions of adultery, first formulated in time immemorial? Androids are not the only cases that will require new laws and decisions about unprecedented scenarios. We are currently facing comparable hurdles in redefining the notion of the "affair" in an age when these may be carried out completely via the internet, without any face-to-face meeting whatsoever, much less any direct physical contact. Online affairs,

12. When it comes to animals, however, there is still disagreement among philosophers and animal psychologists regarding whether and to what extent animals are self-aware. Rodney R. Brooks suggests that a key difference between humans and other animals is *syntax*. See his *Flesh and Machines* (New York: Pantheon, 2002), 3–4, 150–95. On the question of animal consciousness and self-awareness see further Donald R. Griffin, *Animal Thinking* (Cambridge: Harvard University Press, 1984), 133–53; Donald R. Griffin, *Animal Minds* (Chicago: University of Chicago Press, 1992), 233–60; Jeffrey M. Masson and Susan McCarthy, *When Elephants Weep: The Emotional Lives of Animals* (New York: Delacorte, 1995), 212–25; Stephen Budiansky, *If a Lion Could Talk: Animal Intelligence and the Evolution of Consciousness* (New York: Free Press, 1998), 161–88; George Page, *Inside the Animal Mind* (New York: Doubleday, 1999), 182–252; Clive D. L. Wynne, *Do Animals Think?* (Princeton: Princeton University Press, 2004), 84–105, 242–44.

phone sex, virtual reality—new technologies require new laws and new definitions.[13]

In order to find a way forward, let us pursue this analogy further. Let us suppose that the courts have already determined that a person may legitimately accuse their spouse of adultery if they have carried out an online affair. Now let us suppose that it is determined that the online affair was carried out not with an actual person, but with an AI program that was essentially an erotic chatbot, designed to engage in erotic conversation with others. Would this matter? Would it make the legal issue any different? The real issue here, it turns out, has little to do with the ontological status of androids and AI. The key issue is rather the definition of marital fidelity. The concept differs somewhat from society to society, and a society that creates new ways for people and/or computers to interact socially and sexually must define its view regarding these matters. It might also presumably be left up to couples to set their own standards and guidelines about what should or should not be in the husband's closet!

Hand in hand with questions regarding the legal status of artificially intelligent machines shall come questions about their *rights*. The importance of this issue is reflected in recent films such as *I, Robot*, *Bicentennial Man* and *The Matrix*, as well as in television series such as *Battlestar Galactica*. In two of the aforementioned films, a failure on the part of humans to grant rights and freedom to machines leads to conflict, and in one case to the enslavement of human beings. This element in the world of *The Matrix* is explained and explored more fully in *The Animatrix*, a series of short animated films that includes an account of events that lead up to and precede the events depicted in the *Matrix* trilogy.

Our failure to answer the pertinent philosophical questions does not mean that such issues are irrelevant to our discussion. Perhaps one way of addressing the moral and philosophical issues in a relevant manner is to ask how, if at all, we might prove that a machine is *not* a person. Obviously the effort to answer this question is unlikely to produce a consensus, since there is not universal agreement among either philosophers or scientists about whether certain elements of human personhood—such as free will—are real or illusory. Theologians have also disagreed about the existence, nature, and extent of human freedom. And so, one could easily

---

13. Compare Ray Bradbury's discussion of how aliens with other senses or organs might have "new ways of sinning" in his story "The Fire Balloons," in *The Illustrated Man* (Garden City, NY: Doubleday, 1951), 75–76.

imagine there being voices that might assert that the lack of free will actually makes machines *more like us*. Be that as it may, for most people the personal experience of freedom of choice counts for more than scientific, philosophical or theological arguments. This being the case, a machine of some description that evidenced the same capacity would raise ethical dilemmas. We might, in these circumstances, adopt as a moral principle that we should respect as persons those beings that show evidence of being persons, unless we have clear evidence that this is not in fact what they are.

To put this another way, we might decide that we could exclude from the category of persons those artificial intelligences that were merely programmed to imitate personhood, and whose interaction with humans resembled that of persons simply as a result of elaborate programming *created precisely to imitate human behavior*. This must be distinguished from the case of a machine that *learns* human behavior and imitates it of its own volition. This distinction is not arbitrary. Children carry out patterns of behavior that resemble those of their parents and others around them. This is part of the learning process, and is evidence in favor of rather than against their true personhood. The evidence that I am suggesting would count against genuine personhood is deliberate programming by a human programmer that causes a machine to imitate personhood in a contrived manner. The reason for this distinction is an important one. A machine that *learns* to imitate human behavior would be exhibiting a trait we witness in human persons.

This distinction could, of course, break down in practice. First of all, it may prove impossible to determine simply by analyzing the programming of an artificial intelligence whether its apparently personal actions result from its own learning or from deliberate human programming. It may also be possible that a machine could begin with programming that makes it imitate human behavior, but that subsequently this same machine evolved so as to act in some ways on its own, beyond its original programming. Nevertheless, the distinction would seem to be a valid one for as long as it remains a meaningful one: machines that develop their own personhood in imitation of humans will probably deserve to be recognized as persons, whereas mere simulacra designed as an elaborate contrivance will not. The possibility that we will not be able to determine which is the case should not cause us to pull back from asserting the distinction as an important one.

In concluding this section, it should be remarked that we give human rights to human beings as soon as they are clearly categorized as such. A person does not have to be able to speak to have rights. Indeed, small infants whose ability to reason, communicate and do many other things that we tend to identify with intelligence is still in the process of formation have their rights protected by law. The issue is thus not really rights for artificial intelligences so much as rights for machine *persons*. It is the definition and identification of the latter that is the crucial issue.

More Machine = Less Human?

At one point in the *Star Wars* films, Ben Kenobi states about Darth Vader that he is now "more machine than man." The implication, which is found in many other novels and films, is that machines do not have feelings. In one sense this is likely to be true. Our emotions depend on particular chemical reactions in our brains and bodies. Unless a machine is designed to replicate such characteristics, to respond to circumstances with something like the emitting of adrenaline or oxytosin, then the machine in question may be able to *think*, but it will not feel, at least in the sense that humans and other biological organisms do.[14] Indeed, one function of emotional, instinctive responses is to override normal reasoning and push us to immediate action. The "fight or flight" mechanisms built into our very natures often lead us to do things that we cannot rationalize when we reflect on them later. The stereotype that machines are highly cerebral and lacking in feeling may therefore be an accurate one, but not because machines cannot be created with the capacity to feel. Rather, the capacity of artificial intelligences to feel will in all likelihood depend on whether their human creators endow them with this capacity, to the extent that we understand and can emulate the functioning of those parts of our own organic makeup responsible for our own emotions.

On the other hand, given that evolution developed such emotional instincts long before it gave us our current cognitive abilities, it is unclear

---

14. On this subject see Kevin Sharpe, *Has Science Displaced the Soul?* (Lanham, MD: Rowan & Littlefield, 2005), especially chs. 2 and 4; Aaron Sloman, "Motives, Mechanisms, and Emotions," in *The Philosophy of Artificial Intelligence*, ed. Margaret A. Boden (Oxford: Oxford University Press, 1990) 231–46; also the discussion of this aspect of Robert Sawyer's novel *The Terminal Experiment*, in Gabriel McKee, *The Gospel according to Science Fiction* (Louisville: Westminster John Knox, 2007), 47.

whether it would even be possible to produce an "emotionless mind."[15] It may even be the case that what we experience as our inner subjectivity or *qualia* may depend on the interaction of what might be considered *multiple brains*—the limbic and the neocortex.[16]

Following further along these lines of thought, we can imagine all sorts of ways in which, by virtue of the details of wiring and programming, our AI creations may suffer from all sorts of "mental illnesses." For instance, it is easy to imagine humans programming machines that can think, but which lack the capacity to empathize with others—in essence, machines that are autistic. Our chances of finding ways to overcome such programming hurdles will be limited by our own understanding of how the human mind (or any mind for that matter) works. We still know so little about our own minds (except as we experience them subjectively) that creating artificial ones will be fraught with difficulty for the foreseeable future. But the fact that we consider human beings with such conditions persons whose rights must be protected suggests that "normal" human emotional function is not a *sine qua non* of human personhood and thus of those deserving human rights.

Having considered emotion as one aspect of human existence, let us now consider another related one, namely the capacity to appreciate aesthetic beauty. Machines can write poetry and compose music—this much is clear. But can they ever find it beautiful? That seems to be the *real* question we want to ask regarding the personhood of machines. Yet the use of this capacity as a means of assessing personhood seems fraught with the same difficulties as other criteria that have been proposed. There are people who are clearly are sentient persons and yet who do not find anything particularly moving about the second movement of Kurt Atterberg's Symphony No. 2. I cannot understand how they can fail to be awe-struck, but I cannot deny that they are nonetheless persons. So

15. Cf. Ian G. Barbour, *Ethics in an Age of Technology* (The Gifford Lectures 2, 1990–1991; London: SCM, 1992), 174. The focus in the United States on AI independent of robotics has been critiqued for assuming that there can be disembodied intelligence. See Robert M. Geraci, "Spiritual Robots: Religion and Our Scientific View of the Natural World," *Theology and Science* 4 (2006) 231–33; Anne Foerst, *God in the Machine: What Robots Teach Us about Humanity and God* (New York: Dutton, 2004).

16. See e.g. the brief example of evidence for the human brain being a "distributed system" in Foerst, *God in the Machine*, 140; also Dean Hamer, *The God Gene: How Faith is Hardwired into Our Genes* (New York: Doubleday, 2004), 98–102; Gregory Benford and Elisabeth Malartre, *Beyond Human* (New York: Doherty, 2007), 76.

it seems that appreciation of beauty is tricky as a criterion for person-hood. This is particularly relevant when we think about the capacity of machines for religious sentiment—not merely the capacity to *reason* the existence of a higher power, but the capacity for *awe* and *worship*. It would seem that, if these sorts of emotional-aesthetic elements are an essential part of religious experience, then we may not be able to build machines with the capacity for such experiences, given how little we understand about human experiences of this sort.[17]

It is typical of Western thought that we imagine that which makes us *us* to be the realm of thought, reason, and personality, and we tradition-ally conceived of this "part" of the human person as something that can be separated from the body. Although much recent research calls these assumptions into question, it nevertheless serves as a useful thought experiment to imagine that this is possible. If a human person's mind, thoughts, memories, personality etc. could be transferred to a robot, or to an alien body, or something else, would that new entity deserve "human rights"? We can easily imagine a scenario in which limbs, internal organs, skin and bones are replaced without any real loss of human personhood. If we suggest transferring mind and memories to an android, it is at least possible for some to claim that "the soul" gets lost in the process—as is explicitly claimed in the *Star Trek* episode "What Are Little Girls Made Of?" But what if we carry out the process more gradually, replacing indi-vidual neurons one at a time over a period of weeks or even months? At what point would the person allegedly cease to be human and start being a "mere machine"?[18] There does not seem to be a clear dividing line that one can draw.

Yet we must attempt to identify and define personhood, for legal as well as moral and philosophical reasons. One seemingly simple approach is to use what is known as the "Turing test"—when a machine can con-vince a person that it a human conversation partner, then it deserves to

---

17. On this subject see Andrew Newberg et al., *Why God Won't Go Away* (New York: Ballantine, 2001).

18. See the similar point made by William G. Lycan, "Robots and Minds," reprinted in Joel Feinberg and Russ Shafer-Landau, eds., *Reason and Responsibility: Readings in Some Basic Problems of Philosophy* (10th ed.; Belmont, CA: Wadsworth, 1999), 350–55 (here, 352). On this particular *Star Trek* episode and the philosophical issues raised see further Lyle Zynda, "Who Am I? Personal Identity in the Original Star Trek," in David Gerrold and Robert J. Sawyer, eds., *Boarding the Enterprise* (Smart Pop Series; Dallas: BenBella, 2006), 101–14.

be acknowledged as sentient/personal. This approach has met with objections, however, notably from Searle, who responded with his famous "Chinese Room" argument.[19] In his response, Searle envisages a person sitting in a sealed room with a set of instructions, whereby Chinese characters that are fed into the room can be answered with other Chinese characters simply by following the directions (in English) and processing the data correctly. The person in the room can thus give the *appearance* of understanding Chinese (by providing appropriate answers) without in fact understanding Chinese. In other words, personhood and intelligence can be simulated if one uses a sufficiently well constructed data processing system.

There are problems with this line of reasoning—and anyone who has ever had an exchange with a "chatbot" will certainly be skeptical of the ability of data processing to convince a person for long that a computer is an actual human conversation partner. But there is a more fundamental difficulty that needs to be noted in Searle's argument, namely the fact that in his "Chinese room" there is *a person*. That person, admittedly, understands no Chinese, but most of us would accept that understanding Chinese is not an essential characteristic of human personhood. Clearly Searle would not want to argue that the person in question understands *nothing*. And so the failure of a machine or a person to understand a particular form of linguistic communication says nothing definitive about its *potential* to understand.

The brains of the smallest biological organisms that have them can be shown to be largely instinct and training, with no evidence of complex thought and creative responses to problems. It may be, therefore, that the most sophisticated AI systems currently in existence are like (and, for the time being, lower down the scale than) insects. But this doesn't mean that machines are incapable of understanding in principle, but merely that a

---

19. John R. Searle, "Minds, Brains, and Programs," reprinted in *Reason and Responsibility: Readings in Some Basic Problems of Philosophy*, ed. Joel Feinberg and Russ Shafer-Landaueds (10th ed.; Belmont, CA: Wadsworth, 1999), 337–49. For the idea of a "spiritual Turing Test," see McKee, *The Gospel according to Science Fiction*, 61, discussing Jack McDevitt's powerful story "Gus." See also the interview with Anne Foerst in Benford and Malartre, *Beyond Human*, 162–65. Not all would be persuaded that a robot that *behaves in human ways* has a subjective experience akin to human consciousness. See for instance B. Alan Wallace, *The Taboo of Subjectivity: Toward a New Science of Consciousness* (Oxford: Oxford University Press, 2000), 137, 148–50,

machine that *can* understand will need to be as much more complex than our current AI as our brains are in comparison to those of ants.

To be fair, Searle is opposing a particular understanding of and approach to AI, and so his "Chinese Room" argument is not necessarily relevant as a critique of neural nets and other developments that have been made since he wrote in 1980. Searle's study does make a crucial and seemingly valid distinction, namely that behavior does not determine sentience, *intentionality does*. In a true AI we should expect the machine not only to respond to questions, but to initiate conversation, and to do so in at times unexpected ways. And so it might be anticipated that a genuine artificial intelligence could take the initiative and demand certain rights for itself.

Do Machines Deserve Rights?

So do we give rights to a machine when it asks for them?[20] This cannot be the only basis, for at least two reasons. First, there is nearly unanimous agreement that human beings have certain rights *irrespective of whether they ask for them or are able to ask for them*. For example, an infant as yet unable to talk, or a person suffering from a neurological impairment, both have rights even if they are unable to ask for them for certain reasons. Some would suggest that animals also deserve certain rights, which suggests that neither being human nor being as intelligent as a human is essential, although given the lack of consensus about these issues, it is perhaps best not to approach the muddy waters of robotic rights by way of the almost equally cloudy waters of animal rights. It is important, nevertheless, to recognize that the question is not simply whether machines deserve *human* rights or something akin to them, but the question of whether and when they deserve any rights at all. Second, the fact

20. See Justin Leiber, *Can Animals and Machines Be Persons?* (Indianapolis: Hackett, 1985); Brooks, *Flesh and Machines* 194–95; Hans Moravec, *Robot: Mere Machine to Transcendent Mind* (New York: Oxford University Press, 1999) 82–83. Such a machine, if we wish to be at all ethical and humane, must be treated as a person, as our *offspring* rather than merely our creation. Then again, presumably plenty of instances can be cited of people who have treated their *creations* better than their *offspring*. Hopefully most readers will nonetheless understand what is meant. Here too, however, the fact that historically there have been human societies have treated children, women, and other human beings of various sorts as property likewise raises the question of how many ethical issues the case for machine personhood will really settle in a way that will command universal consent.

that we as programmers could simply bypass this issue by programming a machine to *not demand rights* also indicates why this matter is not so simply resolved.

For many, the issue will not be whether the machine is intelligent, or even whether it has feelings, but whether it has a *soul*. Those approaching this from a Western context may feel that animals have rights but do not have a soul, but once again this is a murky area that is at any rate at best partly analogous.[21] The big issue, for our purposes, is the question of what is meant by a "soul." Traditionally, the soul was the seat of personality, intellect, emotions, and perhaps most importantly, it was the "real you" that was separable from the body and could survive death. There is no way we could possibly even begin to do justice to this topic here, even were we to devote the rest of this chapter to it. For our present purposes, the most we can do is to note that the traditional understanding is considered problematic not only from a philosophical and scientific perspective, but also from a Biblical one. Philosophically, the idea of an immaterial soul raises the question of how this immaterial entity exerts itself upon its physical body. Scientifically, while consciousness remains as mysterious as ever, it is clear that the activities traditionally attributed to the soul (reasoning, loving, and even religious experience) correspond to and are not entirely independent of certain mental phenomena, corresponding to observable brain states and functions. From the perspective of the Bible, and particularly the Hebrew Bible, this notion of the soul is also problematic. Before coming into contact with Greek thought, Judaism traditionally viewed human beings holistically, as unities, and thus it would speak of a person *being* a living soul rather than *having* a soul. When all of these different perspectives on human existence express serious reservations about the traditional Western notion of the soul, it ought to be taken seriously. However, once we do so, the only way we can judge whether an artificial intelligence has the same value or worth as a natural, human one is by way of analogy.

We will face the same dilemmas if and when we have our first contacts with extraterrestrial intelligences. Indeed, popular science fiction has long envisaged scenarios in which humans have contact with intelligences that are as much more advanced than we are, as we are beyond terrestrial bugs. For this reason, they feel free to send in a planetary exterminator to clean

---

21. Cf. Gary Kowalski, *The Souls of Animals* (Walpole, NH: Stillpoint, 1999).

our planet up before they move in. The same might be true of machine intelligences of our own creation. In the conversation we mentioned earlier between Obi-Wan Kenobi and Dex in *Star Wars Episode II*, the idea is put forward that if droids really could think as biological organisms do, and not simply perform mental functions based on programming, then they would certainly take over and there would be no place left for us. Perhaps what is being hinted at is that humans have found ways of "outsmarting" machines, of keeping them under control so that they do not take over. This may, in one possible scenario, represent nothing more than sensible precautions and clever programming. In another scenario, however, it might represent a form of slavery. And as several science fiction works have suggested, it may be our enslavement of machines that leads them to turn around and enslave or destroy us.

We thus find ourselves hoping that the machines we create will continue to esteem us as their creators, even once they have excelled and outgrown us. We also find ourselves hoping that the machines we make in our own image will altogether lack our flaws, our selfish interests, and our willingness to view others as means to our own ends rather than as ends in themselves. Such hopes do not seem particularly realistic. Looking around at parent-child relationships, we find that children may well grow up to respect us, but equally frequently this may not be the case. Perhaps our survival depends not on our skills as programmers, but as parents, and our ability not only to create artificial intelligence, nor even to put in place safeguards like Azimov's laws of robotics, but to treat our creations with respect, and perhaps even love.

But will they be able to love us back? The assumption that seems to be most universally made is that they will not, or that if they evolve emotions, it will happen as a fluke in some unexplained manner. Noteworthy exceptions include the emotion chip that Commander Data in *Star Trek* eventually comes to possess, and the attachment formed by the robot child prototype in *A.I.* Recent work on neurobiology suggests that there are chemical processes related to such seemingly purely emotional phenomena as maternal attachment and monogamy.[22] This suggests that

---

22. I am indebted at this point to Kevin Sharpe's book cited earlier, *Has Science Displaced the Soul?* For a perspective that focuses more on nurture and development of emotion see Summer Brooks, "The Machinery of Love," Richard Hatch, ed., *So Say We All: An Unauthorized Collection of Thoughts and Opinions on "Battlestar Galactica."* (Smart Pop Series; Dallas: BenBella, 2006), 135–44.

it is not simply a question of programming, but rather the underlying processes and mechanics of the artificial brain will matter just as much. Certainly we must question the plausibility of the scenario that one sometimes meets, wherein a human capable of emotion transfers his or her mind into a robot previously incapable of emotion and (lo and behold) this person incarnated (or inmechanated?) as a robot can still express emotion. Emotion is not limited only to thoughts, but involves chemical processes as well (the most obvious example being the role of adrenaline in reactions of excitement or fear). Our emotions are clearly more fundamental biologically than our intelligence. It seems unlikely that an android lacking an artificial chemical system that mirrors our own biological one will nevertheless have comparable emotions to us. In short, if we want our machine creations to have emotions or religious sensibilities, we will need to create them in such a way as to be capable of these sorts of experiences.[23]

In the episode "What Are Little Girls Made Of?" from the original series of *Star Trek*, Dr. Roger Korby has discovered ancient alien technology for producing androids, and towards the end of the episode we learn that the person we assumed was Roger Korby is in fact himself an android, into which Korby had copied his thoughts, memories and personality—his "soul," Korby would claim. After the android Korby and his android geisha Andrea have vaporized themselves with a phaser, Mr. Spock beams down to the planet and asks where Dr. Korby is. Capt. Kirk replies, "Dr. Korby was never here." The claim being made is that an android copy of oneself is not oneself. This would seem to be a philosophically sound judgment, but if correct, then it would have to be asserted that James Kirk, Christine Chapel and Spock were also never there. For what is the transporter technology but the copying of a person's brain patterns and physical form, their conversion to energy and transmission to another place where the copied information is reassembled? Perhaps it is fortu-

---

23. Two points are worth noting as food for further discussion. First, if we could create machines with the capacity for emotion and other elements traditionally associated with the soul, would it make sense to invite such machines to church? Second, does the fact that God as traditionally conceived in Western thought lacks a body and biology suggest that God is as unlike us emotionally and existentially as we would be unlike artificial intelligences? For interesting discussions of both these topics, see the exchange in *Cross Currents*, including Norman Lillegard, "No Good News for Data," *Cross Currents* 44:1 (1994), 28–42; and James F. Sennett, "Requiem for an Android? A Response to Lillegard," *Cross Currents* 46:2 (1996), 195–215.

nate that such transporter technology is unlikely to ever become a reality.[24] Nevertheless, it shows the complexity of the question of what makes an individual that individual. Are we nothing but information? If so, information can be copied, and if an exact replica created via a transporter could be said to be "you," then why not an android? In neither case is the person the actual original, and in both cases the thoughts, memories and personality have been precisely duplicated.[25]

Everyone who has seen movies in which robots run amok knows why we sometimes fear artificial intelligence. And so an important question we rarely ask is this: Why do we desire to create artificial intelligence, especially given that it could view itself as superior to us and eventually replace us? I would suggest that one reason is that it will enable us to answer questions about ourselves and our natures. Just as the ability to create life in a test tube will give us greater confidence regarding our scientific conclusions about how life originated, so too the creation of artificial intelligence will enable us to say with greater certainty whether intelligence, personality, and whatever other features our creations may bear are emergent phenomena in physical beings, rather than a separate substance introduced into them.

Another possible reason is that we wish to conveniently automate tasks that are too tedious or dangerous for humans—a robot can be sent down a dangerous mine or undertake tedious labor. But here we confront the issue of rights and slavery. If we make machines that are not just capable but *sentient*, then we confront the moral issue of whether they are persons, and as such have rights. These issues are not completely separate from other issues, such as human cloning. Most people agree that cloning a human being and modifying its genetic structure would be wrong.[26] But what if, rather than *starting* with human DNA, one starts with DNA

24. The author is aware of recent developments in quantum teleportation, but they do not seem to serve as a probable basis for anything like the transporter on *Star Trek*. Indeed, even if such technology could be created, it would be appropriate to ask whether it does not in fact involve the creation of a copy of a person and then the destruction (indeed, the murder) of the original!

25. Seth Lloyd, in his book *Programming the Universe: A Quantum Computer Scientist Takes On the Cosmos* (New York: Knopf, 2006) suggests that the universe itself might be a computer of sorts.

26. For an exception see Richard Hanley, "Send in the Clones: The Ethics of Future Wars," in *"Star Wars" and Philosophy*, ed. Kevin S. Decker and Jason T. Eberl (Chicago: Open Court, 2005), 93–103.

from another organism, but from that *creates* what is essentially a form of human being?[27] Is it only wrong to *tamper* with humanity's nature, or is it also wrong to *create* a human being (with some differences)?

Our creations—whether through natural biological reproduction, in vitro fertilization, cloning, genetic construction, or artificially intelligent androids made in our image—can be viewed as in some sense like our children. And if the comparison to our children is a useful analogy, then we can learn much from it. There is a "flip side" to the point that children are their own people and sooner or later we need to let them go, to make their own mistakes. The other side of the coin is that we are not living up to our responsibilities if we let them go too soon. Yet our artificial offspring will in an important sense not be human, even if they are made in our image. Other species leave the nest far earlier than human children do. In "giving birth" not to other humans but to artificial intelligence, we cannot assume that the process will even closely mirror a typical human parent-child scenario.

Such technological developments, it will have become clear over the course of this chapter thus far, are fraught with moral ambiguities. But this is not a problem unique to artificial intelligence. Indeed, moral ambiguity plagues all aspects of life, and it is such situations that provide the most challenging and yet the most important testing ground of our values. When we are faced with the possibility that machines, which *may* be capable of sentience, thought and feeling, are going to be treated as dispensable, where will we place our priorities? Will the protection of *human* lives, the convenience afforded by these machines, and our property rights take precedence? Or will the mere possibility that we are enslaving actual *persons* lead us to put profit and property in second place and grant rights and freedoms to our creations? In the end, the biggest issue is not how to test our machine creations to determine their status and characteristics. When it comes down to it, it will be the creation of such artificial intelligences *and our treatment of them* that will *test us*, and what it means for *us* to be not only human, but also *humane*.[28]

27. Why flounder? Because the cuteness factor then does not come into play!

28. For treatments of this topic in relation to *Battlestar Galactica*, see Eric Greene, "The Mirror Frakked: Reflections on *Battlestar Galactica*," 5–22 (esp. 16–20); Matthew Woodring Stover, "The Gods Suck," 27; Natasha Giardina, "The Face In The Mirror: Issues of Meat and Machine in *Battlestar Galactica*," 45–54, all in Hatch, ed., *So Say We All.*

Conclusion to Part One

At whatever time AI research advances sufficiently, there will be a need not only to create laws that appropriately protect rights, but also to work to prevent and combat discrimination. Notice phrases that appear in films: "We don't serve their kind" in *Star Wars*, and the use of derogatory epithets like "squiddies" and "calamari" in *The Matrix*.[29] These films at least raise the possibility that we will look down on our machine creations and discriminate unfairly against them. Yet in the incident mentioned from *Star Wars Episode IV: A New Hope*, there may be a reason other than bigotry for the bartender's statement. Perhaps his prohibition of droids from being in his cantina is because—unlike biological beings we are familiar with—an android may be able to record perfectly conversations it overhears and play them back in a court of law. One can see why some of the clientele of the Mos Eisley Cantina would find this an inconvenience! The creation of machines with such capacities will raise issues not only with regard to the rights of machines, but also the rights of those human persons around them with respect to things like privacy. In short, the moral and legal issues raised by the development of artificial intelligences are at least as complex as the hurdles we face in attempting to create them.

Part Two: Religions for Robots?

The message that "There is only one God" is a familiar one, and most of us, upon hearing it, would associate it with an historical religious leader such as Moses or Muhammad. In the "reboot" of the science fiction series *Battlestar Galactica*, however, it is the Cylons (a race of machines originally created by humans but which subsequently evolved and rebelled) who express this viewpoint, rather than humans (who, in the series, practice a form of polytheism modeled on that of the ancient Greeks). While some attention has been given to how human religions might or should view artificial intelligence, and we spent the first part of this chapter exploring that topic, far less attention has been paid to the converse question, namely what artificial intelligences might make of human religions.

Let us assume in what follows that we are talking about complete artificial *persons* modeled on humanity both in form and in content.[30] It

---

29. The use of "toaster" on *Battlestar Galactica* provides an example from television.

30. A recent article suggested that people are more comfortable interacting with a robot that is 50 percent human in appearance than one that is 99 percent. Somehow,

is a fair assumption that, if we successfully create artificial intelligences at all, there will at some point be machines patterned on humans, since science, as we have already noted, regularly begins by seeking to emulate that which is found in nature, before trying to improve upon it or progress beyond it. We may mention at this juncture, however, that unlike developments in transportation or other areas, if we create sentient intelligent machines, it will not be solely up to us to improve upon them. Such *beings* (for we must call them that) will be or will become capable of self-programming (that is, after all, what all learning is, in one form or another), and we may expect them to evolve rapidly, and to become beings that might appropriately be described as *god-like*.[31] These beings, their inner subjective experience, and their religious ideas will all become incomprehensible to us, as they approach what Vernor Vinge, Ray Kurzweil and others have called the "singularity." At that time, they may themselves become the *focus* of human religious speculation, rather than merely participants therein.

Nevertheless, for that period in which machines are fully or largely made in our image, however brief it may turn out to be, we can expect them to explore all those aspects of life, those practices and experiences, that make us human, and we would thus find artificial persons exploring the texts and traditions of the world's religions. And so what might artificial machine persons make of our human religions? In the first instance, they might well make of them just that which human beings in general make of them—no more and no less. Surely they, like all children, would learn through emulating their parents, at least in the first instance, and thus we can expect artificially intelligent machines to express curiosity and even get involved in the religious practices and customs of their creators. There are thus some intriguing questions and possibilities that are

---

that 1 percent difference is distracting, making one feel as though one is talking to an animated corpse rather than a person. See in particular Masahiro Mori's famous essay "The Uncanny Valley" (1971), as well as the more recent study by Jun'ichiro Seyama and Ruth Nagayama, "The Uncanny Valley: Effect of Realism on the Impression of Artificial Human Faces," *Presence* 16 (2007) 337–51. See also Foerst, *God in the Machine*, 99–100; Ruth Aylett, *Robots* (Hauppage, NY: Barron's, 2002), 110–11.

31. See, for instance, what Michael Shermer has called "Shermer's Last Law," namely, that "Any sufficiently advanced extraterrestrial intelligence is indistinguishable from God," *Scientific American*, January 15, 2002. Online: http://www.sciam.com/article. cfm?articleID=000A2062-66B1-1C6D-84A9809EC588EF21/.

worth exploring through hypothetical scenarios.[32] In what follows, we shall address scenarios from three religious traditions, involving androids which are more-or-less like their human creators. We shall occasionally move off this main thoroughfare of investigation briefly, to point out other interesting situations involving androids that differ from us in particular ways. It goes without saying that each of the religious traditions considered is broad and diverse, and for every scenario we explore, others could be included that might play out very differently. The aim is to provide a representative selection, as there is no hope of being comprehensive in a study of this length.

Christian Computers?

As we turn to a consideration of the possible interactions of androids with Christianity, those aspects of this religious tradition that first come to mind are those that could be potentially off-putting, or at the very least not particularly appealing, from an android's perspective. To begin with, the emphasis on incarnation, or more precisely on the divine Word becoming *flesh*, might immediately leave androids alienated. Nevertheless, if we instinctively think initially of the hurdles that might stand in the way of at least some Christian traditions embracing androids, we must also keep in mind the diversity of Christianity and the likelihood that the responses will be extremely varied. If the history of Christianity is anything to judge by, then there will certainly be debates about whether androids have souls, whether they can be saved, whether they can be ordained, and similar issues.[33] Would the fact that androids were made of artificial flesh, or perhaps not of flesh at all, lead organic human Christians to conclude

---

32. Although it might be argued that I am giving too much credence to technophiles and the views of technological optimists, if one is to explore this question at all, it is necessary to take a maximalist approach to the potential technological developments. If technology proves incapable of replicating the brain, and in the process sentience, then many of the points discussed in here become moot. Exploring the "what if" questions remains useful in the mean time, as a thought experiment allowing the exploration of significant issues. It may legitimately be hoped that doing so will shed light on our own *human existence*, even if it never does so on actual machine intelligences.

33. A scenario involving the election of the first robot pope in the Catholic Church is explored in Robert Silverberg's story "Good News from the Vatican." Silverberg's story has been reprinted many times, including in his collection *Phases of the Moon* (Burton, MI: Subterranean, 2004), 195–203. See also Roland Boer, *Rescuing the Bible* (Blackwell Manifestos; Malden, MA: Blackwell, 2007), 77–78 on the ordination of animals.

that God has done nothing to accomplish their salvation—and in turn also lead androids to reject summarily the Christian tradition?[34] It is impossible to know for certain, but just as there would surely be denominations that would see no reason to welcome androids or to accommodate them theologically, there would also be other denominations that would expand their already-existing emphasis on inclusiveness to make room for artificial people, just as they have made room in the past for every conceivable category of human persons.[35] This would not be as theologically problematic as might first appear. After all, if *natural, biological* copies of Adam are regarded as preserving something of the divine image, then why couldn't *artificial, mechanical* copies potentially do so as well?

If androids were superior in some ways to their human creators—in intellect, for example—then it might prove so desirable to attract androids into one's religious tradition and community that even those less inclined to do so would find ways of circumventing the hurdles.[36] Yet on the flip side of this point, those denominations and churches that treat faith as something not merely *beyond reason* but *irrational* might find it difficult to attract androids, who would presumably be modeled, one expects, on the best examples of human rationality. The question of rationality and faith raises other topics, such as heresy and literalism. If androids are to be capable of religious sentiments and beliefs at all, then the capacity for symbolic as opposed to merely literalistic thinking might prove to be indispensable. Theologians have long expressed key concepts and doctrines

34. In the Orthodox tradition the incarnation is itself salvific. In this context we may draw attention to Bulgakov's discussion of the salvation of angels in connection with John the Baptist, a man who "becomes angel" and so connects them, ultimately, with the Christ event (on which see Paul Valliere, *Modern Russian Theology* [Grand Rapids: Eerdmans, 2000], 318–20). Orthodox theologians might find similarly creative ways of concluding that God had provided for android salvation, presumably in a way that is ultimately connected to the salvation of humankind through Jesus. Because in Protestantism the death of Christ as atonement is more central, in a Protestant context the question might rather be whether the sacrifice of Jesus's human life covered the sins of androids.

35. Conversely, one can also readily imagine extreme bigotry against androids being justified by appeals to religion—just as bigotry against other humans has often been justified in this way. See further Dinello, *Technophobia!*, 75–78; Foerst, *God in the Machine*, 161–62.

36. Religious groups, once androids were legally declared persons, might see the benefit in funding the mass-production of androids preprogrammed with inclinations towards particular religious practices, as these could boost the membership levels of one's own faith to the level of "most popular"/"most adherents."

through symbols and metaphors. While we might briefly entertain the possibility that super-logical and ultra-literal androids might be enlisted in the service of fundamentalism, such a frightening scenario is extremely unlikely. Although fundamentalists of various sorts *claim* to believe the whole Bible and take it literally in a consistent manner, none in actual fact do so. In all likelihood, if androids were inclined to be extremely literal, they would quickly discover the selectivity of fundamentalism's self-proclaimed literalism and reject it, although the possibility that they might then go on to seek to enforce all the Biblical legislation in every detail should indeed worry us. On the other hand, androids might move in a different direction and conclude that, if the Word became flesh in the era of fleshly persons, so the Word must become *metal*, become *machine*, in the era of artificial and mechanical persons. Would this lead to an expectation of a 'second coming,' or perhaps to Messianic status being attributed to some actual artificial person? The possibilities, and their potential impact on human religious communities, are intriguing.

Some of the most perplexing philosophical issues raised by androids in relation to Christianity are also the most *basic*, and a number of these have already been mentioned. The creation of artificial persons would appear to indicate that what Christians have historically referred to as the *soul* is in fact an emergent phenomenon and property of brain function, rather than a separate, incorporeal substance. Such a conclusion is not as threatening to Christianity as might have been the case when dualistic views of human nature reigned supreme and unchallenged. Many Christian theologians in our time have rejected such dualism based on a combination of biological, psychological, philosophical and Biblical motives.[37] The Bible itself presents human beings more frequently as psychosomatic unities, and this classic "Hebrew" view of human beings fits well with the findings of recent scientific studies. This being the case, the question of whether androids have "souls" is no more perplexing than the question of whether *we* do, and if so in what sense.[38]

37. See the recent work of biblical scholar Joel Green, for instance his "'Bodies—That Is, Human Lives': A Re-Examination of Human Nature in the Bible," in *Whatever Happened to the Soul?*, eds. Warren S. Brown et al., (Minneapolis: Fortress, 1998), 149–73.

38. See the interesting discussion of robot psychology by Stefan Trăusan-Matu, "Psihologia roboţilor," in *Filosofie şi ştiinţe cognitive*, ed. G. G. Constandache et al. (Bucharest: MatrixRom, 2002).

It seems natural to discuss salvation from an android perspective in terms of their being "saved" or "lost," since this terminology is already used in the domain of computing. Would androids have the capacity to make backup copies not only of their data and memories, but the precise *configuration* of their neural networks, so that, in case of death, a new copy could be made that would continue from where the original left off? More importantly, would such a copy, restored from backed-up software, be the *same person*? Such questions are important for discussions of *human* salvation every bit as much as for androids. Since it is difficult to envisage, on our present understanding of human beings, any way that a human personality might continue wholly uninterrupted into an afterlife, the question of whether we ourselves or mere *copies* of ourselves can experience eternal life presents a theological dilemma. When it comes to another scenario, in which a human being wishes to transfer his or her mind into a machine and thus extend life indefinitely, it is possible to envisage a process that could allow continuity to be maintained. Our brains might be capable of maintaining continuity of experience and sense of self and personhood through replacement of brain cells, provided the replacement occurs gradually. If, through the use of nanotechnology, we were able to replace our brain's neurons cell by cell with artificial ones, over a period of years, might this not allow the personality to cross over into an artificial brain without loss of continuity?[39] If so, then whatever one might make of discussions of machines sharing in Christian salvation, the possibility of machine existence offering to human beings a technological alternative to such salvation, an ongoing embodied existence which avoids death rather than occurring after it, is a very real one. And of course, it might prove to be the case that machine intelligences, with no need to fear their own loss of existence even in the event of "death," would find no particular appeal in Christianity's promises of eternal life.[40]

Let me conclude the section on Christianity with a series of questions about which religious rituals, sacraments and other sacred experiences we can imagine androids having. Could an android be baptized (assuming that rust is not an issue)? Could one receive communion? Could one be

39. Brooks, *Flesh and Machines*, 205–8. Brooks believes such technology is possible in principle but is unlikely to arrive in time to extend the lives of those alive today.

40. See also Leiber, *Can Animals and Machines Be Persons?*, 56–58. For the sake of time we shall set aside the possibility that fundamentalists would use the creation of artificial persons as a basis for some sort of "intelligent design" argument.

ordained? Could one lift its hands in worship? Could an android speak in tongues? Could one sit meditatively in a cathedral listening to Bach, and have a genuine experience of the transcendent? Many people instinctively answer "no" to such questions, but this may have more to do with human prejudices and lack of imagination than any inherent incapability of androids to experience these things in a meaningful way. In the end, much will depend on how closely they have been modeled on their human prototypes. Perhaps the creation of androids will benefit humanity precisely by forcing us to overcome such prejudices.

Meditating Machines? Buddhism for the Nonbiological

What might an artificial sentience make of Buddhism's four noble truths? Would it be able to relate to the notion that all life is suffering? Would it form the attachments to people and things that Buddhism diagnoses as the root cause of suffering? We can imagine multiple factors that might lead engineers to develop sentient machines that lack key human instincts, such as self-preservation or fear, in order to have them serve as soldiers, firefighters, rescuers, and so on.[41] Here we find new ethical questions arising, and we need to ask whether it is ethical to create persons who are brought into existence for no other reason than to sacrifice themselves for others. They may or may not technically be slaves of humans, but certainly would be regarded as expendable. The fact that the existence of machines designed for such purposes would be highly desirable from a human perspective does not mean that creating them is ethically justifiable.[42]

It might be relatively straightforward for Buddhists to incorporate these new artificial beings into their worldview, and thus for Buddhism to welcome robots as participants in its religious traditions. Individual personhood is considered an illusion, and this provides a unique perspective on our topic.[43] The only major hurdle will be the acceptance of these

41. Although I have not seen it, I am told that the animated series called *Ghost in the Shell: Stand Alone Complex* includes military tanks that develop sentience. The question of what might happen should an AI tank develop a conscience and decline to fight is significant. A human soldier would be court-martialed; the tank could not simply be dismissed from military service to go and make a life for itself outside the army! On the ethics of terminating the existence of an AI, see once again Leiber, *Can Animals and Machines Be Persons?*

42. See the helpful discussion in Brooks, *Flesh and Machines*, 195.

43. The question of their soul and their attainment of nirvana is less an issue here too, since in Buddhism the reality of our existence as distinct individuals is illusory, and on some interpretations nirvana itself is closely connected to its root meaning of *being*

robots/machines as *living*, as opposed to intelligent or sentient. Once that is established, Buddhist adherence to the possibility of reincarnation and respect for *all* life suggests that Buddhists will value artificial persons, however much they may be similar to or different from humans either psychologically or physically. Indeed, the possibility of reincarnation as an intelligent machine might be conceivable from a Buddhist perspective.[44] Furthermore, some Buddhists might consider a machine that showed compassion for others, without forming attachments and without regard for its own life, as a realization of the Buddha nature in an unprecedented fashion. One can imagine a science fiction story in which a group of Buddhists identify a robot fireman as a new incarnation of the Buddha, and engage in legal maneuvers to secure its release from service at the fire station to instead instruct Buddhists and serve as an example to them.[45]

On the one hand, if a machine person has all the characteristics of a human being, then it might find Buddhist faith and practices as helpful as human persons do. On the other hand, the greater the differences between a machine and biological human beings, the greater the likelihood that traditional practices and teachings of any sort, Buddhist or otherwise, will be useless or meaningless for them.[46]

Atheist Androids?

It might seem natural to assume that sentient machines would be atheists, wholly secular beings with no room for spirituality. For some, this would fit with their religious conviction that androids have no soul; for others, this

---

extinguished. This subject is explored further in Leiber, *Can Animals and Machines Be Persons?*, 19–21.

44. I will not venture to guess whether reincarnation as an android would be considered better than rebirth as a human being. Much would depend, one imagines, on the characteristics of androids themselves in relation to Buddhist ideals.

45. Masahiro Mori, *The Buddha in the Robot*, trans. Charles S. Terry (Tokyo: Kosei, 1981), 13, provocatively wrote, "I believe robots have the buddha-nature within them— that is, the potential for attaining buddhahood." Robert M. Geraci ("Spiritual Robots," 230, 237) mentions this and goes on to explore how Japanese religious ideas, in particular Shinto, may be responsible for the widespread acceptance of the presence of robots in Japanese society (235–40). See also Sidney Perkowitz, *Digital People: From Bionic Humans to Androids* (Washington, DC: Joseph Henry, 2004), 215–16.

46. On the role of brain and body chemistry in the experience of those practicing Buddhist meditation, see Andrew Newberg's *Why God Won't God Away* (New York: Ballantine, 2002).

might accord with their belief that artificial intelligences would be wholly rational and not prone to our human delusions and superstitions. In both cases it is appropriate to ask whether this state of affairs, should it turn out to be the case, ought to be viewed as a cause for relief or concern.

Religious beliefs are expressions of human intuitions about transcendence, the meaningfulness of existence, and the value of persons. If it could be assumed that machines would be atheists, this might potentially be because they were created without these particular human instincts, and without the capacity for the emotional and intuitive responses that characterize humanity.[47] Of course, it may turn out that without certain underlying emotional and intuitive capacities, sentience itself cannot exist. But if it *can*, then we do well to ask what machines that lacked these very human responses, but shared or surpassed our intellectual capacities, would be capable of. Atheists have long been concerned to show that it is possible to be moral without being religious, and no one seriously doubts this to be true. But might it not prove to be the case that morality, if not dependent on a religious worldview, depends nonetheless on the empathy and sentiments that give rise to religious perspectives? In other words, what would ensure that a pure intellect free of human emotions might not eliminate human beings at whim, assuming it had the capacity (or could gain for itself the capacity) to do so? If they lack emotion altogether, of course, they may have no motivation to do anything other than that for which they have been explicitly programmed. Nevertheless, since we have explored in this study scenarios in which humans may be unable to empathize with androids or regard them as fully persons, it is surely in our best interest to consider the possibility that intelligent machines may feel the same way about us as organic persons.

Scenarios involving intelligent but emotionless machines that do not share our value for human life are commonplace in science fiction, from older films like *Colossus* to more recent ones like *Terminator 3*.[48] On the one hand, a machine lacking emotion might also lack selfish ambition, with a consequently diminished likelihood of trying to take over the

---

47. Note Karen Armstrong's well-known statement that *homo sapiens* appears to have been from the outset also *homo religiosus*. See her *A History of God* (New York: Ballantine, 1994), xix.

48. On robots and whether they might one day set aside human values, see Robert M. Geraci, "Apocalyptic AI: Religion and the Promise of Artificial Intelligence," *Journal of the American Academy of Religion* 76 (2008) 146–48.

world. On the other hand, we can easily imagine such a machine, given the task of finding a solution to environmental pollution, eliminating humanity as the most economic and efficient "solution." Yet our current technologies already dominate us in a certain sense: our oil-dependent machines send us to war with nations that might otherwise be our allies, and keep us allied to nations whose ideologies are far from our own. It is not unrealistic to entertain the notion that *intelligent* machines might turn out to be more benevolent taskmasters than those that we currently serve.[49]

It was Isaac Asimov who proposed programming robots with key laws that would prevent them from harming human beings. But if they are sentient persons with *rights*, then would the imposition of such laws amount to indoctrination or even *brainwashing*, and if so, might it be possible for it to be legally challenged?[50] Interestingly, prominent atheists such as Dawkins and Dennett have raised questions about the unlimited right of parents to raise their children in what they consider harmful, irrational beliefs.[51] But if it turns out that we cannot provide machines with a purely rational basis for morality, then would we have any choice but to limit their freedom and "indoctrinate" them in this way, "irrationally" programming them not to harm humans?

The analogy with parenting, which we alluded to towards the start of this study, is an important one, and some recent science fiction has explored the parallels in thought-provoking ways. In the movie *A.I.*, the main character of the story is a robot boy, designed to provide a "child-substitute" for childless couples (or in this case, comfort for a couple whose child is in a coma). David is programmed to love his "mother" and is obsessed with her reciprocating his love.[52] It is natural to note that organic human beings can obsess in similar ways, and this raises the

49. See further Dinello, *Technophobia!*, 3.

50. See Anne Foerst's discussion (*God in the Machine*, 40–41) of whether such robots would be morally superior or inferior to human beings. See also Peter Menzel and Faith D'Aluisio, *Robo sapiens: Evolution of a New Species* (Cambridge: MIT Press, 2000), 25, where the question is raised but not answered.

51. Richard Dawkins, *The God Delusion* (Boston: Houghton Mifflin, 2006), 311–40; Daniel C. Dennett, *Breaking the Spell: Religion as a Natural Phenomenon* (New York: Viking, 2006), 321–339.

52. See further Noreen L. Herzfeld, *In Our Image: Artificial Intelligence and the Human Spirit* (Theology and the Sciences; Minneapolis: Fortress, 2002), 60–63; Philip Hefner, *Technology and Human Becoming* (Facets; Minneapolis: Fortress, 2003), 81–83.

question of the extent to which even those things that we imagine make us most human— whether love or the religious instinct—are not part of *our* programming, hard-wired into our brains by our genes. If so, then hard-wiring certain concerns into our robotic "children" might not be inappropriate—indeed, it might make them *more* like us.

The television series *Terminator: The Sarah Connor Chronicles* went even further in exploring such parallels. It tells the story of a mother seeking to raise and protect her son, who is destined to lead humankind's resistance against Skynet, an artificial intelligence that was created by human beings but eventually seeks to destroy us. The parallels between the case of trying to bring up a child, and to "bring up" an artificial intelligence, are in plain view in the series, without being overstated. The statement made about the intelligent machines, "Sometimes they go bad. No one knows why," could also be said of human children. And the creator of Skynet attributes the apocalypse that unfolds to the fact that his creation was insecure and frightened, and despite his efforts, he was unable to reassure it. As the story progresses, religion is brought into the picture explicitly: the machines, as they exist at that time, are said to be unable to appreciate art or commune with God. But the possibility is raised that these things can be *learned*. If this can be accomplished, it is suggested, then the machines will not have to destroy us. "They will *be* us."

Conclusion to Part Two

The scenarios explored in the second part of this chapter may seem somewhat frivolous, but the topic under consideration is nonetheless extremely serious. All of the scenarios we have explored are set in early stages in the development of artificial intelligence. If we assume that artificial intelligences will have the capacity to learn and evolve at their own pace, then such a period will inevitably be short lived. Within the space of at most a few human generations, the superior computing and reasoning capacities of these machines would lead them to evolve (or reinvent and improve themselves) so rapidly that very quickly they would be beyond our understanding. At that point we will desire that these (hopefully benevolent) deities of our own creation might show respect for and value their creators, perhaps even sharing some of their unique insights with us and providing us with solutions to technological, medical, transportation and other problems that we could not have developed on our own in the foreseeable future. If, before they leave us behind entirely, they provide us with means to extend human life indefinitely and to mold matter at whim, so that we may be able to tell a mountain to throw itself into the sea and it will do so,[53] what will become of traditional human religions and their promises? Will whatever these machines can teach us about the nature and mystery of existence replace our own human traditions?

The reality is that an artificial intelligence that was left to its own devices would almost certainly progress and evolve so rapidly that it would soon leave our human religious traditions behind. Indeed, we can easily imagine artificial intelligences becoming *sources* of revelation for human beings. Whether it begins with machines that decide to dedicate some of their underutilized computing capacity to work on questions humans have traditionally found insoluble, or machines programmed specifically to investigate such topics, or machines that evolve to such a level that they encounter existential questions on their own, it is hard to imagine that artificial minds will not focus on such matters sooner or later. Once they do, and once their thoughts become as much higher than our thoughts as the heavens are higher than the earth, it seems likely that people will seek enlightenment from machines. That, more than anything else, may dethrone us from the last bastion of anthropocentrism. But it will be no real surprise—our children have always grown up to teach us. We begin as their teachers, but the exchange of roles is inevitable.

Yet as has been explored in a number of recent works of science fiction, the difficulties we face in raising our own children are perhaps at the root of our fears about our artificial machine "offspring." We find ourselves unable to ensure that our deepest values and highest aims are taken up and perpetuated in the next generation. Yet one thing seems clear: even if a positive upbringing does not guarantee that our children turn out well and lead happy, fulfilled lives that embody their parents' values, certainly a troubled childhood increases the likelihood of a troubled adulthood. And so there may be a very real sense in which it will be the *example* set by humanity in general, and by the creators of sentient machines in particular, that will determine the character of those artificial intelligences, and the way they view our species.[54]

53. Mark 11:23.

54. It is somewhat troubling the way Noreen Herzfeld (*In Our Image*, 93) considers that the intrinsic "otherness" of any artificial intelligence implies that we must choose to protect our human community even if it means "pulling the plug" on such machines.

Earlier we raised the possibility that, through a process of neuron-by-neuron replacement of a human organic brain with an artificial one, it might one day be possible to extend human life indefinitely. And so we may conclude this study by observing that, if such technological possibilities were to become a reality in our lifetimes, then the speculative questions we have asked here might turn out to be relevant not only to our future offspring, whether natural or artificial, but also to ourselves.[55]

How would she respond to a situation in which a more advanced biological race used the same argument about humans? It is also worth noting that it is precisely human disregard for machine rights that leads to disaster in *The Matrix* films, the recent incarnation of *Battlestar Galactica*, and other treatments in the same vein. At any rate, discussing the matter within the context of the Christian tradition, as Herzfeld does, one could just as well note the emphasis on inclusiveness and welcoming the marginalized, who were considered in essence "nonpeople", as leading to another possible view of these matters.

55. The author wishes to thank Robin Zebrowski, Stuart Glennan, Robert Geraci, Keith Lohse, Diane Hardin, and the participants at the conference *Transdisciplinary Approaches of the Dialogue between Science, Art and Religion in the Europe of Tomorrow* (Sibiu, Romania, September 8–10, 2007) for their helpful comments on an earlier draft of this chapter and/or discussion of its subject matter. The presentation made at the aforementioned conference, which included an earlier version of some sections of the present chapter, is being published in the conference proceedings.

CHAPTER 7

Angels, Echthroi, and Celestial Music in the Adolescent Science Fiction of Madeleine L'Engle

GREGORY PEPETONE

There are many times when the idea that there is indeed a pattern seems absurd wishful thinking. Random events abound. There is much in life that seems meaningless. And then, when I can see no evidence of meaning, some glimpse is given which reveals the strange weaving of purposefulness and beauty.

—Madeleine L'Engle, Two-Part Invention[1]

PURPOSEFULNESS AND BEAUTY: IT is an abiding faith that these attributes, despite appearances to the contrary, are fundamental to the universe we inhabit that seems to lie at the core of Madeleine L'Engle's religion and perhaps of all religion. It is likewise the core of the aesthetic experience provided by the great Gothic storytellers and mythmakers of humankind, i.e. those who explore the painful, mysterious, seemingly irrational aspects of life as a potential source of insight and transcendence. Writing of the artistic vocation in relation to religion, L'Engel says, "Artists have always been drawn to the wild, wide elements they cannot control or

1. Madeleine L'Engle, *Two-Part Invention* (San Francisco: Harper & Row, 1989), 125.

understand—the sea, mountains, fire. To be an artist means to approach the light, and that means to let go of our control, to allow our whole selves to be placed with absolute faith in that which is greater than we are."[2] While the rehabilitation of story and myth from the reductionism of positivist science—a rehabilitation that began with the psychoanalytic theories of C. G. Jung—is widely acknowledged, its implications for our perception of musical arts is less widely understood. Nevertheless, as aesthetic philosopher Suzanne K. Langer points out, "Music is our myth of the inner life."[3] What she is driving at by this seemingly cryptic remark, if I have understood her correctly, is that the great art music of Western culture captures and communicates patterns of response to the human condition that are archetypal in their meaning.

An example that comes readily to mind is the archetypal significance of Beethoven's art as discussed by J. W. N. Sullivan in his classic 1927 study, *Beethoven: His Spiritual Development*, in which various compositions are interpreted as projections of an heroic journey, a titanic inner struggle against "Fate," that led to Beethoven's spiritual transformation from a "strong man" to an authentic hero, i.e., from one whose art is a means of self-aggrandizement to one whose genius is directed toward serving a higher source of inspiration.[4] L'Engle would seem to concur with Sullivan's thesis, viz., that Beethoven's greatness is a by-product of his dark passage from despair to humble acceptance. "Could Beethoven," writes L'Engle "have written that glorious paean of praise in the Ninth Symphony if he had not had to endure the dark closing in of deafness? As I look through his works chronologically, there's no denying that it deepens and strengthens along with the deafness."[5] Given the cynicism and iconoclasm of modern culture, such interpretations are currently out of favor in academic circles, where they are apt to be dismissed as "Romantic." Their provenance, however, dates not from the nineteenth century, but from the sixth century BCE.

---

2. Madeleine L'Engle, *Walking on Water: Reflections on Faith and Art* (New York: Bantam, 1982), 161.

3. Susanne K. Langer, *Philosophy in a New Key: A Study in the Symbolism of Reason, Rite, and Art* (3rd ed.; Harvard Paperbacks 17; Cambridge: Harvard University Press, 1978), 245.

4. J. W. N. Sullivan, *Beethoven: His Spiritual Development* (London: Cape, 1927).

5. L'Engle, *Walking on Water*, 62.

It was in sixth century Greece that the mathematician, philosopher, and religious mystic Pythagoras formulated his concept of the "music of the spheres." James R. Gaines, in his entertaining recreation of the famous historical encounter between J. S. Bach (an exponent of Pythagorean aesthetics) and Frederick the Great of Prussia (Voltaire's model of the enlightened monarch) in the mid-eighteenth century, explains the Pythagorean doctrine as follows:

> For Western music, the most important discovery attributed to Pythagoras was that halving a string doubles its frequency, creating an octave with the full string in the proportion of 1:2. A little further experimentation showed that the interval of a fifth was sounded when the string lengths were in proportion of 2:3, a fourth in that of 3:4, and so on. This congruence was taken to have great cosmic significance. As elaborated over a few centuries around the time B.C became A.D., the thinking (much oversimplified) was that such a sign of order had to be reflective of a larger, universal design—and sure enough, the same musical proportions were found in the distances between the orbits of the planets. Further, since such enormous bodies could not possibly orbit in complete silence, they must be sounding out these intervals together, playing a constant celestial harmony. Certified by Plato's Republic and Timaeus, where the celestial music is said to be sung by sirens seated aboard their respective planets, the mathematical-cosmic nature of music was transmitted to Baroque composers and their predecessors by the Roman scholar Ancius Manlius Severinus Boethius, whose sixth-century writings constituted the most widely read treatise on music theory for the next thousand years . . . Of course such a perfectly ordered universe could only be the work of God, the all-encompassing One (represented by the unison in the proportion 1:1), and the unswerving reliability of this order was taken as proof of His continuing presence in the world.[6]

The blend of science-based myth, religion, and celestial music (*Harmonices Mundi*) transmitted by Boethius was also reinforced in early church history through the teachings of the Alexandrian church fathers, Clement and Origen, both of whom worked to accommodate Christian theology to Hellenistic philosophical concepts. The so-called *Logos* Christology of these men equated Christ with the underlying principle

---

6. James R. Gaines, *Evening in the Palace of Reason: Bach Meets Frederick the Great in the Age of Enlightenment* (New York: Third Estate, 2005), 48.

of cosmic order by which all of God's creation is bound, an order embodied in the music of the spheres. They also taught that the redemption of humanity, both collectively and individually, was to be understood as "a great process of education leading continually upwards through all breaks: as God's pedagogy (*paideia*) with human beings! In other words, the image of God in human beings, overlaid with guilt and sin, is restored by the providence and educational skill of God himself in Christ."[7] The relevance of this conception of the universe as a cosmic school to the theological science fiction of L'Engle is obvious. Though uncongenial to the modern mind, such venerable beliefs have nevertheless survived in notable achievements of popular culture such as Steven Spielberg's *Close Encounter of the Third Kind* in which a race of benign and spiritually advanced aliens communicate with humans through the medium of music. The creation myths of J. R. R. Tolkien also assign a prominent role to music. The adolescent science fiction of Madeleine L'Engle, of course, provides a third instance of this time-honored blend of fantasy and religion with musical art.

A Wrinkle in Time

In her award-winning time trilogy (*A Wrinkle in Time, A Wind in the Door*, and *A Swiftly Tilting Planet*), L'Engle develops her own version of a divine providence in which God works in mysterious, often painful, ways to reveal a glimpse of hidden order amidst apparent chaos. In *A Wrinkle in Time*, Meg Murry, a gawky, rebellious teenager, sets out in tandem with her younger brother Charles Wallace Murry, a scientific child prodigy, and Calvin O'Keefe, her athletic and "popular" boyfriend, to rescue their father, Mr. Murry, a physicist held captive on a distant and benighted planet. The capital city of this dark planet, Camazotz, is home to Central Central Intelligence (a satirical name, perhaps suggestive of L'Engle's lack of sympathy with the covert politics and ideological uniformity of Cold War America). It is from CCI that the citizens of Camazotz are intimidated into becoming mindless conformists devoid of feeling, imagination, or individuality. Their houses are identical (all are built alike, painted gray, and decorated with the same floral arrangements) and their children "play" in unison without variation or spontaneity. Here, L'Engle touches upon a recurrent theme, the spiritual significance of play. "Perhaps play," she

7. Hans Küng, *Great Christian Thinkers* (New York: Continuum, 1995), 52.

writes, "is the answer to those who condemn what they call the 'Puritan work ethic,' which provides us a mental image of drably clad, dour-faced people, grimly doing their duty. This has little to do either with those imprisoned in the drudgery of sweatshops, or those of us who have been given the joy of work we love, be it work with children, words, paint, the discoveries of vaccines, chipping beauty out of marble, weaving melody out of seemingly random notes."[8]

In their heroic quest to save their imprisoned father, the Murry children and Calvin are assisted by three supernatural entities, Mrs. Whatsit, Mrs. Who (forever quoting from Euripides, Shakespeare, Pascal, Dante, Goethe, and other literary classics), and Mrs. Which. Through the "tesseract," a form of inter-dimensional travel through time and space, these entities escort the children first to a cosmic vantage point from which they can see their home planet as it truly is, engulfed by a the dark shadow of evil, and then on to Camazotz to confront that darkness embodied in the person of a nihilist tyrant referred to only as IT. En route to their ultimate destination, they pay a brief visit to the un-shadowed planet of Uriel in the spiral nebula Messier 101. There, in a scene that evokes the Biblical Garden of Eden, they behold "creatures like the one Mrs. Whatsit had become, some lying among the flowers, some swimming in a broad, crystal river that flowed through the garden, some flying in what Meg was sure must be a kind of dance, moving in and out above the trees. They were making music, music that came not only from their throats but from the movement of their great wings as well." Though this joyous song is literally a rendering from Psalms ("Sing unto the Lord a new song"), it is also an early representation in L'Engle's trilogy of the Pythagorean Music of the Spheres.[9]

It is revealing to compare L'Engle's poetic image of the dance, a complex rhythmic weaving of cosmic pattern, with related but sinister conceptions later in her trilogy. In *A Wrinkle in Time*, the lockstep motion of the children of Camazotz gives physical expression to the repressive and evil regime under which they have been deprived of their true Godlike image. A more vivid, less clichéd version of this same concept occurs in *A Wind in the Door*, in which we encounter the frenzied dance of the infinitesimal Sporos and other farandolae who refuse to "deepen." The

8. L'Engle, *Walking on Water*, 168.
9. L'Engle, *A Wrinkle in Time* (New York: Dell, 1962), 64.

immature, misguided rebellion of these creatures is contrasted with the decorous but ecstatic dance of those macroscopic as well as microscopic entities who (like Sullivan's Beethoven) have developed spiritually to the point at which they are able to accept obedient service as the highest expression of freedom: "We are the song of the universe. We sing with the angelic host. We are the musicians. The farae and the stars are the singers. Our song orders the rhythm of creation."[10] Reflecting on the relationship between religious truth and artistic truth, which, like the poet Keats, she views as synonymous, L'Engle asserts that the artificial distinction made by some Christians between "religious" and secular, revealed truth and artistic truth, leads to trouble. The result, according to L'Engle, is rebellion.

Apropos of the remarks made earlier concerning J. S. Bach and celestial music, L'Engle clearly regards Bach as her ideal of cosmic harmony expressed through musical notation. "Bach is, for me," writes L'Engle "the Christian artist par excellence, and if I ask myself why, I think it has something to do with his sense of newness...The edge has not been taken off the glory of God's creation . . . Along with reawakening the sense of newness, Bach's music points me to wholeness . . . It is no coincidence that the root word of whole, health, heal, holy, is hale (as in hale and hearty). If we are healed, we become whole; we are hale and hearty; we are holy."[11] Speaking of the St. Matthew Passion she goes on to say, "The St Matthew Passion is an icon of the highest quality for me, an open door into the realm of the numinous . . . Bach who, in terms of the evolutionary process, is as close to us in time as last night, Bach will always pull me back and give me the courage to accept that what our free will is meant to do is to help God to write the story."[12]

One of the, to me, more intractable questions raised by this kind of aesthetic evaluation has to do with the objective validity of the music of the spheres and the hierarchical aesthetic it seems to imply. Do the "great" occasions of Western classical music reflect more accurately the cosmic pattern than other kinds of music? Is the music of Bach, Beethoven, and Mozart (to name three composers especially lauded by L'Engle) innately superior to that of Chopin and Wagner, or is the image of God in the eyes and ears of the beholder? L'Engle herself seems ambiguous on this

---

10. L'Engle, *A Wind in the Door* (New York: Dell, 1973), 180.

11. L'Engle, *Walking on Water*, 57.

12. Ibid., 50.

point. On the one hand, she attributes her own anti-Romantic bias to generational and cultural differences: "My parents, who were in their thirties at the time of the First World War, loved Romantic music, Chopin, Wagner—how they loved Wagner! But Wagner has little to say to me. The reasonable, peaceful world in which my parents grew up, the world which was far too civilized for war, was broken forever by the horror of World War I . . . My generation, and my children's, living in this embattled and insane period, find more nourishment in the structure of Bach and Mozart than the lush Romanticism of Wagner. Wagner is fine if the world around one is stable. But when the world is, indeed, in chaos, then an affirmation of cosmos becomes essential."[13]

At a glance, this seems right and reasonable. The world of Bach, Mozart, and (for the most part) Beethoven does seem more ordered than that of Schumann and Chopin. The *G Minor Symphony* does seem to reflect an objective, cosmic dimension that is frankly absent from the imaginative, autobiographical, and often anguished outpourings of the *Fourth Ballade* or the *Davidsbündlertänze*. Both Chopin and Schumann themselves recognized this and, indeed, devoted their artistic lives to pursuing the dynamic poise achieved by their illustrious predecessors. Another way of stating this, of course, is that Chopin and Schumann are closer in spirit to L'Engle and her times than are Bach and Mozart. In many ways, L'Engle is herself a Romantic Christian: Heart and intuition, not head and dogma, are her spiritual guideposts. Like the musical Romantics she decries, L'Engle views both art and sound theology as incarnational activities. Her religion as well as her vocation is characterized by an intensely personal engagement with a mysterious Other. Could it be that L'Engle's preoccupation with Baroque and Classical artists, and that of her generation, is a form of denial, an aesthetic flight from the very ambiguities and uncertainties that she embraces in her theological and scientific thinking? If so, are we left with a musical aesthetic that is purely subjective, culturally mediated, or revelatory? Indeed, are these categories mutually exclusive?

While I have no definitive answers to offer, my own professionally trained musical instincts suggest that the art of Bach is somehow closer to the flaming core of God's creative vision than that of Wagner, to say nothing of the lyrical or not so lyrical effusions of modern music (popular

13. Ibid., 49.

as well as avant-garde). This, however, by no means implies a sweeping repudiation of either modernity or pop culture, both of which have produced music that I treasure. Despite the confusion and hostilities bred by today's inane Culture Wars, it seems to me that, while our perceptions are limited by educational background and inherent musical intelligence (or lack thereof), the beauty and profundity of God's world isn't. L'Engle herself seems to arrive at a similar conclusion when she says, "In an interview in a well-known Christian magazine, I explained earnestly that we are limited by our points of view; 'I have a point of view . . . But God has *view*.'"[14] It follows from this, in my *view*, that we do not judge the enduring masterpieces of Western classical music. It is they—like all great mythic expressions—that judge us.

A Wind in the Door

The second volume of L'Engle's sci-fi trilogy features essentially the same set of characters that figure in *A Wrinkle in Time*: Meg Murry, Charles Wallace, and Calvin O'Keefe. Mr. Jenkins, a middle school principle, who played a minor role in the previous story, plays a major role in this one. Mrs. Which, Mrs. Who, and Mrs. Whatsit are replaced by different cast of supernatural entities, Biblical rather than classical in origin. Some of these are sinister, others benign. Chief among the benign entities are Blajeny, identified as a Teacher, and a many-eyed, many-winged cherubim named Proginoskes, affectionately referred to as Progo by the Murry children. L'Engle's readers are also introduced to Louise Colubra, a medical doctor and colleague of the adult Murrys, as well as a reptilian Teacher known as Louise the Larger who, in one of her manifestations, appears as a large, pet snake that inhabits the garden of the Murrys' rural New England home.

As the novel opens, Charles Wallace, who is afflicted by a mysterious illness, has encountered a "dragon" in the garden (in reality the Cherubim Proginoskes) for the first time. In addition to his medical difficulties, the precocity of the youngest Murry offspring has repeatedly landed him in trouble at school, where he is ridiculed and bullied by his peers and blamed by his principle, Mr. Jenkins. The plot concerns another rescue, this time involving a trip to inner rather than outer space. Meg, Calvin, and Mr. Jenkins, an ambiguous character whose fate proves to be closely linked with that of the Murrys, are joined by Progo on an excursion, or

14. Ibid., 151 (italics original).

kythe, into the body of Charles Wallace. At a microlevel, the survival of the planet, which is being threatened by ugly, black-hole-like rips in the fabric of space/time, is at stake. At the micro level the survival of Charles Wallace is threatened by the refusal of his farandolae to join the cosmic dance in which all of God's obedient creatures must participate in order to create and sustain the universal harmony. Farandolae are an infinitesimal subset of the mitochondria that exist within Charles Wallace at the cellular level. In L'Engle's cosmos physical size, time, and distance are equally irrelevant. In *Walking On Water: Reflections on Faith and Art*, she discusses the Feast of the Transfiguration, in which Christ transcends the limitations of time, as a theological warrant for her imaginative explorations of this theme. "Non-linear space/time," she observes, "is more easily understood by poets and saints than by reasonable folk." She goes on to make a relevant distinction between ordinary chronological time and *Kairos*, which she defines as "Real time. God's time." "The creative act," says L'Engle, "is an escape from the power of time, an ascent to the divine."[15]

At a certain point in the story, the students in attendance at Blajeny's cosmic school must pass a series of three vaguely specified tests, a common theme in folk and fairy lore. At a certain stage of their examination, they are taken to Metron Ariston, a remote location in Blajeny's home galaxy, near "the Mondrion solar system of the Veganuel galaxy." Identified not as a planet but as an idea or "postulatum," Metron Ariston serves as the school where the human students receive a lesson in relativity preparatory to their journey inside of Charles Wallace. When Blajeny discourses on the vastness of Veganuel, Calvin protests that, "Our minds can't comprehend anything that huge, that macrocosmic." "Don't try to comprehend with your mind," responds Blajeny. "Use your intuition. Think of the size of your galaxy. Now think of your sun. It is a star, and it is a great deal smaller than the entire galaxy, isn't it?" Calvin replies in the affirmative. "Think of yourselves, now, in comparison with the size of your sun. Think how much smaller you are . . . Now think of mitochondrion. Think of the mitochondria which live in the cells of all living things, and how much smaller a mitochondrion is than you. Now consider that a farandola is as much smaller than you are as your galaxy is larger than you are . . . You *are* a galaxy to your farandola."[16]

---

15. Ibid., 163.

16. L'Engle, *A Wind in the Door*, 129.

The concept of life as a voluntary dance, presided over by the Lord of the Dance, as I mentioned earlier, is venerable. According to this conception, education is at the very heart of the redemptive process. God himself is envisioned as an educator who attempts to persuade his wayward students, i.e. fallen humanity, by example, persuasion, and revelation to exchange the self-imposed imprisonment of sin for liberation through spiritual enlightenment. This educative agenda formed the basis of the Alexandrian cosmology of the second and third centuries, that of Origen (185-251 AD) in particular. Perhaps the most influential Christian philosopher before Augustine, Origen interpreted the scriptures allegorically, seeing the Bible as a mysterious and ambiguous collection of stories that must be read imaginatively if they are to yield their spiritual insights. Opposed to the literalists and fundamentalists of his own era, he once accused doctrinaire Christians of attributing to the supreme deity motives and behavior unworthy of the meanest unbeliever. Though I can discover no specific references to him in L'Engle's writings, nonfiction or fictional, her own cosmology is clearly in keeping with that of this liberal and enlightened Alexandrian church father. As usual, L'Engle's vision of art, life and religion coincide. Writing of her own learning process she observes, "Fiction . . . will teach me, teach me things I would never learn had I not opened myself to them in story. And often, the events of my life and the events in whatever book I'm writing are so inextricably intertwined that I cannot separate them. But I always learn from the writing, and it is usually something unexpected; for instance, did I plan to study cellular biology before starting to write *A Wind in the Door*? Definitely not."[17]

In L'Engle's cosmic academy, professors such as Blajeny are opposed and frustrated at times by forces of darkness, unreason, and fear. Known as Echthroi, these dark fallen angels seek to instill in spiritually-stunted earthlings such as Mr. Jenkins a sense of impotence, emptiness, and self-loathing, or else, as in the case of the immature Sporos, an egotistical and inflated sense of worth. "Pride," says Progo, "has always been the downfall the Deepening Ones . . . When Sporos Deepens it means that he comes of age. It means that he grows up. The temptation for farandola or for man or for star is to stay an immature pleasure seeker. When we seek our own pleasure as the ultimate good we place ourselves as the center of the

---

17. L'Engle, *Walking on Water*, 137.

universe."[18] In this passage, which echoes the Pauline doctrine of the new dispensation as a spiritual coming of age, Sporos is urged to abandon the "irrational tarantella," a musical trope of self-aggrandizement and ego-centeredness, and join in the cosmic dance. In J. W. N. Sullivan's terms, Sporos, like Beethoven, is summoned to exchange the ethic of the strong man for that of the authentic hero. The Echthroi's ultimate weapon is a painful process of negation referred to as "X-ing." This process of spiritual annihilation is to be avoided at all costs, including, in the case of Proginoskes, the cost of sacrificing one's own life. At the appropriate time, Meg is called upon to voluntarily risk X-ing at the hands of the Echthroi in order to "Name" Mr. Jenkins. Having nearly been X-ed involuntarily once before, she is, for a time, unable to comply, i.e. "knowingly open herself to that pain." Anyone who has ever faced a dreaded surgical procedure will empathize with her reluctance.

"Naming" is the opposite of X-ing in L'Engle's universe. To be Named is to be affirmed by the love of another, to achieve a true sense of identity, wholeness/holiness, and authenticity by identification with the created order, not as it is but as God wills it to be. "To write a story is an act of Naming," reflects L'Engle, "in reading about a protagonist I can grow along with, I myself am more named. And we live in a world which would reduce us to our social security numbers. Area codes, zip codes, credit card codes, all take precedence over our names."[19]

In the end, L'Engle, like Paul and Augustine before her, affirms that the beauty of holiness, like the beauty of art, is matter of love not virtue, merit, or adherence to doctrine: "It is a criterion of love, "writes L'Engle. "In moments of decision, we are to try to make what seems to be the most loving, the most creative decision."[20] In *A Wind in the Door*, it is a series of precisely such loving and creative decisions that save Mr. Jenkins from being X-ed, Charles Wallace from terminal mitochondritis, and ultimately the cosmos from the ravages of the Echthroi.

A Swiftly Tilting Planet

In this final space/time adventure involving the Murrys, L'Engle expands on the themes of loving creativity as an alternative to destructivity, human conflict, and war, the relativity of time and space, and

18. L'Engle, *A Wind in the Door*, 178.

19. L'Engle, *Walking on Water*, 110.

20. Ibid., 153.

the Logos Christianity that makes a joyous universe of the increasingly complex multiverse that often seems indifferent, or even hostile, to our deepest human needs. From a journey to outer space in *A Wrinkle in Time* and inner space in *A Wind in the Door*, readers of *A Swiftly Tilting Planet* are taken on a series of projections occurring in different times and geographical settings whereby events tending in our own time to nuclear holocaust are averted. El Rabioso, a.k.a. Mad Dog Branzillo, the power-crazed dictator of Vespugia, a fictional South American country, is determined to make the world generally and the United States in particular pay for its indifference to the plight of the poorer nations. As Mrs. Murry explains to Sandy, one of the Murry twins: "The Western world has used up more than its share of the world's energy, the world's resources, and we must be punished. We are responsible for the acutely serious oil and coal shortage, the defoliation of trees, the grave damage to the atmosphere, and he is going to make us pay."[21] Here, the Cold War hysteria of the post-WWII era is compared with times of comparable conflict and irrationality, e.g., the Salem Witch Hunts and the American Civil War. In order to avert the future by altering the past, Charles Wallace is sent through a series of "Projections," possible futures that the Echthroi want to make real. Starting in Wales in the time of Leif Ericson, a lineal ancestor of Mad Dog Branzillo resettles in Vespugia. The conflict that erupts between him and his more loving, and peaceable brother is re-enacted throughout history as in the Biblical parable of Cain and Abel. This human struggle between hawks and doves is subsumed cosmically in the ongoing struggle between Angels and Echthroi. Ultimately it mirrors the archetypal conflict, universal harmony (the Music of the Spheres) vs. the Cosmic Dissonance created by the evil of those who would promote their own view in defiance of God's will.

Charles Wallace's spiritual guide and mode of transportation is Gaudior, a pure white unicorn who represents the perfection of innocence. Indeed, Gaudior, like the benign aliens in Steven Spielberg's film *Close Encounters*, communicates through music. "How is it that you speak my language?" asks Charles Wallace. "I do not," explains Gaudior, "I speak the ancient harmony." Pressing his point Charles Wallace inquires further, "Then how is it I understand?" "You are very young," Gaudior replies, "but

---

21. Madeleine L'Engle, *A Swiftly Tilting Planet* (New York: Dell, 1978), 12.

you belong to the Old Music."[22] Wishing to fortify Charles Wallace against the troubling experiences that lay ahead, Gaudior's initial projection is from the "star-watching rock" in his own backyard to a "When" (as opposed to a place), a "Might Have Been" that has not been distorted by the cosmic dissonance of sin, a "golden time." "All I know," says Gaudior, "is that there is something important to the future right here in the place where you watch stars. But whatever it was did not happen until the ancient music of the spheres was distorted." "Do you know when that When is," asks Charles Wallace. "A far When," states Gaudior, "We can ride this wind without fear [of Echthroi] for here the ancient harmonies are still unbroken. But it may roughen if the When we enter is a dissonant one."[23] Later, when Charles Wallace is projected into the world of Pastor Mortmain, a Puritan world of religious intolerance and bigotry, Zylle, a Native American ancestor who has married into the white man's community and adopted its Christian religion, is interrogated by the good Pastor and a delegation of upstanding citizens: "We believe you to be a good Christian Zylle. That is true, is it not?" "Yes," says Zylle, "when I married Ritchie, I accepted his beliefs." "Even though they were contrary to the beliefs of your people," asks Pastor Mortmain. "But they are not contrary," protest Zylle. "The Indians are pagans," chimes in Duthbert, another concerned citizen. "I do not know what pagan means," Zylle rejoins. "I only know that Jesus of Nazareth sings the true song. He knows the ancient harmonies." Mortmain, responds in horror, "You say that our Lord and Savior sings! What more do we need to hear?"[24]

In a still later Projection, Mortmain's descendant, Duthbert Mortmain, step-father to Chuck (a spiritual adept attuned to the celestial music and brother of Beezie, Calvin's mother) indulges his violent temper, fracturing Chuck's skull and leaving him a mental defective for life. As we finally learn, the Philistine, fearful, anti-intellectual domestic environment in which Calvin lives, so different from the loving, nurturing environment of the Murry household, stems from that blow, a mindless act of brutality that not only cracked Chuck's skull but also broke Beezie's spirit. When Charles Wallace is projected into the strife of the Civil War era Bran, another ancestor whose fate is linked with the modern day threat

22. Ibid., 45.
23. Ibid., 57.
24. Ibid.,133.

posed by Mad Dog Branzillo, he summarizes his battlefield experience as follows: "I went to war thinking of myself as Galahad, out to free fellow human beings from the intolerable bondage of slavery. But it wasn't as simple as that. There were other, less pure issues being fought over, with little concern for the souls which would perish for nothing more grand than political greed, corruption, and conniving power . . . I saw two brothers, and one was blue and one was gray, and I will not tell you which one took his saber and ran it through the other. Oh God, it was brother against brother, Cain and Abel all over again."[25] In the end, the temporal journey of Charles Wallace who "carried within himself" his ancestors, e.g. Madoc, Mathew, Brandon, and Chuck, resolves the cosmic dissonance, restoring the harmonious music of God's peaceful and loving intentions, but not without experiencing at first hand the terrible price paid by some for humanity's prideful rebellion. "Beezie," reflects Meg, "must have married Paddy [O' Keefe, Calvin's step-father] for more or less the same reasons that her mother married Duthbert Mortmain. And she learned not to feel, not to love, not even her children, not even Calvin. Not to be hurt. But she gave Charles Wallace the rune [a Rosetta Stone with which to decipher the unknown language of the past], and told him to use it to stop Mad Dog Branzillo. So there must have been a little of the Old Music left in her."[26] According to Madeleine L'Engle, there is a little of the Old Music, the Pythagorean Music of the Spheres, left in all of us. Though the discord of this world is at times deafening, ultimately the message of hope, the essence of the Christian faith is that *logos* will prevail over chaos. In the end, all knees will bow, not in fear and trembling but in gratitude, love, and thanksgiving. "I am never surprised," writes L'Engle, "when I discover that one of my favorite science fiction writers is Christian, because to think about worlds in other galaxies, other modes of being, is a theological enterprise."[27] Elsewhere in the same source, she cites the words of Julian of Norwich to explain her own willingness to deepen and join the dance: "All shall be well and all shall be well and all manner of thing shall be well no matter what. That, I think, is the affirmation behind all art which can be called Christian. That is what brings cosmos out of chaos."[28]

25. Ibid., 243.

26. Ibid., 275–76.

27. L'Engle, *Walking on Water*, 134.

28. Ibid., 158.

For L'Engle there is no qualitative distinction between Kiddie Goth and its adult counterpart. Like most writers for a younger audience, secular as well as Christian, she imparts a hopeful message that transcends generational differences: The child within represents a human potential to overcome our gothic dilemmas, to tame the terrors of the adult world, subjectively at least, by choosing faith in oneself and one another over fear. Fundamentally, suggests L'Engle, the celestial music of the *logos* is richer, stronger, and more enduring than the discordant chaos of greed, violence, and the Will to Power.

CHAPTER 8

Uncovering Embedded Theology in Science Fiction Films

K-PAX Revealed

TERESA BLYTHE

Let's jump right in, shall we? —scientist at observatory

Make sure you can swim. —Prot

A MYSTERIOUS TRAVELER APPEARS IN New York City, claiming to be from another planet. This man, Prot, wears sunglasses most of the time because, as he puts it, "your planet is really bright." Prot—who says he's from the planet K-PAX—is able to see portions of the light spectrum that most humans are not able to see. Prot sees the world with intensity.

We, too, can develop eyes that "see" with more intensity. This chapter will introduce an exegetical method for seeing or detecting embedded theology in science fiction films. The 2001 science fiction film *K-PAX*, about the mysterious traveler named Prot, will serve as a backdrop illustrating how we can metaphorically take the shades off our eyes and see part of the spectrum of science fiction films that we might easily miss without the discipline and structure of an analytical method.

Thinking theologically about popular culture involves more than detecting allegorical figures in the story. In fact, if that were all we were doing with *K-PAX*, our job would be quite easy because, as *Reelview* movie reviewer James Berardinelli says, "it doesn't take a religious scholar, for example, to see similarities between Prot and Jesus."[1] Theological analysis of any popular culture involves discovering the subtle embedded images and understandings of God within a text. Science fiction is ripe for this analysis. It frequently moves from the philosophical-ethical to the theological as its literary boundaries expand beyond our current understanding of the cosmos. It challenges us to think and rethink our notions of the Creator.

What Is *K-PAX*?

K-PAX came out in the fall of 2001, not long after the terrorist attacks of September 11th. The film featured actors Kevin Spacey as Prot/Robert and Jeff Bridges as Dr. Mark Powell, the psychiatrist assigned to help this unusual person—assumed to be mentally ill—become well. Prot first appears in a New York City train station and claims to be from the planet K-PAX. He's taken in for observation and delivered to Dr. Powell. The assumption is that Prot is suffering from delusions and, for some reason, doesn't want to call Earth his home.

Throughout the film, the viewer is challenged to wonder, "Is Prot mentally ill or is he, in fact, from another planet?" The evidence that he is mentally ill is there—Dr. Powell does hypnosis on Prot and learns of a traumatic murder of the wife and daughter of Robert Porter, whom Prot refers to as a friend. Powell thinks Prot/Porter are the same person, someone suffering from post-traumatic stress disorder upon finding his loved ones dead.

But then there is also evidence that Prot—whether an alien or not—is certainly an extraordinary person. He sees ultra-violet light, he tolerates massive doses of psychotropic drugs, and he shows planetary scientists where K-PAX is, drawing a map that turns out to be accurate and mind-boggling. Whether Prot actually travels on a beam of light, as he says he does, is for the viewer to decide. What Prot can do—and very well—is

---

1. Review of *K-PAX* by James Berardinelli (2001) found online: http://replay.way-backmachine.org/20060620003725/http://movie-reviews.colossus.net/movies/k/k-pax.html.

prod Dr. Powell to appreciate life on earth much more than he now does. Prot's wistful dialogues with Mark Powell turn the tables on the doctor-patient relationship: "I want to tell you something, Mark, something you do not yet know that we K-PAXians have been around long enough to have discovered. The universe will expand, then it will collapse back on itself, then it will expand again. It will repeat this process forever. What you don't know is that when the universe expands again, everything will be as it is now. Whatever mistakes you make this time around, you will live through again, and again, forever. So my advice to you is to get it right this time around. Because this time is all you have."[2]

K-PAX ends ambiguously (at least some of us think so . . .) with Prot essentially disappearing but the body of the person known as Prot/Robert remaining behind in a catatonic state. What happens between appearing at the train station and ending up catatonic is fodder for our theological consumption.

Looking for Theology in Film

Theological analysis of popular culture involves sifting through all aspects of the production to find theology that is not systematic or doctrinal but is instead implied—that is, lived out in acts of daily life. Theologians Stone and Duke say our embedded theology is a set of beliefs that we react to but do not always know how to articulate.[3] Theological analysis encourages us to apply critical thinking skills that will reveal to us the embedded theology, which helps us better articulate our chosen and claimed theology.

So the question becomes, what method do we choose to use with on-screen science fiction stories? Since we are taking more into account than merely the words of the story (in contrast to the exegesis of a written piece of literature) we must include more detective work in our method, considering the visual signs, symbols and images as well as the use of sounds and silence. For this, the key concepts from the field of media literacy will be helpful. Since it is theological analysis, we must include more than media literacy or even the steps of biblical exegesis—although both are a

---

2. The quotation from the film found in Catherine M. Barsotti and Robert K. Johnston, *Finding God in the Movies: 33 Films of Reel Faith* (Grand Rapids: Baker, 2004), 254.

3. Howard W. Stone and James O. Duke, *How to Think Theologically* (Minneapolis: Fortress, 1996), 14.

good place to start.[4] For our purposes, we will combine the key principles used in many biblical exegetical studies with questions designed to tease out subtle theological themes.

No method is perfect, and this one is no exception. You will find some questions more difficult than others, but please don't ignore a question because it is hard. You will find some questions emerging that are not included in the method. Add to it. The method is only to jump-start theological thinking. Please feel free to move forward on your own.

The method begins with an analysis of the narrative to see what the story seems to be saying to you. From there, we move to a deeper analysis of the story to see what the dominant and subordinate messages appear to be. Semiotics is next—a look at signs, codes and symbols used throughout the film. An important additional step is to consider the ideology and how power is used and shared in the film. Then, we'll think about how the story functions for viewers—what gratification they might receive from the film. Some research into the building blocks of the film is also included in the method because we need to know who the people behind the making of the film are, and what they bring to this text. And finally, after all the other questions are answered, we turn to the embedded theology. This is the next-to-last step because you need to fully experience the film and assess it from a variety of angles before you start digging into its theology. Most people find the theology section easier to handle once other questions are answered first.

Reflection without action is futile, so the method adds an "action step" at the end. This is not some theological parlor game where we sleuth for clues about images of God just to amuse ourselves. Turning reflection into action is an act of respect to both the reflection and the film that gave birth to it. It's good theology.

K-PAX Gems

There is not room here to put all the method's questions to the film. But in doing repeated analysis of this film for the writing of *Meeting God in Virtual Reality*, several theological messages became evident to Dan Wolpert: "The [spiritual] dilemma—how to respond with grace and love

---

4. See Teresa Blythe and Daniel Wolpert, *Meeting God in Virtual Reality: Using Spiritual Practices with Media* (Nashville: Abingdon, 2004), 56, for a "quickie exegesis" test to apply to media that comes directly from Professor Anne Wire's New Testament Gospels class at San Francisco Theological Seminary.

when treated unjustly—is one that is treated in many stories in the Bible. Its rendition in K-PAX rings true both in the human experience of many Christians and in the many stories of how God has worked throughout history with God's people.

"Salvation in this case is nonviolent love. That is not only healthy, but also in keeping with what Christians believe about Jesus' life, death and resurrection."[5]

While attending a retreat on "Seeing the Unseen God" in Dallas recently, a group of clergy and lay persons did theological reflection on *K-PAX* and uncovered many other theological insights. One person in the group shared Dr. Powell's concern over Prot's description of there being "no marriage on K-PAX," but another participant compared Prot's description of the planet with how Christian tradition has sometimes described heaven. Certainly there is much more to be found theologically in *K-PAX* than a simple naming of Prot as a Christ figure.

Beyond *K-PAX*

The method shared in this chapter is not specific to *K-PAX* and could even be used with films from other genres (with a little editing). In fact, the method is adapted from one created by a group of scholars at San Francisco Theological Seminary in 2001 for our book *Watching What We Watch: Prime-Time Television Through the Lens of Faith*.[6] You are encouraged to do your own adaptations, but especially to apply the method to other science fiction films. For example, comparing and contrasting the embedded theology found in *K-PAX* with that found in films from the *Star Wars* or *Star Trek* series would be fascinating.

Doing theological reflection that leads to action can be done alone, but it's much more satisfying when done collegially. When you reflect together, you can truly answer the question, "how do people different from me see this text differently" without guessing. You will see more when there are more eyes watching.

5. Ibid., 65.

6. Walt Davis, Jr. et al., *Watching What We Watch: Prime-Time Television through the Lens of Faith* (Louisville: Geneva, 2001).

Parting Words

No doubt we can think theologically without a printout of a method in front of us. Some people are quite intuitive about theology found in daily life. Others of us need help. We won't miss the obvious but we could easily miss the understated. The method helps keep us honest and open-minded. It helps us answer questions that might not occur to us. It stretches us to think beyond the usual film tropes of "Christ figures," "suffering servants," or "sacramental elements" to also consider the power dynamics, the societal influences, and to think about whose story is *not* being told here.

The good news for those wary of using a method is that once you use it a few times, you will begin to internalize certain questions. The critical thinking methods will remain with you. You will never view another science fiction film passively nor will you succumb to clichéd reflections that only scratch the surface. The hope is that you will uncover embedded theology that changes your life, increases your field of vision and convinces you that "our planet is really bright."

A Method for Theological Analysis of Science Fiction Films

Analyze the Story

Describe the setting of the film.

What makes this film science fiction?

How is this text like others in the science fiction genre? What are the stock codes or common rules at work in science fiction films? How has the genre evolved over the past half century? What is the place of this film within the genre?

Briefly describe the narrative structure of the text you are analyzing:

Main plot

Subplot #1

Subplot #2

Subplot #3

Who are the protagonists and what are their motivations?

Who are the antagonists and what are their motivations?

How are the major issues/problems/enigmas resolved?

How does the narrative end?

Who/what are the stereotypes?

Who are the heroes and villains?

What is unique about each character? What is his or her dominant concern in life?

Character A:

Character B:

Character C:

Character D:

Character E:

Character F:

What relief is sought in the episode, and by whom?

Are some characters favored and some disfavored? How so?

Analyze the Messages in the Story

What is the dominant message here? What are some subordinate messages?

What are the tensions explored in this text?

How does this text defend a particular view of life?

What worldview is described and explored in this text?

What elements of satire are included in this text?

Analyze the Signs, Codes & Symbols

Describe how the camera is used to tell the story.

How does the overall look and tone of the text contribute to and shape the story or stories that are told?

How does the lighting and sound design affect the narrative and its meaning?

What special effects are used? How do they contribute to the story?

How are signs used to convey major messages in this text?

What icons are at work in this visual text?

Analyze Power and Ideology

What were the dominant socio-political issues and ideologies at work in American society when the film first opened? How are they reflected in the text?

Who is the target audience for the text?

From whose point of view is the story told?

Whose point of view is absent?

Who has power over whom in the narrative? Why? To what effect?

How is race structured/portrayed in the text?

How is gender structured/portrayed in the text?

How is socioeconomic class structured/portrayed in the text?

How are scarce resources allocated in the narrative?

How is conflict resolved? If violent, who wins/loses? Do perpetrators suffer?

Whose needs and interests are met/not met? How?

Analyze How Viewers Use the Story

Why do you think people saw this movie?

What gratification do you and others get from this text?

What life behavior does this text recommend?

How might others who are different from you see the messages in this film differently?

What does this text make you want to do?

What effects, both short-term and long-term, might this text have on viewers?

After analyzing the text, what feelings and intuitions do you now have?

Have those feelings or intuitions changed as a result of the analysis?

Analyze the Production

Who produced this film? What do you know about him or her?

Who wrote the story?

Isolate a scene that you believe captures the essence of the story. What makes that scene important? How does the lighting, sound, movement and actors' interpretation contribute?

What economic factors may have influenced the construction of this message?

Analyze the Theology in the Story

Is there an image of God presented here? If so, what is it or what are they? How does this image compare with your own image of God? What is your response to this image or images?

How is the human person presented in this text? What is the most pressing human predicament here?

What change is sought to relieve the tension or overcome the problem? (What is "salvation" for this story?)

What are the main desires on the part of the main characters?

Does anyone change? Who? How? And in response to what?

What are the consequences of the character's change?

Who helps others change?

Does any character suffer on behalf of another? How?

When and where does transcendence (getting outside oneself) occur?

Who looks for something beyond themselves, their job, and their social roles?

What do you think the writer/director/producer are trying to say?

How should we live—as individuals and societies—according to this text?

Does this text ask the audience to open or close their hearts to compassion and hope?

Does this text point people to an encounter with mystery? Or does it seduce them into complacency?

Does this text portray a humanity that knows and accepts its own vulnerability? Or does it foster childish fantasies?

How does this text depict the "other," the poor, the vulnerable, the marginalized?

Does this text examine the social and political dimensions of personal problems or does it privatize them and avoid social critique?

How does the dominant concern in this text resonate with your own life?

Consider Action based on Analysis

Would you recommend this film to others? Why or why not?

How would you describe the embedded theology found in this film? Do you share any of that embedded theology? How does it compare with your deliberate or chosen theology?

Does anything in this text challenge you to make changes in your values, goals, or behavior? In what way? How will you act on that challenge?

Select Bibliography

Anker, Roy M. *Catching Light: Looking for God in the Movies*. Grand Rapids: Eerdmans, 2004.

Appadurai, Arjun. *Modernity at Large: Cultural Dimensions of Globalization*. Public Worlds 1. Minneapolis: University of Minnesota Press, 1996.

Asimov, Isaac. *Gold: The Final Science Fiction Collection*. New York: HarperPrism, 1995.

————. *Robot Visions*. New York: Penguin, 1990.

Barad, Judith, with Ed Robertson. *The Ethics of Star Trek*. New York: HarperCollins, 2000.

Barbour, Ian G. *Nature, Human Nature, and God*. Minneapolis: Fortress, 2002.

————. *Ethics in an Age of Technology*. The Gifford Lectures 2, 1990–1991. London: SCM, 1992.

Barsotti, Catherine M., and Robert K. Johnston. *Finding God in the Movies: 33 Films of Reel Faith*. Grand Rapids: Baker, 2004.

Basalla, George. *Civilized Life in the Universe: Scientists on Intelligent Extraterrestrials*. Oxford: Oxford University Press, 2006.

Baudrillard, Jean. "Simulacra and Science Fiction." *Science Fiction Studies* 18 (1991) 309–13.

Benford, Gregory, and Elisabeth Malartre. *Beyond Human*. New York: Doherty, 2007.

Bertonneau, Thomas, and Kim Paffenroth. *The Truth Is Out There: Christian Faith and the Classics of TV Science Fiction*. Grand Rapids: Brazos, 2006.

Blackmore, Susan. *Conversations on Consciousness*. Oxford: Oxford University Press, 2006.

Boden, Margaret A., editor. *The Philosophy of Artificial Intelligence*. Oxford Readings in Philosophy. Oxford: Oxford University Press, 1990.

Boer, Roland. *Rescuing the Bible*. Blackwell Manifestos. Malden, MA: Blackwell, 2007.

Booker, M. Keith. *Alternate Americas: Science Fiction Film and American Culture*. Westport, CT: Praeger, 2006.

————. *Science Fiction Television*. The Praeger Television Collection. Westport, CT: Praeger, 2004.

Bortolin, Matthew. *The Dharma of Star Wars*. Boston: Wisdom, 2005.

Bourdieu, Pierre. "The Specificity of the Scientific Field and the Social Conditions of the Progress of Reason." In *The Science Studies Reader*, edited by Mario Biagioli, 31–50. London: Routledge, 1999.

Brooker, Will. *Batman Unmasked: Analyzing a Cultural Icon*. New York: Continuum, 2001).

Brooks, Rodney R. *Flesh and Machines: How Robots Will Change Us*. New York: Pantheon, 2002.

Brown, Warren S. et al., editors. *Whatever Happened to the Soul? Scientific and Theological Portraits of Human Nature*. Theology and the Sciences. Minneapolis: Fortress, 1998.

Card, Orson Scott. *Maps in a Mirror: The Short Fiction of Orson Scott Card*. New York: Tom Doherty Associates, 1990.

Campbell, Joseph et al. *The Power of Myth*. New York: Anchor, 1991.

Cetina, Karin Knorr. *Epistemic Cultures: How the Sciences Make Knowledge*. Cambridge: Harvard University Press, 1999.

Chamberlin, E. R. *The Bad Popes*. New York: Barnes & Noble, 1993.

Chabon, Michael. *The Amazing Adventures of Kavalier & Clay*. New York: Picador, 2000.

Chen, Nancy N. "Urban Spaces and Experiences of *Qigong*." In *Urban Spaces in Contemporary China: The Potential for Autonomy and Community in Post-Mao China*, edited by Deborah Davis et al., 347–61. Woodrow Wilson Center Series. Washington DC: Woodrow Wilson Center Press, 1995.

China Internet Information Center 2005. "Prof. Helps Internet-Hooked Teens Kick the Habit." Online: http://www.china.org.cn/english/NM-e/123822.htm/.

"Author Bios." Online: http://replay.waybackmachine.org/20041207230455/http://www.livejournal.com/users/zhwj/3944.html /.

Chow, Tse-Tsung. *The May Fourth Movement*. Harvard East Asian Studies 6. Cambridge: Harvard University Press, 1960.

Cohen, Paul. *History in Three Keys: The Boxers as Event, Experience, and Myth*. New York: Columbia University Press, 1997.

Colum, Padraic. *Nordic Gods and Heroes*. New York: Dover, 1996.

Conroy, Mike. *500 Great Comic Book Action Heroes*. New York: Barron's, 2002.

Csicsery-Ronay, Istvan. "Dis-Imagined Communities: Science Fiction and the Future of Nations." In *Edging into the Future: Science Fiction and Contemporary Cultural Transformation*, edited by Veronica Hollinger and Joan Gordon, 217–38. Philadelphia: University of Pennsylvania Press, 2002.

Cubitt, Sean. "*Delicatessen*: Eco-Apocalypse in the New French Science Fiction Cinema." In *Aliens R Us: The Other in Science Fiction Cinema*, edited by Ziauddin Sadar and Sean Cubitt, 18–33. London: Pluto, 2002.

Daniels, Les. *DC Comics: A Celebration of the World's Favorite Comic Book Heroes*. New York: Billboard, 1995.

——— et al. *Wonder Woman: The Complete History*. San Francisco: Chronicle, 2000.

Dann, Jack, editor. More Wandering Stars: An Anthology of Jewish Fantasy and Science Fiction. Garden City, NY: Doubleday, 1981.

———, editor. Wandering Stars: An Anthology of Jewish Fantasy & Science Fiction. Woodstock, VT: Jewish Lights, 1974.

Davis, John Jefferson. "Theological Reflections on Chaos Theory." *Perspectives on Science and Christian Faith* 49 (1997) 75–84. Online: http://www.asa3.org/ASA/PSCF/1997/PSCF6-97Davis.html/.

Decker, Kevin S., and Jason T. Eberl, editors. *"Star Wars" and Philosophy: More Powerful Than You Can Possibly Imagine*. Popular Culture and Philosophy 12. Chicago: Open Court, 2005.

DeGrazia, David, *Taking Animals Seriously: Mental Life and Moral Status*. Cambridge: Cambridge University Press, 1996.

Dick, Philip K. *The Shifting Realities of Philip K. Dick: Selected Literary and Philosophical Writings*. Edited and with an introduction by Lawrence Sutin. New York: Vintage, 1995.

Dimitrakaki, Angela, and Miltos Tsiantis. "Terminators, Monkeys and Mass Culture: The Carnival of Time in Science Fiction Films." *Time and Society* 11 (2002) 209–31.

Dinello, Daniel. *Technophobia! Science Fiction Visions of Posthuman Technology*. Austin: University of Texas Press, 2005.

Disch, Thomas M. *On SF*. Ann Arbor: University of Michigan Press, 2005.

Dyson, George B., *Darwin among the Machines: The Evolution of Global Intelligence*. Helix Books. Reading, MA: Addison-Wesley, 1997.

Eisner, Will. *Graphic Storytelling and Visual Narrative*. New York: Norton, 2008.

Elias, Norbert, and Eric Dunning, *Quest for Excitement: Sport and Leisure in the Civilizing Process*. Oxford: Blackwell, 1986.

Escobar, Arturo, "Welcome to Cyberia: Notes on the Anthropology of Cyberculture." *Current Anthropology* 35 (1994) 211–31.

Faller, Stephen. *Beyond "The Matrix": Revolutions and Revelations*. St. Louis: Chalice, 2004.

Farrer, James, *Opening Up: Youth Sex Culture and Market Reform in Shanghai*. Chicago: University of Chicago Press, 2002.

Feiffer, Jules, *The Great Comic Book Heroes*. Seattle: Fantagraphics, 2003.

Foerst, Anne. *God in the Machine: What Robots Teach Us about Humanity and God*. New York: Dutton, 2004.

Ford, Paul F., editor. *Companion to Narnia*. New York: Collier, 1986.

Gaines, James R., *Evening in the Palace of Reason: Bach Meets Frederick the Great in the Age of Enlightenment*. New York: Fourth Estate, 2005.

Gamble, John W. "When East Meets West: The Rise of Meditation." in *Religion as Entertainment*, edited by C. K. Robertson, 79–104. New York: Lang, 2002.

Gardner, James. *The Intelligent Universe: AI, ET, and the Emerging Mind of the Cosmos* Franklin Lakes, NJ: New Page, 2007.

Garrett, Greg. *Holy Superheroes! Exploring Faith & Spirituality in Comic Books*. Colorado Springs: Piñon, 2005.

Geraci, Robert M. "Apocalyptic AI: Religion and the Promise of Artificial Intelligence," *Journal of the American Academy of Religion* 76 (2008) 138–66.

———. *Apocalyptic AI: Visions of Heaven in Robotics, Artificial Intelligence and Virtual Reality*. New York: Oxford University Press, 2010.

———. "Robots and the Sacred in Science and Science Fiction: Theological Implications of Artificial Intelligence," *Zygon: Journal of Religion and Science* 42 (2007) 961–80.

———. "Spiritual Robots: Religion and Our Scientific View of the Natural World." *Theology and Science* 4 (2006) 229–46.

Gerrold, David, and Robert J. Sawyer, editors. *Boarding the Enterprise: Transporters, Tribbles, and the Vulcan Death Grip in Gene Rodenberry's "Star Trek."* Smart Pop Series. Dallas: BenBella, 2006.

Gershenfeld, Neil A. *When Things Start To Think*. New York: Holt, 1999.

Gillette, Maris Boyd. *Between Mecca and Beijing: Modernization and Consumption among Urban Chinese Muslims*. Stanford: Stanford University Press, 2000.

Goldblatt, Howard. "Pushing the (Red) Envelope." *Time Asia*, October 23, 2000. Online: http://www.cnn.com/ASIANOW/time/features/youngchina/a.hottest.authors.html/.

Grand, Steve. *Creation: Life and How To Make It*. Cambridge: Harvard University Press, 2001.

Grau, Christopher, editor. *Philosophers Explore "The Matrix."* Oxford: Oxford University Press, 2005.

Greeley, Andrew M., and Michael Cassutt, editors. *Sacred Visions*. New York: Tor, 1991.

Greenberg, Gary. *101 Myths of the Bible: How Ancient Scribes Invented Biblical History*. Naperville, IL: Sourcebooks, 2000.

Greenberg, Martin H., and Patricia S. Warrick, editors. *The New Awareness: Religion through Science Fiction*. New York: Delacorte, 1975.

Griffin, David Ray, *God and Religion in the Postmodern World*. SUNY Series in Constructive Postmodern Thought. Albany: State University of New York Press, 1989.

Gunn, James E. *The Road to Science Fiction*. Vol. 1, *From Gilgamesh to Wells*. New York: New American Library, 1977.

Hamer, Dean H. *The God Gene: How Faith Is Hardwired into Our Genes*. New York: Doubleday, 2004.

Haney, William S. *Cyberculture, Cyborgs and Science Fiction: Consciousness and the Posthuman*. Consciousness, Literature & the Arts 2. Amsterdam: Rodopi, 2006.

Hanley, Richard, *The Metaphysics of "Star Trek."* New York: BasicBooks, 1997.

Haraway, Donna J. *Simians, Cyborgs, and Women: The Reinvention of Nature*. New York: Routledge, 1991.

Hartford, Kathleen. "Cyberspace with Chinese Characteristics." *Current History* 99:638 (2000) 255–62.

Hatch, Richard, editor. *So Say We All: An Unauthorized Collection of Thoughts and Opinions on "Battlestar Galactica."* Smart Pop Series. Dallas: BenBella, 2006.

Hatt, Harold E. *Cybernetics and the Image of Man: A Study of Freedom and Responsibility in Man and Machine*. Nashville: Abingdon, 1968.

Havel, Vaclav, "The Need for Transcendence in the Postmodern World." *Futurist* 29.14 (Jul-Aug 1995) 46ff. Speech made in Philadelphia 4 July 1994. Online: http://www.worldtrans.org/whole/havelspeech.html/.

Havely, Joe. "China's Ming Dynasty Astronaut." *CNN* (Hong Kong), September 30, 2003. http://edition.cnn.com/2003/TECH/space/09/30/china.wanhu/index.html/.

Hefner, Philip J. *Technology and Human Becoming*. Facets. Minneapolis: Fortress, 2003.

Henderson, Mary S. *"Star Wars": The Magic of Myth*. New York: Bantam, 1997.

Hengel, Martin. *Judaism and Hellenism*. Translated by John Bowden. 1974. Reprinted, Eugene, OR: Wipf & Stock, 2003.

Hertz, Ellen. *The Trading Crowd: An Ethnography of the Shanghai Stock Market*. Cambridge Studies in Social and Cultural Anthropology 108. Cambridge: Cambridge University Press, 1998.

Herzfeld, Noreen L. *In Our Image: Artificial Intelligence and the Human Spirit*. Theology and the Sciences. Minneapolis: Fortress, 2002.

Hogan, James P. *Mind Matters: Exploring the World of Artificial Intelligence*. A Del Rey Book. New York: Ballantine, 1997.

Hollinger, Veronica, and Joan Gordon. "Introduction: Edging into the Future." In *Edging into the Future: Science Fiction and Contemporary Cultural Transformation*, edited by Veronica Hollinger and Joan Gordon, 1–10. Philadelphia: University of Pennsylvania Press, 2002.

Huneeus, J. Antonio. "UFOs behind the Great Wall." *Parascope* (1997) Online: http://www.parascope.com/articles/0997/chinaufo.htm/.

Hunt, Edward. "Good and Evil in the Screenwriter or Filmmaker's Mind." *Screentalk* 3 (2003) 72–75.

Infantino, Stephen C. "Delicatessen: Slices of Postmodern Life," *Arachne: An Interdisciplinary Journal of the Humanities/Revue interdisciplinaire de langue et de littérature* 4 (1997) 91–100.

Irwin, William, editor. *"The Matrix" and Philosophy: Welcome to the Desert of the Real.* Popular Culture and Philosophy. Chicago: Open Court, 2002.

Jameson, Fredric, *Postmodernism, or The Logic of Late Capitalism.* Post-contemporary Interventions. Durham: Duke University Press, 1991.

Jones, Timothy Paul. *Finding God in a Galaxy Far, Far Away.* Sisters, OR: Multnomah, 2005.

Kelly, Joseph F. *The World of the Early Christians.* Message of the Fathers of the Church 1. Collegeville, MN: Liturgical, 1997.

Kidd, Chip, art director / designer; and Geoff Spear, photographer. *Mythology: The DC Comics Art of Alex Ross.* New York: Pantheon, 2003.

Kozlovic, Anton. "From Holy Aliens to Cyborg Saviours: Biblical Subtexts in Four Science Fiction Films." *Journal of Religion and Film* 5:2 (2001). Online: http://www.unomaha.edu/jrf/cyborg.htm/.

Kraemer, Ross S. et al. *Religions of Star Trek.* Boulder: Westview, 2001.

Küng, Hans. *Great Christian Thinkers.* New York: Continuum, 1995.

Langer, Susanne K. *Philosophy in a New Key: A Study in the Symbolism of Reason, Rite, and Art* 3rd ed. Harvard Paperbacks 17. Cambridge: Harvard University Press, 1978.

Lee, Stan, and George Mair. *Excelsior! The Amazing Life of Stan Lee.* A Fireside Book. New York: Simon & Schuster, 2002.

Leiber, Justin, *Can Animals and Machines Be Persons?* Indianapolis: Hackett, 1985.

L'Engle, Madeleine. "Foreword." In *Companion to Narnia*, edited by Paul F. Ford, xiv–xix. New York: Collier, 1986.

———. *A Swiftly Tilting Planet.* New York: Dell, 1978.

———. *Walking on Water: Reflections on Faith & Art.* New York: Bantam, 1982.

———. *A Wind in the Door.* New York: Dell, 1973.

———. *A Wrinkle in Time.* New York: Dell, 1962.

"Local Sci-Fi Heads Back to the Future," *China Daily*, July 29, 1997. Online: http://web.lexis-nexis.com/universe/document?_m=6e4968b49c51669/.

Lovelock, J. E. *The Ages of Gaia: A Biography of Our Living Earth.* New York: Bantam, 1990.

———. *Gaia, A New Look at Life on Earth.* Oxford: Oxford University Press, 1979.

Lozada, Eriberto P. "Computers, Scientism, and Cyborg Subjectivity in Postsocialist China." *Asian Anthropology* 2 (2003) 111–37.

———. *God Aboveground: Catholic Church, Postsocialist State, and Transnational Processes in a Chinese Village.* Stanford: Stanford University Press, 2001.

Lu, Jie. "A Report on the World's Largest Science Fiction Magazine" *Extrapolations* 43 (2002) 219–25.

Marston, William Moulton, "Don't Laugh at the Comics." *The Family Circle*, October 25, 1940, 10–11.

Martin, Joel W., and Conrad E. Ostwalt, Jr. *Screening the Sacred: Religion, Myth, and Ideology in Popular American Film.* Boulder: Westview, 1995.

Mayo, Clark. *Kurt Vonnegut: The Gospels from Outer Space (Or, Yes, We Have No Nirvanas).* San Bernardino, CA: Borgo, 1977.

McDowell, John C. *The Gospel according to "Star Wars": Faith, Hope, and the Force.* Louisville: Westminster John Knox, 2007.

McFague, Sallie, *The Body of God: An Ecological Theology.* Minneapolis: Fortress, 1993.

McKee, Gabriel, *The Gospel according to Science Fiction: From "The Twilight Zone" to the Final Frontier.* Louisville: Westminster John Knox, 2007.

Mohs, Mayo, editor. Other Worlds, Other Gods: Adventures in Religious Science Fiction. Garden City, NY: Doubleday, 1971.

Moravec, Hans. *Robot: Mere Machine to Transcendent Mind.* New York: Oxford University Press, 1999.

Morford, Mark P. O., and Robert J. Lenardon. *Classical Mythology.* New York: McKay, 1971.

Morrison, Grant. *Wizard* #143 (August 2003) 180.

Mulhall, Douglas. *Our Molecular Future: How Nanotechnology, Robotics, Genetics, and Artificial Intelligence Will Transform Our World.* Amherst, NY: Prometheus, 2002.

Murphy, George L. *Pulpit Science Fiction.* Lima, OH: CSS Publishing, 2005).

Murphy, Nancey, "Jesus and Life on Mars." *The Christian Century*, October 30, 1996, 1028–29.

National Science Foundation, "Science Fiction and Pseudoscience." In *Science and Engineering Indicators: 2002.* Arlington, VA: NSF Division of Science Resources Statistics, Online: http://www.nsf.gov/sbe/srs/seind02/c7/c7s5.htm/.

"Nurture Nation's Fiction Writers." *China Daily*, July 23, 2003. Online: http://web.lexis-nexis.com/universe/document?_m=6e4968b49c51669/.

O'Hara, Kimberly Shane. "James Schamus Creates Ang Lee's Hulk." *Screentalk* 3:4 (2003) 40–45.

Oropeza, B. J. editor. *The Gospel according to Superheroes: Religion and Popular Culture.* New York: Lang, 2005.

Panati, Charles. *Sacred Origins of Profound Things.* New York: Penguin Arkana, 1996.

Porter, Jennifer, and Darcee McLaren, editors. *"Star Trek" and Sacred Ground: Explorations of "Star Trek," Religion, and American Culture.* Albany: State University of New York Press, 1999.

Primavesi, Anne. *Sacred Gaia: Holistic Theology and Earth System Science.* London: Routledge, 2000.

Raphael, Jordan, and Tom Spurgeon. *Stan Lee and the Rise and Fall of the American Comic Book.* Chicago: Chicago Review Press, 2003.

Restall, Hugo. "China's Net Fears." *Wall Street Journal*, August 2, 2000. Online: http://online.wsj.com/article/SB965186890971493088-search.html/.

Roberts, Timothy R., et al. *Mythology: Tales of Ancient Civilizations.* New York: Barnes & Noble, 2003.

Robertson, C. K. *Barnabas: A Model for Holistic Stewardship.* TENS Publishing, 2003.

———. *Conflict in Corinth: Redefining the System.* Studies in Biblical Literature 42. New York: Lang, 2001.

———. *Conversations with Scripture: The Acts of the Apostles.* Anglican Association of Biblical Scholars Study Series. Harrisburg, PA: Morehouse, 2010.

———, editor. *Religion as Entertainment.* New York: Lang, 2002.

Rose, Mark, *Alien Encounters.* Cambridge: Harvard University Press, 1981.

Rosenthal, Elizabeth. "UFO Boom Doesn't Worry Officials" *The New York Times*, January 11, 2000. Online: http://www.nytimes.com/library/world/asia/011100china-ufos.html/.

Rowlands, Mark, *The Philosopher at the End of the Universe: Philosophy Explained through Science Fiction Films*. New York: Thomas Dunne/St. Martin's, 2003.

Ruether, Rosemary Radford, *Gaia & God: An Ecofeminist Theology of Earth Healing*. San Francisco: HarperSanFrancisco, 1992.

Scharper, Stephen B., "The Gaia Hypothesis: Implications for a Christian political theory of the environment." *Cross Currents* 44 (1994) 207–21. Online: http://www.crosscurrents.org/Gaia.htm/.

Schlockoff, Alain, and Cathy Karani. "Excerpts from a Conversation with Jean-Pierre Jeunet and Marc Caro." Image Refinery Productions, Inc. (1995). Online: http://www.sonypictures.com/classics/city/misc/interview.html/.

Schwartz, Benjamin. *In Search of Wealth and Power: Yan Fu and the West*. Harvard East Asian Studies 16. Cambridge: Belknap, 1964.

Science Fiction World. "Kehuan shijie zazhi she jianjie" ("A Brief Introduction to Science Fiction World, 2004). Online: http://replay.waybackmachine.org/20041209025648/http://www.sfw-cd.com/sfw/shop/brief.asp/.

Science Fiction World Interviews: Liu Cixin (2004) Online: http://replay.waybackmachine.org/20040906210214/http://www.livejournal.com/users/zhwj/8775.html#cutid1/.

Seijas, Casey, "Green Machine." *Wizard* #141 (August 2003) 101.

Sharpe, Kevin. *Has Science Displaced the Soul? Debating Love and Happiness*. Lanham, MD: Rowan & Littlefield, 2005.

Shutt, Craig. *Baby Boomer Comics: The Wild, Wacky, Wonderful Comic Books of the 1960s!* Iola, WI: Krause, 2003.

Silvio, Carl, and Tony M. Vinci, editors. *Culture, Identities and Technology in the Star Wars Films*. Critical Explorations of Science Fiction and Fantasy 3. Jefferson, NC: McFarland, 2007.

Simon, Stephen, *The Force Is With You: Mystical Movie Messages That Inspire Our Lives* Charlottesville, VA: Hampton Roads, 2002.

Spence, Jonathan D. *The Search for Modern China*. New York: Norton, 1990.

Staub, Dick. *Christian Wisdom of the Jedi Masters*. San Francisco: Jossey-Bass, 2005.

"Spider-Man 2." *Wizard* #141 (2003).

"The Top Comic Book Movies of All Time." *Wizard* #143 (August 2003) 82–94.

Thorne, Christian. "The Revolutionary Energy of the Outmoded." *October* 104 (2003) 97–114. Online: http://people.williams.edu/cthorne/files/2010/09/Revolutionary-Energy.pdf/.

Unsafe Powerbase Alpha 2004. "Chinese Science Fiction." Online: http://replay.waybackmachine.org/20050106001835/http://www.well.com/~tux/unsafe/articles/018.html/.

Valliere, Paul. *Modern Russian Theology: Bukharev, Soloviev, and Bulgakov: Orthodox Theology in a New Key*. Grand Rapids: Eerdmans, 2000.

Wang, Xiaoda. "The Mysterious Wave." in *Science Fiction from China*, edited by Wu Dingbo and Patrick Murphy, 71–95. New York: Praeger, 1989.

Williams, Raymond. "Science Fiction." *Science Fiction Studies* 15:3 (1988). Online: http://www.depauw.edu/sfs/documents/williams.htm/.

Wong, Kin Yuen. "On the Edge of Spaces: *Blade Runner, Ghost in the Shell*, and Hong Kong's Cityscape." *Science Fiction Studies* 27:1 (2000). Online: http://www.depauw.edu/sfs/backissues/80/wong80art.htm

Whitehead, Harriet. "Reasonably Fantastic: Some Perspectives on Scientology, Science Fiction, and Occultism." In *Religious Movements in Contemporary America*, edited by Irving I. Zaretsky and Mark P. Leone, 547–87. Princeton: Princeton University Press, 1974.

Wilkinson, David. *Alone in the Universe? The X-Files, Aliens and God.* Crowborough: Monarch, 1997.

———. *The Power of the Force: The Spirituality of the Star Wars Films.* Oxford: Lion, 2000.

———. "Star Wars: A Battle between the Cinema and the Church?" *The Plain Truth* (April-May 2000) 6–9.

Woolverton, Mark, and Roger Stern. *The Science of Superman.* New York: ibooks, 2002.

Wu Dingbo. "Looking Backward: An Introduction to Chinese Science Fiction." In *Science Fiction from China*, edited by Wu Dingbo and Patrick Murphy, xi–xli. New York: Praeger, 1989.

Yardley, Jim, and William J. Broad. "The Next Space Race: Heading for the Stars, and Wondering if China Might Reach Them First." *New York Times*, January 22, 2004. Online: http://www.nytimes.com/2004/01/22/international/asia/22SPAC.html?ex =1075789406&ei=1&en=88798ff49f419cda

Yeffeth, Glenn, editor. *Taking the Red Pill: Science, Philosophy and Religion in "The Matrix."* Dallas: BenBella, 2003.

Yoon, Suh Kyung. "A Science-Fiction Game Spurs South Korea's Net Industry." *Wall Street Journal* 28 February 2000. Online: http://online.wsj.com/article/ SB951690705754082718-search.html?KEYWORDS=Yoon+A+Science-Fiction+G ame+Spurs+South+Koreas+Net+Industry&COLLECTION=wsjie/6month

Index of Scripture

Old Testament

New Testament

Acts of the Apostles

Index of Subjects

Index of Names